Human Trafficking

Recent Titles in the
CONTEMPORARY WORLD ISSUES
Series

The Minimum Wage: A Reference Handbook
Oren M. Levin-Waldman

Juvenile Justice: A Reference Handbook, second edition
Donald J. Shoemaker and Timothy W. Wolfe

The Global Water Crisis: A Reference Handbook
David E. Newton

Youth Substance Abuse: A Reference Handbook
David E. Newton

Global Pandemic Threats: A Reference Handbook
Michael C. LeMay

Same-Sex Marriage: A Reference Handbook, second edition
David E. Newton

DNA Technology: A Reference Handbook, second edition
David E. Newton

Modern Sport Ethics: A Reference Handbook, second edition
Angela Lumpkin

Marijuana: A Reference Handbook, second edition
David E. Newton

Gun Control in the United States: A Reference Handbook, second edition
Gregg Lee Carter

The Right to Die: A Reference Handbook
Howard Ball

Student Debt: A Reference Handbook
William Elliott III and Melinda K. Lewis

Food Safety: A Reference Handbook, third edition
Nina E. Redman and Michele Morrone

Books in the **Contemporary World Issues** series address vital issues in today's society such as genetic engineering, pollution, and biodiversity. Written by professional writers, scholars, and nonacademic experts, these books are authoritative, clearly written, up-to-date, and objective. They provide a good starting point for research by high school and college students, scholars, and general readers as well as by legislators, businesspeople, activists, and others.

Each book, carefully organized and easy to use, contains an overview of the subject, a detailed chronology, biographical sketches, facts and data and/or documents and other primary source material, a forum of authoritative perspective essays, annotated lists of print and nonprint resources, and an index.

Readers of books in the Contemporary World Issues series will find the information they need in order to have a better understanding of the social, political, environmental, and economic issues facing the world today.

Human Trafficking

A REFERENCE HANDBOOK

Alexis A. Aronowitz

ABC-CLIO™

An Imprint of ABC-CLIO, LLC
Santa Barbara, California • Denver, Colorado

Copyright © 2017 by ABC-CLIO, LLC

Human Trafficking: A Reference Handbook
Library of Congress Cataloging in Publication
Control Number: 2016052706

ISBN: 978-1-4408-3484-4
EISBN: 978-1-4408-3485-1

21 20 19 18 17   1 2 3 4 5

This book is also available as an eBook.

ABC-CLIO
An Imprint of ABC-CLIO, LLC

ABC-CLIO, LLC
130 Cremona Drive, P.O. Box 1911
Santa Barbara, California 93116-1911
www.abc-clio.com

This book is printed on acid-free paper ∞

Manufactured in the United States of America

This book is dedicated to Gert-Jan, Julius,
Marilyn, Jay, and Andrée
and their children, Jenna, Jeboa, Shavon,
Tony, and Jason
my sources of love, support, and friendship,
past, present, and future

Recruiters came to a town in Syria offering paid work in restaurants and hotels in Lebanon. A young woman, anxious to leave her war-torn country, accepted the offer. Upon arriving in Lebanon, she was forced into prostitution with more than 70 other women and girls, many of whom were from Syria. The victims were locked in hotels, raped and tortured, and forced to service as many as 20 clients each day.

Halfway around the world, a Bangladeshi man was brought to a palm oil plantation seeking work. His passport was confiscated by the contracting company that withheld his salary to pay for his recruitment fees.

In Canada, a 13-year-old adolescent was deceived by a young girl she had met online. The girl, her boyfriend, and another man forced the adolescent into prostitution and "sold" her to clients in cities around Canada (U.S. Department of State, 2016).

There are an estimated 21 million people who are victims of forced labor in the world today (ILO, 2012). The United Nations identifies human trafficking as the third most profitable crime after drugs and arms trafficking, estimating that it generates US$32 billion in profit for the traffickers. It is not just a problem affecting developing nations. In 2016, the U.S. Department of State's Office to Monitor and Combat Trafficking in Persons identified 188 countries with a significant trafficking problem (U.S. Department of State, 2016). The United Nations found that between 2010 and 2012, victims of 152 different nationalities were identified in 124 countries worldwide (UNODC, 2014).

The image of a trafficked victim is one of foreign women being brought into a country and enslaved in the sex industry. Sex trafficking is perhaps the most well-known form of trafficking, but it is not the only form. Where criminals can profit off of the exploitation of a person's labor, human trafficking will thrive. Exploitation occurs not only in the unregulated sex sector, but also in the more common and legitimate sectors such as construction, food service, the restaurant and hotel industry, domestic service, agriculture, and fishing. Other less common forms of human trafficking have been identified. These include the trafficking of persons for the purpose of organ removal, forced begging or other criminal activities, and children for use as child soldiers and child brides (Aronowitz, 2009).

Who are those who fall prey to traffickers and why is it so difficult to identify victims of trafficking? They are rarely ideal victims who fit a perfect victim profile (Christie, 1986). They sometimes agree to travel abroad using false identity papers and know they will be residing and working illegally in the country of destination. Some even know they are going to work in prostitution. They are sometimes nationals of the country in which they are exploited. They frequently refuse to cooperate with law enforcement. This picture will vary from country to country as well as within countries across different markets.

And who are the people who so viciously exploit the victims? Studies of victims' testimonies, data produced by international organizations and government agencies, newspaper articles, and police files show a varied picture. The image of traffickers as "dark, swarthy men" may be more fiction than fact. The United Nations reports a growing involvement of women in the business of human trafficking (UNODC, 2012; 2014). Studies of police files also show differences in the level of organization and roles of traffickers. A trend that is being observed is the involvement of former trafficking victims as traffickers. Why and how this happens will be the addressed in Chapter 2 of this book.

When the author began her career in the field of human trafficking for the United Nations Interregional Crime and Justice Research Institute (UNICRI) in 2000, there was limited awareness of human trafficking. Researchers were being told by national law enforcement agencies in different countries that foreign women were working illegally as prostitutes but that human trafficking did not exist. No one questioned how these young women and girls were able—without help—to migrate from villages in their country to destinations thousands of miles away and establish themselves as prostitutes in a country with which they were unfamiliar and did not speak the language.

The situation began to change. The UN Convention on Transnational Organized Crime and its supplementing protocols on migrant smuggling, human trafficking, and the arms trade were open for signature in Palermo, Sicily, on December 12, 2000. At the same time, in 2000, the U.S. Government passed the Victims of Trafficking and Violence Protection Act (TVPA), which has undergone a number of reauthorizations since its entry into law. Each year, more countries ratify the UN Convention on Transnational Organized Crime and the Trafficking Protocol, pass national legislation, train police officers, and witness governments, civil society, and the private sector join hands to combat the problem.

The purpose of this book is to dispel myths about human trafficking and provide the reader with a more nuanced understanding of the phenomenon. The reader will learn more about the complexity and weaknesses in the definition of human trafficking, why it is so difficult to identify trafficked victims, who these victims are, and how traffickers recruit and control them. The reader will understand criticisms of the trafficking data and the factors in society that fuel and facilitate the trafficking problem. Attempts to combat the problem from a number of different angles will be addressed. A chronology of the significant events and dates, a glossary of terms, and profiles of some of the most important persons and organizations working in the field of human trafficking will provide the reader with a starting point for further research. The chapter on perspectives gives a voice to individuals working in the anti-trafficking field, providing insight into the impact they have made in the understanding of and fight against human trafficking. An annotated bibliography of print and Internet sources allows the reader to continue research into the topic.

Acknowledgments

This book could not have been written without the support of my ABC-CLIO editor, Robin Tutt, who graciously and professionally guided me through the process. You made it enjoyable! I would like to express my gratitude to my colleagues Aaron Cohen, Elif Isitman, Ivonne van de Kar, Joanne van der Leun, Glynn Rankin, Dina Siegel, Patsy Sörensen, Klaus Vanhoutte, Rebecca Surtees, and Ron Weitzer, who shared their expertise in the contributions in the Perspectives chapter. Your ideas have helped shape my thinking and understanding about human trafficking.

Thanks to my students who have studied human trafficking with me at Leiden University College, The Hague, Jacobs University, Bremen, John Jay College of Criminal Justice, New York City, and The University of Illinois at Chicago. You have kept me inspired and challenged as we both learn more about trafficking problems in your countries. Special thanks go to Alexandra van Walraven and Maya Alba Heller. Your many interesting ideas and the information you collected have made their way into the Profiles chapter.

I would like to express my gratitude to University College Utrecht for having provided research time to work on my book, and to Leiden University College for the research clinics in which students have assisted me with my book and other research on human trafficking.

Above all, I would like to thank my husband, Gert-Jan, who took care of life, while everything got put on hold to complete this book and other projects. I could not have done it without your support. My deepest thanks go out to my family, who are a constant reminder that life exists beyond the printed page.

References

Aronowitz, Alexis. 2009. *Human trafficking, human misery: The global trade in human beings.* Westport, CT: Praeger.

Christie, Nils. 1968. "The ideal victim." In Fattah, E.A. (Ed.), *From crime policy to victim policy.* New York: St. Martin's Press.

ILO (International Labour Organization). 2012. *ILO global estimate of forced labour.* Geneva, Switzerland: International Labour Office.

UNODC (United Nations Office on Drugs and Crime). 2012. *Global report on trafficking in persons.* Vienna, Austria.

UNODC. 2014. *Global report on trafficking in persons.* Vienna, Austria.

U.S. Department of State. 2016. *Trafficking in persons report 2016.* Washington, DC.

Human Trafficking

The twentieth century has been a century of progress in almost every area of human rights. This makes the persistence of slavery in today's world even more egregious. Even as laws banning slavery and its prohibition are enshrined in international instruments, notably the Universal Declaration of Human Rights, it is still practised in many forms: traditional chattel slavery, bonded labour, serfdom, child labour, migrant labour, domestic labour, forced labour and slavery for ritual or religious purposes.
—Kofi Anan, Secretary-General of the United Nations
(United Nations, 1999)

The taking and enslaving of human beings has a history that dates back to ancient Greece and the Roman Empire and remained common throughout the medieval period. African slaves were traded by Europeans in the middle of the 15th century, and the first slaves were brought to the United States in the 17th century. Unlike the seizure of slaves as spoils of war,

---

Slaves are brought to market for trade. Slaves were first introduced to North America at Jamestown, Virginia, in 1619. The U.S. Congress banned the international slave trade in the United States in 1808, but the illegal importation of slaves continued. Slavery was formally abolished in the United States on December 6, 1865, with the passage of the Thirteenth Amendment. (Photo by © CORBIS/Corbis via Getty Images)

common to many conquering nations, chattel slavery, defined as slavery in which persons are bought and sold as commodities, is the most common form of slavery. Slavery transcends jurisdictional boundaries and time and has been defined as "one of the most ubiquitous and pervasive features of all human civilizations, across time and space" (Newman, 2013, 24). Slavery continues to adapt and evolve.

Slavery in Ancient Times

Slavery existed in ancient societies and has been documented as existing as early as 4000 BCE in Mesopotamia. Slaves—spoils of war—were used in agriculture and to contribute to food production, to tend stock, and work in mines. Slavery took two forms—as punishment for the transgression of laws, for having taken up arms against the community, or for the purpose of organizing laborers to contribute to the survival of the community (Newman, 2013).

Slavery continued to be practiced more than 2,000 years later during the reign of King Hammurabi (ca. 1792–1750 BCE). Many of the laws defined in the Code of Hammurabi dealt with slavery where persons in a state of slavery were viewed as merchandise. Distinction was made between chattel slavery (persons who were captured or punished for criminal violation of the law could be enslaved forever) and those who were obtained as a result of debt bondage. These slaves were to be freed by their owners after a period of three years. Male slaves were provided rights to marry free women, own property, and buy their freedom. These rights were not available to female slaves (Newman, 2013).

The Greeks, too, maintained slaves, as can be seen in the existence of "slave societies." Unlike other societies, where slaves were marginalized, in ancient Greece (fifth to the third centuries BCE), slavery was the focal point of economic production (Berlin, 1998). Slaves were put to work in industrial, agricultural, and domestic labor. Slavery was so pervasive in Ancient

Athens that slaves outnumbered freemen by approximately two to one. After 594 BCE, all slaves were non-Greek captives of war acquired generally at markets. Women and female children were purchased for the purpose of sexual exploitation (Newman, 2013).

Between 27 BCE and 476 CE, slavery was documented as well in ancient Rome, and the Roman Empire "became the largest slave society in the ancient world" (Newman, 2013, 35), comprising approximately a third of the population in Italy and 10–15 percent in the remainder of the empire. According to Roman law, slaves were viewed as property, not as persons. While both male and female slaves were expected to participate in agricultural, domestic, and trade labor, female slaves were expected to reproduce offspring, who themselves became slaves. Three quarters of Rome's total population of enslaved laborers were the children of female slaves (Newman, 2013).

The Trans-Atlantic Slave Trade

While Europeans were taking slaves in West Africa and the New World in the 15th through the 17th centuries, the Trans-Atlantic slave trade "that developed during the early modern period was more brutal and exploitative than that which had previously existed in Europe, Africa or the Middle East" (Newman, 2013, 39). African slaves were taken to the Americas to work on plantations cultivating crops of tobacco, rice, sugarcane, and coffee, and work in the mines in the colonies in Brazil, the Caribbean islands, and Central and North America (Newman, 2013). The provision of African slaves to European merchants was facilitated, in part, by Africans themselves, who enslaved criminals or conducted raids for the purpose of enslaving and selling captives to European traders. A system of racial division arose that allowed for white European masters to continue to oppress African and Amerindian slaves in the colonies. Slaves were demonized as "blacks" or "heathens" (as opposed to "whites" or "Christians"), which designated their position as both inferior and a slave (Newman, 2013). Slaves were bought and sold at markets as property, and the children born of slaves also became the property of the slaveholders.

The Trans-Atlantic slave trade continued into the 19th century. The passage to the New World was particularly brutal, with many slaves dying during the passage (for a graphic portrayal, see Steven Spielberg's depiction of the voyage of African slaves to the New World in his film *Amistad*, based on the true story of the slave ship *La Amistad*). It is estimated that between the 15th and the 19th centuries, nine and a half million Africans were shipped as slaves to the New World.

The Abolition of Slavery and the Rise of the White Slave Trade

The 1815 Declaration Relative to the Universal Abolition of the Slave Trade was the first international instrument to condemn slavery. Its goal was to eliminate slavery by obliging states to make it a crime. Around the late 19th and early 20th centuries, concern over slavery in general, and the morality of women in particular, led abolitionists to protest the movement of women across international borders for the purpose of prostitution—what later came to be known as "white slavery." The most commonly used definition is "the procurement—by use of force, deceit or drugs—of a white woman or a girl against her will for prostitution" (Doezema, 2000, 25). There is documented evidence (an investigation on the "Importation and Harbouring of Women for Immoral Purposes" in the United States from 1908 to 1909) that foreign women and girls were being brought into the United States in the early 1900s for the purpose of prostitution (League of Nations, 1927). The trade in foreign women is documented in various European cities and the United States in the late 1800s and early 1900s (Picarelli, 2007). Around the turn of the century, focus on white slavery in Europe (Paris, London, and Budapest) resulted in the 1904 International Agreement for the Suppression of the "White Slave Traffic" not only to protect women and girls from being traded into prostitution, but also to regulate and repatriate migrant women. The movement against white slavery was driven by a combined desire to eradicate both prostitution and slavery.

Six years later, in 1910, the International Convention for the Suppression of the White Slave Trade was signed by 13 countries (United Nations, 1951). The focus of this International Convention was on white women, in particular from European countries, to the exclusion of male children, men, or migrants from countries outside Europe. Due to criticism, the emphasis was shifted from "white slavery" to traffic in women and children (reflecting also a shift from the national to the international level) (Kangaspunta, 2008).

During this time (early 1900s), the existence of organized forced prostitution in the United States resulted in the enactment in 1910 of the federal statute known as the White Slave Traffic Act or the Mann Act (18 U.S.C.A. § 2421 et seq.) aimed at preventing men from forcing women into prostitution or transporting them across state lines for consensual sex. The term "white slavery" referred to the fact that women, obtained through deceit, force, or drugs, were coerced or tricked into prostitution (Doezema, 2000) and then held against their will and forced to work in brothels (Aronowitz, 2012).

The League of Nations (the predecessor to the United Nations), established after World War I, led the effort to convince the world that individual human rights were a legitimate concern in international law (Bales and Robbins, 2001). Slavery was first defined in the Slavery, Servitude, Forced Labour and Similar Institutions and Practices Convention of 1926 (Slavery Convention of 1926), agreed upon by the League of Nations. The Slavery Convention of 1926 defines slavery as "the status or condition of a person over whom any or all of the powers attaching to the right of ownership are exercised" and provides a further definition that "includes all acts involved in the capture, acquisition or disposal of a person with intent to reduce him to slavery, all acts involved in the acquisition of a slave with a view to selling or exchanging him, all acts of disposal by sale or exchange of a slave acquired with a view to being sold or exchanged, and, in general, every act of trade or transport in slaves" (Slavery Convention of 1926, http://www1.umn.edu/humanrts/instree/f1sc.htm). It was not until the middle of the 20th century (December 10, 1948) that the most important document to focus on human rights—the Universal Declaration of Human Rights—was adopted by the General Assembly of the United Nations. Article 4 states: "No one shall be held in slavery or servitude, slavery and the slave trade shall be prohibited in all their forms" (United Nations, http://www.un.org/en/documents/udhr/index.shtml).

Trafficking in Women and Children

The International Convention for the Suppression of the Traffic in Women and Children (United Nations, 1950) was signed by 33 states in Geneva in 1921. Mirroring the offences mentioned in the 1910 Convention on White Slave Traffic, this later convention requested countries to take measures to prosecute persons engaged in the traffic in children of both sexes. Furthermore, emphasis was placed on the need to protect individuals during the migration process and countries were encouraged to raise awareness of the dangers of being trafficked (United Nations, 1950, art. 7). The emphasis still remained upon women and children and for the purpose of sexual exploitation (Kangaspunta, 2008).

Trafficking in Persons

The United Nations Convention for the Suppression of the Traffic in Persons and of the Exploitation of the Prostitution of Others (adopted in 1949) entered into force in 1951. It was the first legally binding international instrument to address human trafficking, but still focused on trafficking in women for forced prostitution. This convention was followed by the Beijing Platform for Action in 1995, which called for the effective suppression of trafficking in women and girls for the sex trade (Kangaspunta, 2008).

A number of instruments were passed dealing with the protection of children from sexual exploitation (Optional Protocol to the Convention on the Rights of the Child on the Sale of Children, Child Prostitution and Child Pornography, which entered into force in January 2002; see http://www.ohchr.org/EN/ProfessionalInterest/Pages/OPSCCRC.aspx) and forced labor (International Labour Organization [ILO] Convention 182 on the Worst Forms of Child Labour entering into force in 2000; see http://www.ilo.org/dyn/normlex/en/f?p=NORMLEXPUB:12100:0::NO:12100:P12100_ILO_CODE:C182).

It was not until 2000 that the next international legally binding instrument addressing human trafficking was crafted and open for signature. The UN Protocol to Prevent, Suppress and Punish Trafficking in Persons, Especially Women and Children, Supplementing the United Nations Convention Against Transnational Organized Crime entered into force in 2003. This instrument extended the definition of human trafficking beyond the sexual exploitation of women and girls to include different forms of exploitation—and for the purpose of organ removal—against all victims. It is also the first international instrument against crime "that balances law enforcement action with the rights of victims" (Kangaspunta, 2008, 40), focusing on the prevention of the crime, the prosecution of offenders, and the protection of victims (Kangaspunta, 2008; UNODC, 2004).

Over the years, our understanding of the concept of human trafficking has undergone a metamorphosis. While earlier attention was drawn to foreign women and girls in forced prostitution, the current international definition recognizes that all forms of exploitation experienced by men and boys, as well as women and girls, constitute the crime of human trafficking.

What Is in a Definition?

The history of slavery spans 6,000 years. It has taken on various forms, and while we refer to human trafficking as "modern-day slavery," human trafficking is a very specific subset of the broader phenomenon of slavery. Definitions matter, as they are the basis for our legal codes and guide the collection of data. Data help us understand a problem and are the basis for the creation of policies and practices to address it.

The many definitions that are used to describe the different forms of abuse share a great degree of commonality. At the same time, it is important to draw distinctions in order to avoid what legal scholar Janie Chuang (2014) calls "exploitation creep"—labeling certain practices as more severe and extreme than they are. By "[r]ecasting all forced labor as trafficking, and all trafficking as slavery, 'exploitation creep' re-labels abuses as more extreme than is legally accurate" (Chuang, 2014, 4), and this will dramatically affect the number of victims estimated or recorded. Not all persons in forced labor are trafficked and not all trafficked persons are enslaved.

Slavery, as defined by the 1926 Slavery Convention, is "the status or condition of a person over whom any or all of the power attaching to the rights of ownership are exercised." This describes the form of chattel slavery common during the Atlantic Slave Trade. A leading authority on slavery, Kevin Bales, has defined slavery as "a state marked by the loss of free will where a person is forced through violence or the threat of violence to give up the ability to sell freely his or her own labor power" (Bales and Robbins, 2001, 32). This definition is based upon definitions of slavery in international agreements and scientific theory. The three key dimensions in this definition are (1) control by another person, (2) the appropriation of labor power, and (3) the use or threat of violence. According to Bales, slavery manifests itself in human trafficking, bonded labor, and forced labor. Weitzer (2015a) argues that Bales has included forms of exploitation that do not reach the level of slavery.

There are different forms of slavery and exploitation. According to Anti-Slavery International, *bonded labor* is the most prevalent, yet the least understood form of slavery. Millions of low-caste laborers are believed to be trapped in debt bondage in South Asia. As a result of a loan, and exorbitant interest fees and housing costs added on to the loan, laborers are often trapped into working for little or no money to repay the debt, which continues to accrue without ever being absolved. Families may be forced to work 14–16 hours a day. Children are generally prohibited from attending school and bonded slave laborers are often subjected to physical abuse (female bonded laborers may be subjected to sexual assaults). Debts can be passed on from one generation to the next and entire families can be enslaved for a debt incurred by a (distant) family member. The individual or family cannot change employers and literally becomes the "property" of the debt lender (see Anti-Slavery International, no date, and Upadhyaya, 2008, for a report on bonded labor in India, Nepal, and Pakistan). Debt bondage is a form of slavery practiced widely in South Asia.

The ILO defines *forced labor* as "all work or service which is exacted from any person under the menace of any penalty and for which the said person has not offered himself voluntarily" (Art. 2, para.1 of the ILO Convention on Forced Labour No. 29). Forced labor is a more general concept than slavery or human trafficking, and while slavery, bonded labor, and human trafficking almost always include elements of forced labor, forced labor is not necessarily the same as human trafficking or slavery.

The Supplementary Convention on the Abolition of Slavery, the Slave Trade and Institutions and Practices Similar to Slavery of 1956 defined *serfdom* as "the condition or status of a tenant who is by law, custom or agreement bound to live and labour on land belonging to another person and to render some determinate service to such other person, whether for reward or not, and is not free to change his status." This Supplementary Convention also prohibits other practices, which together with debt bondage and serfdom are identified as "servile status" (Weissbrodt, 2002, 6). These prohibited practices include the following:

- A woman is promised or given in marriage, without the right to refuse, on payment of a consideration in money or in kind to her parents, guardian, family, or any person or group.
- The husband of a woman, his family, or his clan has the right to transfer her to another person for value received or otherwise.
- On the death of her husband, a woman is liable to be inherited by another person.
- A young person under the age of 18 years is delivered by either or both of his natural parents or guardian to another person, whether for reward or not, with a view to the exploitation of the child's labor.

The least common form of slavery in the world today is *chattel slavery*, in which a master "owns" his slave. Slaves are considered the property of the slave owner—they can be bought, sold, inherited, or traded. This type of slavery still exists in the East African country of Mauritania, which was the last country to ban slavery in 2007 (see the websites of Fight Slavery Now and Anti-Slavery International for more on chattel slavery in Mauritania).

According to Allain and Bales (2012, 2), trafficking (which will be defined in detail in the following section) "is not in itself slavery, but a process by which slavery can be achieved."

Returning to the three elements in Bales's definition of slavery (loss of free will, appropriation of labor power, and violence or threat of violence), and taking into account other forms of exploitation, Bales and Robbins (2001) examine the degree to which the elements of loss of freedom, appropriation of labor power, and violence or threats of violence are present. According to them, all three elements are present in "white slavery," debt bondage, child prostitution, forced prostitution, and sexual slavery. This is not the case for other forms of prostitution, forced marriage, and trafficking for the purpose of organ removal. It is clear from their interpretation that not all forms of exploitation are tantamount to slavery.

Weitzer (2015a) argues that Bales has wrongly identified forced and bonded labor as slavery cases. Bales (2004, 9) has defined debt bondage as a situation in which "people give themselves into slavery as security against a loan or when they inherit a debt." This view is supported by the ILO, which views the use of a bond or debt as a form of coercion (Weitzer, 2015a). Equating the occurrence of a debt with a situation that is inherently harmful or coercive assumes—perhaps falsely— or ignores the fact that some individuals voluntarily assume a debt in order to travel or seek employment abroad (Weitzer, 2015a; Aronowitz, 2015a). A study of Brazilian sex workers in Spain found that while many of the women working in the sex industry in Spain would be considered trafficking victims according to Brazilian law, they rejected this label and "they perceived their migratory trajectories and sex work as paths for the improvement of their lives" (Piscitelli, 2012, 301). In a study on prostitution in Amsterdam, one researcher was told by a Romanian sex worker that when she came to the Netherlands 15 years earlier, her facilitator paid for her trip to Amsterdam, secured the necessary paperwork, found her an apartment, and paid her travel expenses. In exchange, she had to pay him half of her earnings for a period of one year. According to Dutch law, she would have been identified as a victim of trafficking in a situation of debt bondage and (financial) exploitation. She reported never viewing herself as a victim of human trafficking and seeing this as a financial arrangement to facilitate her move to and employment in the Netherlands (unpublished bachelor's thesis, Raluca Ciausoiu, University College Utrecht, May 2015).

A further point made by Weitzer (2015a) is the fact that bonded labor in a wealthy country is, for some migrants, seen as preferable to unemployment or what is available on the free labor market at home. It is not a debt bondage relationship that should be the determining factor, but "the precise nature of the contractual relationship and whether it is honored in practice, coupled with the subsequent working conditions—criteria that determine whether a debt is truly coercive, fraudulent, unpayable or exploitative or instead simply a mutually agreed loan to be repaid" (Weitzer, 2015a, 22).

It is not difficult to see how various forms of exploitative labor (debt bondage, forced labor) and human trafficking are conflated with slavery. Chuang (2014) is right to be concerned with "exploitation creep."

Defining Human Trafficking

In November 2000, the General Assembly of the United Nations adopted the Convention Against Transnational Organized Crime, aimed at preventing and combating transnational crime perpetrated by organized criminal groups. Three important Optional Protocols supplement this convention. The first is the Protocol Against the Smuggling of Migrants by Land, Sea and Air, Supplementing the United Nations Convention Against Transnational Organized Crime (hereafter referred to as the UN Smuggling Protocol). The second is the Protocol to Prevent, Suppress and Punish Trafficking in Persons, Especially Women and Children, Supplementing the United Nations Convention Against Transnational Organized Crime (hereafter referred to as the UN Trafficking Protocol). The third is the Protocol Against the Illicit Manufacturing of and Trafficking in Firearms, Their Parts and Components and Ammunition,

Supplementing the United Nations Convention Against Transnational Organized Crime (the UN Firearms Protocol).

More than 100 countries took part in negotiating the terms and definitions of the protocols. The convention and supplementing protocols were open for signature in Palermo, Italy, in December 2000. The UN Trafficking Protocol entered into force on December 25, 2003. As of November 2016, 170 countries, including the United States, have ratified the Trafficking Protocol.

The UN Trafficking Protocol is the first international, legally binding instrument defining human trafficking, including trafficking for forms of sexual exploitation, forced labor, and organ trafficking. Article 3 of the protocol defines trafficking in persons as:

> the recruitment, transportation, transfer, harboring or receipt of persons, by means of the threat or use of force or other forms of coercion, of abduction, of fraud, of deception, of the abuse of power or of a position of vulnerability or of the giving or receiving of payments or benefits to achieve the consent of a person having control over another person, for the purpose of exploitation. Exploitation shall include, at a minimum, the exploitation of the prostitution of others or other forms of sexual exploitation, forced labor or services, slavery or practices similar to slavery, servitude or the removal of organs.

Trafficking must comprise three constituent elements:

(1) An *action* (recruitment, transportation, transfer, harboring, or reception of persons),

(2) through *means* of threat or use of force, coercion, abduction, fraud, deception, abuse of power, or vulnerability, or giving payments or benefits to a person in control of the victim,

(3) *goals* (for exploitation or the purpose of exploitation, which includes, at a minimum, exploiting the prostitution

of others, other forms of sexual exploitation, forced labor or services, slavery or similar practices, and the removal of organs).

One element from each of these must be present for trafficking to occur.

The consent of a victim of trafficking in persons to the intended exploitation is irrelevant where any of the means set forth in the definition have been used. It is important to understand that consent is negated when threats, force, abduction, deception, fraud, or buying or receiving a child from the parent or guardian is present. A commonly mistaken perception is that if individuals agree to leave their country to seek illegal employment in a destination country, they are not trafficked persons. If this consent is obtained through any of the means stated earlier, the consent is no longer valid. Furthermore, special protection is extended to persons under the age of 18. The recruitment, transportation, transfer, harboring, or receipt of a child for the purpose of exploitation is considered trafficking in persons, even if this does not involve any of the means set forth earlier.

A misperception exists that trafficking in human beings requires the movement of people—either within a country or across international borders. Returning to the definition, the act in human trafficking is the recruitment *or* transportation *or* transfer *or* harboring *or* reception of persons through means, for the *purpose* of exploitation. This definition allows for numerous acts to be identified as human trafficking. For example, the child sex tourist who approaches a hotel concierge as well as the hotel staff who contacts the child's parent(s) or guardian, the taxi driver who brings the child back to the hotel, and the concierge who brings the child to the tourist's room are all involved in the act of the trafficking of a child for the purpose of sexual exploitation. Furthermore, the definition does not require that the exploitation has to have occurred. If a person is recruited, transported, transferred, harbored, or received (with the means outlined in the definition, unless in the case of a child) for the purpose of exploiting the individual's labor or services, an act of human trafficking has occurred.

How Does Trafficking Differ from Smuggling?

Trafficking is often confused with smuggling. The news often refers to the trafficking of human beings (similar to the trafficking of drugs), when in fact reference should be made to smuggling. While these two crimes share some similarities, they differ on a number of important aspects. The smuggling of migrants has been defined in Article 3 of the UN Smuggling Protocol (2000) as "the procurement, in order to obtain, directly or indirectly, a financial or other material benefit, of the illegal entry of a person into a State Party of which the person is not a national or a permanent resident." Inherent in the definition of smuggling is the crossing of international borders. Generally, migrants pay the total sum of their journey prior to departure, and upon entering the destination country, their relationship with the smuggler is terminated. Trafficked victims, on the other hand, have often incurred a debt for their transportation costs and this debt binds them to the trafficker. Either they are forced to work to repay the debt or are sold to other traffickers.

There is a smuggling–trafficking–migration nexus. International trafficking often occurs within the context of (il)legal migration or smuggling. Both smuggled persons and victims trafficked internationally may leave their country of origin willingly. Both may face hardship in their travels to (and attempt to enter) a destination country. In 2014, 218,000 irregular migrants (the term is used for those with irregular and sometimes illegal status) attempted to cross the Mediterranean and enter the European Union (Office of the United Nations High Commissioner for Refugees [UNHCR]). According to a report by Amnesty International (2014), in the first nine months of that year, over 2,500 people died trying to enter the European

Union on makeshift boats from Northern Africa. Three months later, the total had risen to 3,419 dead (Wieners, 2015). The decomposing bodies of victims who were likely Syrian refugees (among them 60 men, 8 women, and 3 children between the ages of two and eight) were found in the back of a truck in Austria (Smith-Spark and Karimi, 2015), a day after a tragic incident involving the death of hundreds of migrants who drowned off the coast of Libya when their boats capsized (BBC, 2015b). Since 2001, more than 2,300 undocumented immigrants have died crossing the desert in the state of Arizona in the United States (Trevizo, 2015). The International Organization for Migration's Missing Migrants Project recorded 5,571 migrant deaths worldwide in 2015 (with many more unaccounted for). In the first ten months of 2016, the deaths of 5,585 migrants were recorded. Unlike trafficked persons, those irregular migrants (smuggled persons) who survive the journey are free to leave once they reach their destination. However, similar to trafficked victims, they may be subject to exploitation once they enter a destination country, as their irregular status often precludes them from legal employment.

These two phenomena are intertwined and not always mutually exclusive. Persons beginning a journey, having paid everything prior to departure and hoping to be smuggled into a destination country, may find themselves victims of human trafficking—as was the case with two participants in the first study on human trafficking from the Philippines carried out by the United Nations Interregional Crime and Justice Research Institute (Aronowitz, 2004). The binary distinction human smuggling and human trafficking may be a false division, as there is "victimization in smuggling and agency in trafficking or a mixture of choice and compulsion" in the two (Weitzer, 2015b, 225).

The important differences between trafficked victims and smuggled persons are their legal status and the benefits to which they are entitled in the destination country. Trafficked persons are (or should be considered) victims, and in many countries are entitled to special protections. These include shelter, legal assistance, psychosocial care, and a period of reflection (for more on this, see, for example, the European Commission's publication "The EU Rights of Victims of Trafficking in Human Beings," 2013, and the U.S. Justice for Victims of Trafficking Act of 2015). Undocumented migrants, unless they are granted asylum, are considered violators of immigration law and subject to arrest and deportation. Table 1.1 clarifies the differences between trafficked victims and smuggled persons.

Table 1.1   Differences between Human Trafficking and Smuggling

Trafficking	Smuggling
Force is used or consent is obtained through fraud, deception, or coercion (actual, perceived, or implied), unless under 18 years of age, the person being trafficked may or may not cooperate	The person being smuggled generally cooperates and consents to the smuggling
Forced labor and/or exploitation	There is generally no actual or implied coercion (smuggled persons may be subject to coercion or force during the transportation phase, but not upon entry into the destination country)
Persons trafficked are victims	Persons smuggled are violating the law, and by law they are not victims
Enslaved, subjected to limited movement or isolation, documents may have been confiscated	Persons are free to leave, change jobs, etc.
Need not involve the actual or physical movement of the victim	Facilitates the illegal entry of person(s) from one country into another
No requirement to cross an international border, trafficking can occur within a country	Smuggling always crosses an international border
Persons are exploited in labor/services or commercial sex acts (i.e., must be "working")	Person must be attempting illegal entry or only be in country illegally

Source: Aronowitz, 2009, 8 (based on U.S. State Department, Human Smuggling and Trafficking Center [modified]).

How Straightforward Is the Definition of Human Trafficking?

The definition of human trafficking appears straightforward; however, certain key terms—"coercion," "exploitation," "abuse of power," "vulnerability," and "control"—are left undefined (Weitzer, 2015a) and continue to be debatable. Returning to the definition of the Trafficking Protocol of the United Nations, trafficking in persons is defined as an action, the means, and for the purpose of exploitation. The concepts of "coercion," "deception," and "of a position of vulnerability" continue to provide challenges to those trying to understand the complexities of human trafficking.

Coercion is a complex issue. Physical coercion rarely occurs during the recruitment phase and is more commonly found in the exploitation phase as a way of maintaining control over trafficked persons. Coercion, however, is not always physical and, in the case of human trafficking, is often more psychological. Traffickers use threats of contacting immigration authorities (if workers are undocumented migrants), of informing parents that their daughters are working in prostitution, or threatening to harm the families or children of trafficked persons. This psychological terror is much more effective than using physical harm in ensuring compliance of trafficked persons. It also causes enforcement authorities and judges to raise questions about whether persons are in fact trafficked when, according to them, "victims could have escaped at any time . . . they weren't chained to the bed . . . no guards were present." Until those coming into contact with trafficked persons realize that many are controlled through psychological coercion, they are less likely to be rescued and provided services.

Deception in the recruitment process, and subsequent exploitation in prostitution, can best be understood along a continuum. It is true that many persons willingly leave with their recruiters or traffickers. They may have consented to entering a country illegally and working as a laborer, domestic servant, or even in prostitution. But the consent is obtained through a web of lies regarding the victim's future life or employment opportunities. This can best be understood when examining victim consent from complete coercion to full deception on a continuum. On the far left of the continuum are victims who are obtained through force or coercion. These persons may have been kidnapped or coerced into cooperating with the trafficker due to threats of harm to themselves or a family member. As one moves along the continuum to the right, there is complete deception as victims are promised jobs as nannies, domestic workers, or employees in a legitimate business. Further along the continuum are victims who were deceived through half-truths—they were told they would be working as exotic dancers or as escorts, but were promised that they would not be forced to have sexual contact or intercourse with customers. Those on the far end of the continuum are women (or men) who have been recruited as prostitutes in their country of origin, to knowingly work in prostitution in the destination country. They agree to the nature of the (sex) work; the deception involves the exploitative working conditions to which they are exposed—excessive hours, six to seven days a week, receiving little or no pay, and often having to seek permission to call home or seek medical care. All of these persons are victims of trafficking, although it is easy to see why those victims falling on the left side of the continuum (abducted or coerced) are more easily identified and evoke more sympathy than those who are deceived about the conditions of the work. This victim continuum is portrayed in Figure 1.1.

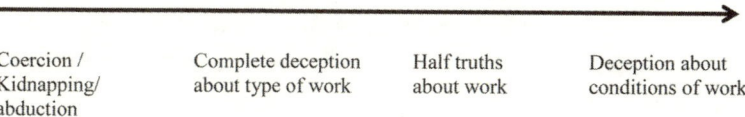

| Coercion / Kidnapping/ abduction | Complete deception about type of work | Half truths about work | Deception about conditions of work |

Figure 1.1   Victim Continuum.

Source: (Aronowitz, Alexis A. 2015. "Victims of Human Trafficking: A Complex Issue." *Dossier of Analysis: Human Trafficking*, Centro de Estudios Internacionales—CEI Facultad de Ciencias Sociales Universidad de los Andes. http://cei.uniandes.edu.co/index.php/component/docman/cat_view/5-dossier?Itemid=)

Abuse of a position of vulnerability is another term that is not clearly defined in the UN Trafficking Protocol. According to a report by the United Nations Office on Drugs and Crime (UNODC; Gallagher, 2013, 3), abuse of a position of vulnerability exists in "any situation in which the person involved has no real and acceptable alternative but to submit to the abuse involved." Vulnerability can be understood within the context of personal (individual) or external factors. Some vulnerabilities such as age (young children and, to a lesser extent, older people), poverty, disability (both mental and physical), cultural and religious beliefs (in certain parts of West African countries, voodoo or juju is used to control victims), gender, and sexuality (women and transgender persons) are intrinsic to the victims. Other vulnerabilities, such as irregular or illegal migration status or lack of social networks and isolation, may be created by the trafficker to maintain control over the victim. Individual vulnerabilities may make persons susceptible to trafficking. It is the abuse of these vulnerabilities by traffickers and exploiters that make trafficking occur. Traffickers threaten to report the trafficked person's illegal migration status to immigration authorities, or threaten to disclose a victim's involvement in prostitution to the family. In this manner, offenders make the victim dependent upon the trafficker (Aronowitz, 2015b). "In the context of trafficking, 'vulnerability' is typically used to refer to those . . . factors that increase the susceptibility of an individual or group to being trafficked. These factors are generally agreed to include . . . inequality, discrimination and gender-based violence" (Gallagher, 2013, 15). It is not, however, the vulnerability to abuse, but the "*abuse* of vulnerability as a *means by which trafficking is perpetrated*" (Gallagher, 2013, 15).

Exploitation is not defined in Article 3 of the UN Trafficking Protocol, which only states that exploitation "includes, at a minimum, exploiting the prostitution of others, other forms of sexual exploitation, forced labor or services, slavery or similar practices, and the removal of organs." The definition fails to fully explain what is meant by "forced labor" or practices "similar to slavery."

What Contributes to Human Trafficking?

The root causes that facilitate trafficking are numerous and differ from one context to the next, influencing the type of trafficking found in different countries or regions. Trafficking is driven by economic, social, cultural, and other factors, among them, political factors, globalization, and demand (Shelley, 2010; Aronowitz, 2009; Cameron and Newman, 2008; UNODC, *Toolkit*). There are other factors that are not root causes but clearly facilitate human trafficking. These are corruption, the involvement of criminal networks, and legal loopholes in work visas. The remainder of this section will examine these factors in more detail.

Push and Pull Factors

Trafficking often occurs within the context of migration. Migration, whether legal or illegal, is driven by "push" (reasons to leave a certain country) and "pull" (reasons to go to a certain country) factors. The reasons why people leave their country of origin (push factors) either through legitimate or illicit channels are the same. Countries of origin are traditionally developing nations or those in a state of transition. Migration (and trafficking) takes place from rural to municipal areas within a country and from poorer to wealthier, more stable countries, internationally.

The root causes of migration—both licit and illicit—lie in the unstable political, social, and economic conditions in countries or origin. Rapid growth of the population, high unemployment, abject poverty, internal conflicts resulting in civil disorder and widespread violence, unstable or oppressive political regimes, and grave violations of human rights have all been identified as root causes of migration and displacement (Cameron and Newman, 2008; Bales, 2007; Anti-Slavery International, 2003). Push factors include the following:

- Inadequate employment opportunities combined with poor living conditions, a lack of basic education, and poor health services
- Political and economic insecurity that may be caused by mismanagement, nepotism or political corruption, conflict, environmental disaster, or structural adjustment policies resulting in rising cost of living, in higher unemployment, and a lack of public services
- Discrimination (ethnic, gender, or caste) excluding certain persons from the employment sector
- Dissolution of the family (possibly as the result of sickness, HIV/AIDS, the death of one or both parents), which may compel the remaining family member(s) to migrate or send children away to work and help support the family

To this list, the European Police Agency (EUROPOL) has added other factors to include the abuse of human rights violations, the collapse of social infrastructure, and other environmental conditions, including conflict and war (EUROPOL, 2009).

The "pull" of promises of a better future is powerful.

The following have been identified as pull factors (Anti-Slavery International, 2003; EUROPOL, 2009):

- Increased ease of travel (cheaper and faster travel opportunities, easier access to passports)
- Higher salaries and improved standard of living in larger cities and countries abroad (greater possibilities for acquiring new skills and greater access to education, increased job opportunities, and mobility)
- Established migration routes and ethnic, national communities in destination countries

- Active demand for migrant workers in destination countries, combined with the existence of recruitment agencies and persons willing to facilitate jobs and travel
- High expectations of opportunities in other countries boosted by global media and Internet access and stories of returning migrants or those whose families have profited from the remittances

Additionally, other factors such as less discrimination or abuse than in the destination country, the enforcement of minimum standards and individual rights, as well as the demand for cheap labor, sexual services, and workers in the sex industry contribute to the pull of migrants to a country (EUROPOL, 2009).

In an exploratory test of a theory of global trafficking, Bales (2007) compiled 76 variables measuring economic activity, food production, energy consumption, basic health measures, population profile, political and civil liberties, censorship, government corruption, conflict, and social unrest, among others. Combining his own assessment of the level of slavery and human trafficking in the country, Bales empirically tested which variables were significant predictors of trafficking *from* (the push factors) and *to* (the pull factors) a country. The research identified the following "push" predictors, rank ordered, "from" a country: (1) government corruption, (2) high infant mortality, (3) a very young population, (4) low food production (an indication of poverty), and (5) conflict and social unrest (Bales, 2007).

The "pull" factors predicting trafficking "to" a country were less conclusive. The permeability of the country's border is a strong indicator of a "pull" factor, and this may be related to government corruption, particularly within border control or immigration agencies. Other factors, rank ordered, predicting the "pull" of a country were the male population over the age of 60, (low) governmental corruption, food production, energy consumption, and (low) infant mortality—all indicators of economic well-being of the destination country (Bales, 2007).

These factors will be discussed in greater detail in the remainder of this chapter.

Poverty

The root or structural causes contributing to human trafficking are numerous. One of the most salient factors is poverty. "Poverty and wealth are relative concepts which lead to both migration and trafficking patterns in which victims move from conditions of extreme poverty to conditions of less-extreme poverty" (UNODC, *Toolkit*, 424). Trafficking flows are generally from poor to wealthier countries, from rural to urban centers. The inability to feed, clothe, educate, and provide the most basic needs for one's family is a strong motivating factor for people to seek employment (or marriage) with the promise of a better life. According to the most recent statistics of the World Bank, in 2013, an estimated 767 million people were living below the international poverty line of US$1.90 per person per day (World Bank, 2016).

"Poverty is a driving factor in all forms of human trafficking on the African continent, the world's poorest according to rankings on the United Nations Development Program's (UNDP) Development Index. Of the 43 countries ranked low on UNDP's Development Index, 35 of these countries are in Africa. The eighteen countries scoring lowest on the Development Index (ranked 170–187) are in Africa" (Aronowitz, 2015a). Salah (2001) attributes the trafficking of women and children in Africa to abject poverty, inequality, and the absence of programs for the creation of employment. Those most affected are children in rural areas. "The director of UNICEF for West and Central Africa states that poverty is a 'major and ubiquitous' causal factor behind child trafficking" (Cameron and Newman, 2008, 22). Millions in Africa live below the poverty line, and child trafficking goes hand in hand with poverty and child labor.

Those that fall prey to human trafficking in a country tend to be the most vulnerable—usually the socially deprived characterized by low income, poor education, and lack of employment. These are typically circumstances of the poor, even though available data show that it is not necessarily the poorest in a country who are trafficked. Research, however, shows that many of the victims assisted by international organizations and NGOs invariably come from some of the most poverty-stricken countries (Bangladesh, Mali, Moldova, and Nepal) (Omelaniuk, 2005).

Extensive research has been undertaken on victim support provided in Southeastern Europe. There, it is shown that trafficked victims come from the poorer countries of the region—Moldova, Romania, Albania, and Bulgaria. Albania and Moldova are the poorest in the region, and are also primary source countries for trafficked persons (Omelaniuk, 2005; Limanowska, 2003, 2005). In South Asia, Bangladesh, and Nepal, two of the most poverty-stricken countries in the region, are the major source countries (Dottridge, 2002). Poverty is seen as the key factor in human trafficking in West and Central Africa and for rural trafficking in China (Dottridge, 2002; IOM, 2005).

EUROPOL has identified Bulgaria, Moldova, Romania, The Russian Federation, Ukraine, and Nigeria as major source countries for trafficking into Europe (Shelley, 2014), with Moldova, Romania, and Bulgaria being among the poorest countries in Europe.

An additional contributing factor related to poverty is that weak economies may motivate governments to encourage or even facilitate migration (to obtain remittances sent home by overseas foreign workers). This can be observed in countries where the personal remittances received are a large percentage of the GDP. In Nepal, personal remittances comprised 29 percent of the country's GDP in 2013 (World Bank, *Personal remittances, received [% of GDP]*).

Migration

Poverty, coupled with the desire or ability to migrate, is another powerful factor contributing to human trafficking. Migration can occur within a country (from rural to urban areas) or across country borders. High U.S. labor demand, limited country quotas, and the prioritization of family reunification over employment-based immigration make many migrants from less developed countries ineligible for legal entry into the United States. Migrants trying to enter "Fortress Europe" from Africa, or migrants from Malaysia and Indonesia attempting to enter Australia, meet similar obstacles. Faced with increased border patrols and heightened security at the United States, European, Canadian, and Australian ports of entry, illegal migrants increasingly rely on smugglers (and traffickers) to enter these countries. Those migrants entering or residing in a country without proper documentation—irregular migrants—are most at risk of being subjected to forced labor and exploitation, but regular migrants are also routinely denied both their human and labor rights (Anti-Slavery International, 2003). The dimensions of human trafficking cannot be accurately measured (see Chapter 2), but it is a fact that in the United States (based upon U.S. Government statistics), most confirmed victims of labor trafficking cases were identified as undocumented aliens (67%) or qualified aliens (28%) (Banks and Kyckelhahn, 2011).

Migration is intimately linked with globalization and gender inequality. In many countries, women are the first to migrate. Migration is often both easier and cheaper for women than for men. Educational and skills requirements are lower for women than for men migrating to the Middle East from Indonesia or Bangladesh. Women pay lower fees than do men and they are in greater demand in the Middle East as domestic servants (Aronowitz, 2009).

Globalization

Globalization, market liberalization, and privatization have created an increasing need for cash incomes to purchase the most basic needs, including those (in many countries) once provided by the state. Often, this demand cannot be satisfied in the local labor markets, obliging families to send family members out into the global workplace. An increasingly globalized world, easily accessible through television and the Internet, provides ready access to information about actual or potential opportunities in large cities, neighboring countries, or other destinations such as Australia, Canada, Europe, or the United States (Heyzer, 2002). As a result of globalization and access to television, Internet, or stories from persons who have returned from travel, people are exposed to different standards of living, and as a result become more aware of their relative poverty (Cameron and Newman, 2008).

Globalization "has caused increasing economic and demographic disparities between the developing and developed world" (Shelley, 2010, 2). "Unequal development is also a hallmark of globalization" (Shelley, 2010, 45). According to the ILO, there are an estimated 232 million international migrants around the world. This figure is expected to rise with globalization, income inequality, conflicts, and demographic changes (ILO, *Labour Migration*). Globalization has resulted in an unprecedented mobilization of unskilled and low-skilled labor to fill labor-deficit markets for domestic work, agriculture, construction, and manufacturing. At an ever increasing rate, migrant workers from less developed countries in South and East Asia often fill short-term labor contracts in more developed Asian, European, and Gulf State countries. In some Gulf State countries, foreign nationals comprise more than half the work force (Saudi Arabia 50.6%, Oman 74.6%, Bahrain 76.7%, Kuwait 83.2%, United Arab Emirates 85.0%, and Qatar 94.3%; Baldwin-Edwards, 2011, 9). Migrant labor supports the economies in both the sending and receiving countries, and is, in itself, beneficial. It can, however, easily lead to situations of abuse, trafficking, and conditions paramount to slavery.

Globalization goes hand in hand with free trade and the ideology of free markets accompanied by a decline in state intervention and regulation. Those who advocate globalization argue that reducing international regulations and trade barriers will increase investment, trade, and development. While globalization has contributed to the transfer of knowledge between countries, foreign investment, and international trade, at the same time it has contributed to deepening rural poverty and a rapid increase in global slavery (Kara, 2009).

The very conditions that promote a globalized environment, however, aid in the expansion of crime. Crime groups "have exploited the enormous decline in regulations, the lessened border controls, and the resultant greater freedom, to expand their activities across borders and to new regions of the world. These contacts have become more frequent, and the speed at which they occur has accelerated" (Shelley, 2006, 43–44).

Globalization has also greatly contributed to the rapid and tremendous growth in tourism facilitating the ease with which child sex tourists can find new markets in exotic places. ECPAT, the nonprofit organization to end prostitution, pornography, and trafficking in children, reports that child sex tourism is particularly prevalent in Central and South America (Mexico) and Asia (India), with Costa Rica, Cambodia, Thailand, and Brazil as some of the most popular sex tourist destinations for child sex tourism (Aronowitz, 2009; Godoy, 2007), with new destinations opening (see also ECPAT's Child Sex Tourism Fact Sheet at http://www.defenceforchildren.nl/images/13/1313.pdf).

Gender Inequality

Human trafficking is highly gender-specific, affecting girls and women worldwide. Gender is a social and cultural construction influencing a society's expectation of the roles and behaviors associated with a person's sex (either male or female). Gender is a social construction "that significantly contributes to a person's life chances and participation in society" (Cameron and Newman, 2008, 38).

Gender roles are specific to a society and influence the treatment of individuals, their interaction with other individuals in society, and their employment opportunities. Trafficking often affects women and female children due to the fact that fewer resources are provided for their education, medical care, the development of job skills, and employment opportunities in many societies in Africa and Latin America as well as parts of Asia (Shelley, 2010). In societies where resources are limited (India, Nepal, Central and West Africa), parents choose to educate their sons (Cameron and Newman, 2008).

Strict gender discrimination and patriarchal views toward women place strong emphasis on chastity and honor in certain countries, which in turn places women at extreme risk of trafficking, and it enhances victims' fear of coming forward with accusations of exploitation. In 2006, Iran publicly hung a 16-year-old victim of trafficking for sexual exploitation. She was convicted of "engaging in acts incompatible with chastity" (Hepburn and Simon, 2014, 199).

A study of trafficking among Nigerian girls and women in Edo State, conducted by the Nigerian NGO, Girls Power Initiative, attributes the reason why girls are more susceptible to trafficking abroad than boys and young men to a number of factors. First and foremost, there is a demand for their sexual services that makes them marketable commodities. Girls are expected to sacrifice their education and assume domestic responsibilities taking care of their parents and siblings. Since they leave the family upon marriage, they are regarded as a poor investment, and this makes it easier for the parent(s) to send them out to work. Additionally, domestic work is regarded as a preparation for marriage. Because girls are more willing to make a sacrifice to support their families, parents prefer to send their daughters abroad. Low rates of education among young girls—due to the fact that their parents were unwilling or unable to educate them—result in high rates of unemployment. According to Antonio Maria Costa, former director of the UNODC, "When families (in Asian villages) sell their daughter, it's not out of poverty necessarily, it may be cultural" (Heinrich, 2007). All of this combined provides a "pool of girls to be trafficked abroad" (the study by Girls Power Initiative, 2002, an NGO operating in Edo State, cited in Okojie, 2003, 14).

The custom of early and arranged marriage of young girls, particularly to an older man, may be viewed as a manner to relieve the poverty of her family, but puts young girls at risk of being trafficked (UNICEF, 2003). In other countries, female children are viewed as an economic liability, when the family must produce a dowry to the groom upon marriage. Further, there is a demand for young girls (virgins) in many African (Tlou, 2002) and South Asian countries (UNDP, 2007), fueled by the false belief that sex with a virgin can cure sexually transmitted diseases or HIV/AIDS (UNDP, Trafficking).

In some societies, female children are seen as a bartering tool and a way out of poverty or to pay off debts for families. About 40 and 49 percent of young girls in Central and Western Africa, respectively, are "sold" for early marriage (UNICEF, 2003). In Afghanistan, it has been reported that men whose opium crops have failed or been destroyed and who are unable to repay loans to drug warlords give their young daughters away in marriage as payment for debt (U.S. Department of State, 2014). Research carried out by an Afghani schoolteacher and local television reporter found that "opium weddings" are not uncommon in parts of Afghanistan. In two of Nangarhar's districts, she interviewed more than 100 families and found approximately half the weddings were arranged as repayment for opium debts. Girls tend to be young teenagers, often promised to older men. Among the new brides were children as young as five who are used as domestic servants in their in-laws' home until they are old enough to consummate the marriage. The researcher documented cases of suicide among the young girls (Yousafzai et al., 2008).

A further factor discriminating against girls and women is tied to rules of inheritance. The fact that girls and women are excluded from inheriting and owning land in many countries results in their marginalization, poverty, and high risk of being trafficked (Dottridge, 2002).

According to the Asian Development Bank (2003, 47), the feminization of poverty in South Asian countries puts women at greater risk of being trafficked. Evidence exists that women are disproportionately poor and "disproportionately excluded from development through deeply rooted gender-based discrimination." More recent data from the United Nations Development Program's Human Development Report show that despite the fact that women's life expectancy is higher than men's in the eight countries in South Asia, the quality of their life is poorer. Women have less access to education, and if they are employed, their earning power is limited and they earn considerably less than men. In Afghanistan, men earn six times more than women, in Pakistan men earn more than four times and in India men earn more than three times the salary of women. The Asian Development Bank concludes that "it would appear that there is considerable feminization of poverty in South Asia" (2003, 47).

What puts women at greater risk of trafficking during a migration experience is the fact that industries are gendered. Women and girls tend to be trafficked into the more informal sectors of

Table 1.2 Indicators Comparing Gender Gaps for Countries in South Asia

Country	Life Expectancy		Years Schooling		GNI PPP 2013	
	F	M	F	M	F	M
Afghanistan	62.2	59.7	1.2	5.1	US$503	US$3,265
Bangladesh	71.5	69.9	4.6	5.6	US$1,928	US$3,480
Bhutan	68.7	68.0	–	–	US$5,419	US$7,942
India	68.3	64.7	3.2	5.6	US$2,277	US$7,833
Maldives	79.0	76.9	5.4	6.2	US$7,504	US$12,608
Nepal	69.6	67.3	2.4	4.2	US$1,857	US$2,554
Pakistan	36.5	65.7	3.3	6.1	US$1,707	US$7,439
Sri Lanka	77.4	71.2	10.7	9.4	US$5,078	US$13,616

GNI PPP is gross national income (GNI) converted to international dollars, using purchasing power parity (PPP) rates.

Source: UNDP Human Development Reports Table 5: Gender-related development index (GDI). http://hdr.undp.org/en/content/table-5-gender-related-development-index-gdi

prostitution or domestic service, whereas men and boys tend to be trafficked into more traditional labor sectors. For example, Togolese boys are trafficked into farm labor, while girls from Togo are trafficked into domestic service (it was found that the boys were released after a period of time, whereas the girls escaped their traffickers after prolonged periods of mental and physical abuse); Nepalese boys are trafficked to India to work in garment factories, while Nepalese girls are trafficked to the same country to work in prostitution. Both are exploited, but their experiences are very different (Cameron and Newman, 2008).

Social Hierarchy and Discrimination (Minority Status)

Article 1 of the United Nations Minorities Declaration refers to minorities as based on national or ethnic, cultural, religious, and linguistic identity (UN Office of the High Commissioner for Human Rights). If susceptibility to trafficking is impacted and increased by powerful factors, like disenfranchisement, poverty, lack of education, and access to the job market, then it follows that minority populations are likely to be prime targets for human traffickers (Box, no date). Poverty, compounded by discrimination and systemic inequality, severely limits minority group job prospects, resulting in an increased likelihood of exploitation. Trafficking and exploitation has been documented among the Roma in Albania, Romania, and Bulgaria (Omelaniuk, 2005, 5) and indigenous people in Bolivia, Paraguay, and Peru (Bedoya et al., 2009). From the Gaugaz in Moldova to the Roma in Europe, to the Hill Tribes in Northern Thailand and the Rohingya from Burma, to indigenous peoples in Bolivia, Paraguay, and Peru (Bedoya et al., 2009), ethnic minorities have faced challenges in almost every country in which they reside. Due to marginalization in many aspects of their lives, ethnic minorities and those of low social caste are at particular risk of being trafficked and exploited, and suffer once again as services (health, educational, and employment opportunities, among others) to these groups are often limited.

Discrimination against non-Muslim foreign workers (many are Hindus from India and Nepal, Buddhists from Sri Lanka, or Catholics from the Philippines) in the Gulf States is a factor contributing to the exploitation of foreign workers, who make up a large percentage of the workforce in many of these countries. Historically, mistrust of foreign workers has existed in the region, as they were perceived to influence the security and structure of society and endanger the cultural identity of their host country (Abella, 1995; Kapiszewski, 2006). Nationals are concerned about the negative influence of foreign workers on the national identities, values, and cultures of their countries, and in particular, fear foreign teachers and domestic helpers/nannies who might educate and raise the children "without proper attention being given to Islamic and Arabic values" (Kapiszewski, 2006, 12). Additionally, foreign workers in the region are not just feared, but are also despised. When asked how Qataris view foreign workers who are there building the infrastructure in the country for the 2022 World Soccer Cup, Sharan Burrows, General Secretary of The International Trade Union Confederation, replied, "I don't think they [the Qataris] see them [foreign guest workers] as human" (see the documentary *Qatar's World Cup*, https://vimeo.com/95215527, accessed on March 3, 2015).

The black Hratine are the "slave caste" in Mauritania to white descendants of the Moors. The Hratine may be born into slavery or bought, sold, and traded. Children of slaves are considered property of the slave owners, and it is for this reason that Anti-Slavery International refers to this as descent-based slavery. Women, who often work in the master's household, face double discrimination as women and as members of the slave caste (see Anti-Slavery International at http://www.anti slavery.org/english/slavery_today/descent_based_slavery/slavery_in_mauritania/default.aspx).

Traditional Practices

In many parts of the world, traditional practices contribute to the exploitation of persons, often children. Polygamy has been described as a "value system" in many countries in sub-Saharan Africa and is practiced particularly in rural areas. It helps maintain a high level of fertility and has contributed to what Hayase and Liaw (1997, 293) refer to as the "explosive population growth in sub-Saharan African countries since the 1950s." A widow often remarries another male in the family of her deceased husband, usually a brother. The large number of children produced within these polygamous marriages can put a financial strain on the family, which may influence the decision to place (some of) the children with other families. The majority of trafficked children in sub-Saharan Africa come from large, poorly educated, and often polygamous families, where opportunities for education and training are limited for children (ILO, 2001). Parents who cannot support their children are often willing to "give" them to traffickers in the false belief that the child will be given an education, training, or a job (ILO, 2001; UNICEF, 2002; Aronowitz, 2015a).

The trafficking of children in West and Central Africa is promoted by historical and cultural patterns of child fosterage, or placing children outside the home. The placement of children outside the home is based on cultural values, is done to foster extended family solidarity and to further the educational and vocational training of the child (Howard, 2011; De Lange, 2009; Aronowitz, 2006; Manzo, 2005; Bazzi-Veil, 2000). This historical practice of child apprenticeship, known as child fosterage or "vidomegon" ("putting a child in a home," often a female child), contributes to the internal displacement and trafficking of children, which is met with, if not acceptance, then less outrage than the trafficking of children abroad (Aronowitz, 2006). Children are introduced to work at very young ages, and as a result of this are taught social values. It is a common belief that the life and education of a child is the responsibility of the extended family; thus, it is not uncommon for children to grow up in the family of relatives or third persons, particularly if these persons are living in better circumstances and are able to provide the child with better educational and work opportunities (Aronowitz and Peruffo, 2003).

The voluntary placement of children (which often leads to their trafficking) is the result of poverty and the desire to provide a better life for their children (Verbeet, 2000). The child's biological parents may receive a financial incentive from the receiving family or promises are made to pay the child, but this rarely occurs. The practice of child fosterage, according to Truong (2006, 64), "has been distorted into a commercial transaction." Rather than being a practice of placing the child for the benefit of the child's future, it has been corrupted to one of viewing the child as an income-generating opportunity. Whether the child is placed for economic or altruistic purposes, child fosterage can easily lead to the exploitation of children who are located in homes with no supervision. "This 'strategic fostering out of children' is said to be a stronger causal factor in child trafficking than poverty" (Aronowitz, 2006, 27, referencing e-mail correspondence between Anne Kielland and Human Rights Watch, cited in Human Rights Watch, 2003, 13; Kielland cites a report by Bazzi-Veil, "Traffic des enfants en Afrique de l'Ouest et du Centre"; World Bank; Aronowitz, 2015a).

Another traditional practice is linked to voodoo, or the West African practice of juju, to traffic hundreds of young Nigerian women into prostitution in Western European countries. Large numbers of Nigerian girls began arriving in the Netherlands as unaccompanied minors in the early 1990s. They were granted asylum. After a few years, they began surfacing throughout the Netherlands in various red-light districts in prostitution. Stories emerged of voodoo practices binding the girls to their traffickers and causing them to be terrified of cooperating with the authorities. In Nigeria, a lock of hair, a fingernail clipping, or piece of (intimate) clothing was used in a ritual performed by a priest. This binds the victims to their traffickers. Victims are forced to swear an oath, and failure to respect the oath results in misfortune befalling the girls or their families (Aronowitz, 2015a; referencing Van Dijk, 2001; Aghatise, 2005; Siegel and De Blank, 2010). It is alleged that the trafficked women are so fearful of these oaths that Italian police note that compared to other foreign women trafficked into prostitution in Italy, Nigerian women are subjected to much less physical supervision and control (Aghatise, 2005). What is clear is that local religious traditions, the belief in magic, and rituals played a role in the trafficking of young Nigerian women to Europe, although it is not clear to what degree voodoo played a part in the control of these young girls in prostitution in the Netherlands. It is better understood as a symbolic action to seal a promise (Van Dijk, 2001), but one that appears to have frightened young women into submission.

A traditional practice in another very different part of the world has been linked to the sexual abuse of young boys in Afghanistan—*Bacha bazi*, the practice of dressing prepubescent boys in women's clothing to have them dance at parties before all-male audiences (after which the boys may be given to the highest bidder to be sexually abused). This practice has been closely linked to tribal leaders and members of the Pashtun ethnic group. The Pashtun traditional practice of *halekon*—taking boys from their families to integrate them into the collective fighting groups or using them as apprentices—has a long history (Martin and Shaheen, 2014). During this process, they are also sexually objectified and abused (Londoño, 2012a,b). Pashtun literature praises the love of older men for beautiful young boys (Schut and Van Baarle, 2014; De Lind van Wijngaarden and Rani, 2011; HTT, 2009; Reynolds, 2002). The socially acceptable practice by mujahedeen of keeping young male sexual partners during the war greatly facilitated the practice and the widespread acceptance of *bacha bazi* among certain members of society. This intimate association between men and young boys is further exacerbated by the strict patriarchal attitudes and segregation and marginalization of women in Afghan society (Aronowitz, 2015a).

In the West African country of Niger, one of the poorest countries in the world (ranked lowest of all 187 countries on the United Nations Human Development Index for 2014), the practice of *Wahaya* is practiced mainly in the Tahoua region, and more particularly in the Illela, Bouza, Madaoua, and Konni districts. This practice contributes to the exploitation of young girls. In a predominantly Islamic country, where men are allowed to marry up to four wives, the practice of *Wahaya* allows for the buying and selling of young girls to become the "fifth wife," although they have no access to the legal rights accorded the first four legitimate wives. In a study of the *Wahaya* practice, women reported being sold between the ages of 9 and 11. More than 8 in 10 girls (83%) were under the age of 15 when they were sold. These girls and women, often of the slave caste, are used as domestic and sexual slaves, and exploited as property by dignitaries (mostly wealthy men or religious leaders). In addition to providing sexual services to the master, *Wahayu* (the plural of *Wahaya*) are subjected to physical abuse by the legitimate wives of the slave owner. Although a *Wahaya* has no legal rights, any child born to her is recognized by her owner and may become an heir to his fortune (Abdelkader and Zangaou, 2012).

Demographic Factors

Demographic inequality in certain parts of the world creates a gender imbalance with a lack of eligible women for marriage, forcing men to seek wives outside their community. This situation in China can be attributed to the government's family planning policy (commonly known as the one-child policy), coupled with a preference for male children. Chinese families, preferring a male child to carry on the family name and inheritance, may abandon or abort female fetuses or put the child up for adoption to foreigners (Davis, 2006). This skewed sex ratio of 117 males to 100 females in China is expected, by 2020, to result in a surplus of 40 million men in China looking for wives. With lower social and economic status males unable to compete for suitable mates, they must find alternative means of finding a bride (Bielke, 2004). According to the U.S. Department of State (2014, 132), this skewed sex ratio "may serve to increase the demand for prostitution and for foreign women as brides for Chinese men—both of which may be procured by force or coercion. Women and girls from Burma, Vietnam, Mongolia, Cambodia, Laos, and North Korea are recruited through marriage brokers and transported to China, where some are subsequently subjected to forced prostitution or forced labor."

Gender imbalances in Bangladesh, India, Nepal, and other South Asian countries can be attributed to a different factor. "The negative sex ratio can be attributed to excess mortality of women and girls resulting from both direct and indirect discrimination in the provision of food, care, medical treatment, education, and above all physical and sexual violence" (Asian Development Bank, 2003, 49).

A second demographic factor contributing to a greater likelihood of trafficking in a country or region is the explosive population growth, affecting the developing world. Annual population growth is highest in a number of sub-Saharan African countries, among them Angola, Benin, Burkina Faso, Burundi, Cameroon, Eritrea, Ethiopia, The Gambia, Guinea, Guinea Bissau, Liberia, Madagascar, Malawi, Mali, Mozambique, Niger, Nigeria, Senegal, South Sudan, Tanzania, Togo, Uganda, Zambia, and Zimbabwe (see World Bank, *Population Growth* at http://data.worldbank.org/indicator/SP.POP.GROW). Every one of these countries, with the exception of Zambia, scores low on the Human Development Index (Zambia is rated as a Medium development country, South Sudan is not rated; see UNDP's *Human Development Reports*, Table 1: Human Development Index and its components at http://hdr.undp.org/en/content/table-1-human-development-index-and-its-components).

A large percentage of the population in African countries is below the age of 15 (41%), compared to the population under 15 in the rest of the world (26%) (Population Reference

Bureau, http://www.prb.org/DataFinder/Geography/Data.aspx?
loc=246). A very young population in countries with high
unemployment puts children at risk of being exploited by recruiters with promises of employment. According to the ILO
(2010), at 25.3 percent, sub-Saharan Africa boasts the highest proportion of children engaged in child labor of any region in the world. Approximately, one child in every four is a
child laborer. High population growth only partly explains the
high level of trafficking in this region of the world. According
to the ILO, "the AIDS pandemic, recurrent food crises, and
political unrest and conflict clearly exacerbate the problem"
of exploitative child labor (ILO, no date, Child Labor in Africa, http://ilo.org/ipec/Regionsandcountries/Africa/lang—en/
index.htm).

Gender imbalances may also be "created" in certain industries, what the U.S. Department of State (2015) refers to as
extractive industries. Where large concentration of men work,
the demand for commercial sexual services increases. Peruvian
and Bolivian girls are said to have been trafficked to mining
areas in Peru, while sex trafficking of women and girls near
gold mines have been reported in Suriname and Guyana. Children are sexually exploited near mines in Madagascar.

Political Instability and Conflict

Political instability contributes to migration from a country
putting (irregular) migrants at the mercy of smugglers and traffickers. Regional conflicts were the cause of migration from
areas such as Kosovo (the former Yugoslavia), the Congo, and
Dafur (Sudan). Political and religious persecution has been the
push factor from nations such as China and Russia (Aronowitz,
2001; Cameron and Newman, 2008). As a result of war and
political instability and insecurity in Iraq, the United Nations
estimates that millions have been displaced, either internally or
into neighboring countries (UNHCR, 2015), resulting in dev-
astating health care, increased infant mortality, and an increased
lack of access to clean water and sanitation (Watson Institute,

2015). The United Nations Refugee Agency, UNHCR, estimates that 4,013,000 people have fled their country (Jones and Shaheen, 2015).

The situation is as pressing for Syrians, with the UNHCR registering over 4 million (4,015,070) refugees in Egypt, Iraq, Jordan, Lebanon, and Turkey. Daily news reports thousands of Syrian refugees attempting to enter the European Union through Macedonia. The UN refugee agency, the UNHCR, has expressed concern for "thousands of vulnerable refugees and migrants, especially women and children, now massed on the Greek side of the border amid deteriorating conditions" (BBC, 2015a).

Migration, internally displaced persons, and migrant smuggling tends to increase during times of conflict. And while it is impossible to document the degree to which trafficking increases during times of war or armed conflict, anecdotal evidence supports the allegation. This is due, in part, to the collapse of State institutions and border controls, and an increase in lawlessness—all factors that increase the risk of trafficking in persons, in particular, women and children.

According to the United Nations, the breakdown of law and order, combined with the increased demand for sexual services by members of the military and/or fighting factions, can lead to a situation where a conflict area becomes a destination for human trafficking. Organized criminal groups take advantage of the chaotic conditions to run trafficking operations, knowing that the chances of detection are minimized (UNICRI, 2006). Forms of trafficking vary according to the nature of the armed conflict and "the specific political and economic factors on the ground." While in many cases, children and women are used for prostitution, male children have been used as soldiers and suicide bombers in Afghanistan, Iraq, Pakistan, Syria, and Yemen (U.S. Department of State, 2015). A common thread, however, is that women and children, who constitute the majority of internally displaced persons, are the most vulnerable to traffickers (UNICRI, 2006; Hepburn and Simon, 2013).

The link between prostitution and the military is well documented. Military servicemen deployed far from home have been a "long-standing source of demand for sexual services from local populations" (Burke, 2013; citing Fisanick, 2010). American soldiers, during the Vietnam War, used military-inspected and certified prostitutes during "rest and recreation" breaks in Thailand, Vietnam, and the Philippines (Allred, 2005, 64). U.S. military stationed in South Korea drew "entertainers" from Southeast Asia (Omelaniuk, 2005). According to one expert, the U.S. military deployed abroad in combat and peacekeeping operations may be "one of the largest sources of demand for sexual services around the world, some of which would likely be provided by trafficked women" (Allred, 2005, 65).

War and Peacekeepers

In order to support countries trying to stabilize and rebuild after war, international assistance initiatives provide monitoring, maintenance, the establishment of peace, and prevention of resurgent violent conflict. Peacekeeping operations support and monitor the building of peace, while peace enforcement operations create conditions of peace but are allowed to use force. Both of these are forms of Peace Support Operations (PSOs) (Johnston, 2004). The UN staff are a small minority of peacekeeping missions. The majority of soldiers serving in these missions are "on loan" from troop-contributing countries. These troops are members of their own military and the United Nations has no disciplinary authority over them (Allred, 2006).

According to the United Nations Interregional Crime and Justice Research Center, the links between human trafficking and PSOs are threefold. First, the international community is the only or primary source of law enforcement, and therefore the primary authority for combating human trafficking. Second, in most PSO situations, the staff is paid a wage much higher than that earned by the communities they serve. This advantage may make them the primary source of demand for domestic labor and trafficked persons in brothels. Last, members of PSOs have been directly implicated in human trafficking (UNICRI, no date). The United Nations Department for Peacekeeping Operations has recognized that these operations "trigger human trafficking rings in the regions in which they operate because of the mass influx of a relatively wealthy, predominantly male peacekeeper population potentially interested in purchasing sexual and other services from trafficked women and girls" (Johnston, 2004, 41).

United Nations observer, peacekeeping, stabilization, or disengagement forces are currently serving in the following countries—Americas: Haiti; Africa: Abyei, the Central African Republic, Côte d'Ivoire, Darfur, The Democratic Republic of Congo, Liberia, Mali, South Sudan, and Western Sahara; Europe: Cyprus and Kosovo; Middle East: Lebanon, "Middle East," and Syria; Asia: India and Pakistan (for a complete list of UN Missions, see the website of the UN Department of Peacekeeping Operations at http://www.un.org/en/peacekeeping/operations/current.shtml). While most of the deployed soldiers serve without incident, there have been documented cases or allegations of peacekeeping troops from Cambodia, East Timor, Morocco, Nepal, Pakistan, South Africa, Tunisia, Uruguay, and countries in West Africa involved in allegations of pedophilia, prostitution, and rape, while commanders failed to investigate or protect whistleblowers (Allred, 2006). The arrival of peacekeepers in post-conflict countries was found to be responsible for the rise in childhood prostitution (Allred, 2006).

The 50,000 peacekeepers that were deployed to Bosnia and Herzegovina in the early 1990s were directly responsible for the trafficking in women for prostitution, which "sprang up overnight outside the gates of the UN compounds." According to a regional human rights officer in Bosnia after the war, "The sex slave trade in Bosnia largely exists because of the UN peacekeeping operation. Without the peacekeeping presence, there would have been little or no forced prostitution in Bosnia"

(Allred, 2009, 306; quoting David Lamb, UN Human Rights Investigator in Bosnia during 2000 and 2001). Investigations were carried out to determine the involvement of the UN policing officials in the sex slave trade in Bosnia, and enough evidence was found to justify a full-scale criminal investigation into the matter. In addition to visiting brothels where trafficked women were kept, cases were reported of members of the Stabilization Force (SFOR) and International Police Task Force members involved in the actual trafficking of women. In three cases, International Police Task Force monitors purchased women and their passports from traffickers and brothel owners (testimony of Martina Vandenburg of Human Rights Watch to the U.S. House Committee on International Relations 2002, and documented in Bolkovac's 2011 book, *The Whistleblower*).

By patronizing brothels in which trafficked victims were held, or purchasing them directly from brothel owners, military and civilian contractors operating under UN impunity abused the human rights of their trafficked victims, and also further supported organized crime, which ran the brothels and trafficked the women. Revenues generated through trafficking are used to corrupt law enforcement and to invest in the further growth of the trade (Shelley, 2003b).

The Washington-based Center for Strategic and International Studies, in its report "Barracks and Brothels," wrote, "The United Nations has an especially troubling track record of peacekeeper involvement in trafficking as well as in other forms of sexual exploitation in conflict and post-conflict regions. Yet decision makers at the UN seem to fear that creating a taboo against trafficking for peacekeepers will negatively affect the UN's ability to attract peacekeepers" (Mendelson, 2005, ix). Chapter 2 of this book addresses measures that have been taken by the UN Department of Peacekeeping Operations to rectify the problem.

Technology

By November 2016, almost 3.5 billion people (almost 46 percent of the world's population) were connected to the Internet (http://www.internetlivestats.com/internet-users/). The use of the Internet and social media are rapidly expanding and are being used for the recruitment of victims, advertising their services, live streaming of sexual abuse of children, and as a forum to connect people with common interests (such as pedophiles looking for the best vacation spot to find and abuse children). Meetings between victims and clients are organized through dedicated websites, as are the meetings between men and mail order brides who, too, may become victims of trafficking. Technological advances, such as disposable mobile phones and messages that disappear (as in Snapchat), have made it easier for criminals to conceal their activities. According to EUROPOL, "[a]nonymity and the mass audience of online services increases both the discretion and profitability of these services, making it very hard to identify criminals using traditional police techniques" (EUROPOL, 2011, 11).

An example of the ease and profitability of Internet operations is documented in the story of an undercover report by ITN news on the trade of Czech women to the United Kingdom. Reporter Chris Rogers established an Internet cover operation, EUrotica, in the United Kingdom, and then traveled to the Czech Republic to discuss with traffickers the possibility of securing women for his U.K. brothels. The girls, he was told, were for rent for a period of six months. The rental price for a woman, who would be delivered to the United Kingdom, was 5,000 British pounds—3,000 of which was to be paid upfront and the remainder upon delivery of the woman. Half of her earnings would be paid to the brothel owner in the United Kingdom, the other half to the traffickers in the Czech Republic. To provide an idea of the huge amount of money generated by prostitution, Rogers told CNN that within two hours of launching his website, the Internet company had received 400 bookings for prostitutes, and within a week, 1,000 bookings had been made. If only half of the bookings were realized, his "organization" would have made 20,000 pounds in a two-week period (Aronowitz, 2009; Rogers, 2008).

The Internet and affordable global travel have facilitated the ease with which men are now able to find a foreign wife. In a report on Internet recruitment, carried out for the Council of Europe in 2007, a simple Google search turned up 128,000 "suspect" Internet sites advertising modeling, dating, escort, and marriage services. What made the sites suspect is the fact that women came from poor and often rural areas in countries known as source countries for human trafficking, or marriage sites used "subtle, but often blatant sexualized photographs of the women . . . to appeal to men" (Council of Europe, 2007, 32). This is not clear proof of trafficking, but trafficked victims may be hidden amongst the more legitimate offers on such sites (Hughes, 2004).

The company, A Foreign Affair, at www.loveme.com, boasts on its Internet site that it is not a "Mail Order Bride company, but the largest and most respected International Introduction and Singles Tour Company in the industry," offering upcoming singles tours to cities in Colombia, Dominican Republic, Peru, Ukraine, China, Thailand, and The Philippines, among others (http://www.loveme.com)—poor countries from which women are often trafficked into exploitation.

Mail order bride agencies are not per se "fronts" for the recruitment of trafficked victims. However, in her testimony on Human Trafficking: Mail Order Bride Abuses before the U.S. Senate, Hughes (2004) argued that with agencies maintaining a database with extensive information on single women—and their families—who have expressed a desire to go abroad, it is not difficult to imagine how these agencies could use that information to coerce women into prostitution and thus be involved in trafficking. In her testimony before the U.S. Senate, one expert reported that workers in the St. Petersburg (Russia) Psychological Crisis Center for Women had heard of Russian women being recruited by marriage agencies, and then trafficked into prostitution. This same pattern was confirmed by NGOs operating in countries of the former Soviet Union (Aronowitz, 2009).

The demand for child pornography is enormous, and law enforcement and researchers believe the production and trade in child pornography is increasing, facilitated by the growing use of the Internet (Wolak, 2005). According to the international police agency, INTERPOL, one company in the United States that sold access to child pornography sites at US$29.95 each grossed US$5.5 million in five months of operation (Tomiuc, 2003).

High speed Internet access has allowed for the real-time streaming of live sex shows that may use children or trafficked persons. The international and borderless nature of the Internet means that a viewer may be on one continent, while watching a live sex show or the sexual abuse of a child on another (Hughes, 1998).

Traffickers who recruit and use victims (in particular, children) for pornography via websites may differ from traffickers who use the Internet to recruit women via escort services, dating, or marriage, or employment websites (in which there must be personal contact between the trafficker and the victim). In the case of trafficking for pornography via the Internet, the victim does not even have to leave his or her home, and may, in fact, be unaware of the sexual exploitation (Council of Europe, 2007). Child sex offenders may groom children to perform sexual activities online while they are being recorded. "Webcam Child Sex Tourism" occurs "when adults pay or offer other rewards in order to direct and view live streaming video footage of children in another country performing sexual acts in front of a webcam" (Terre des Hommes, 2014, 1). Children either work out of their homes (often forced by parents to perform), from Internet cafés, or from cyber dens (Internet companies owned by traffickers forcing the children to perform). Contact is established through one of the estimated "40,000 public chatrooms where one can encounter paedophiles with 100% certainty" (Terre des Hommes, 2014, 2).

In order to address the demand side of webcam child sex tourism, Terre des Hommes launched "Sweetie-1000"—a sting operation in the guise of a 3-D computer-generated model resembling a 10-year-old girl from the Philippines. To get a sense of the size of the global demand for webcam child sex tourism, the researchers conducted extensive field research into public online chat rooms. Four researchers spent a combined total of 1,600 hours in a sample of 19 public chat rooms, over the course of 10 weeks. Over 20,000 predators from all over the world initiated contact, seeking webcam sex shows from what they thought was a 10-year-old female Filipina child. As a result of their proactive investigation, 1,000 predators from 71 different countries were identified (Terre des Hommes, 2014).

Alternatively, the offender may use Internet chat sites to recruit children who they later anticipate meeting and exploiting. The television reality show *NBC Dateline* ran a series of undercover sting operations in various cities portraying adult men who had been chatting online with what they thought was a minor. These men showed up at the home of the minor—who, in fact, was an adult volunteer working for the Internet watchdog agency Perverted Justice—anticipating a sexual liaison, only to be recorded by hidden cameras. Some of the men had sent suggestive or explicitly sexual material to the "child," prepping him or her for the encounter. As of November 2016, 623 persons have been convicted (for more, see the Perverted Justice website at http://www.perverted-justice.com/).

Supply and Demand

Whether for labor or sexual exploitation, human trafficking cannot be fully understood without looking at the question of supply and demand. There is an almost endless supply of persons willing to leave a country in search of a better future for themselves and their family. In an empirical econometric analysis of determinants of sex trafficking, the ILO (Danailova-Trainor and Belser, 2006) identified the most important supply factor contributing to human trafficking. Especially for females, supply into the sex market is influenced by youth underemployment or unemployment in a country. A statistical correlation exists between the level of female youth unemployment and the number of victims trafficked out of a country.

Throughout history and across countries, demand has always existed for prostitution and workers in the commercial sex market as well as domestic servants and slaves. In highly developed nations, and as societies progress, there is the demand for cheap, unskilled labor—construction, domestic service, home health care, the agricultural, and food processing sectors (Heyzer, 2002; Shelley, 2010). While Danailova-Trainor and Belser (2006) claim that demand for trafficked victims is higher in countries that are more open to globalization, this has been disputed by Heller et al. (2016), who found that economically free countries are not associated with higher levels of human trafficking, and that they are more likely to enact and enforce anti-trafficking policies.

Traditional market theories state that demand influences the supply (to meet the demand); however, this may not be the case in human trafficking. Anderson and O'Connell Davidson (2003, 41), in a multicountry study of the demand side of human trafficking for commercial sexual services and domestic labor, found that demand for such services was "a socially, culturally and historically determined matter . . . intimately related to questions concerning supply and vulnerability . . . supply generates demand rather than the other way around." The availability of a service, they argue, generates demand— whether it is for prostitutes, lap dance clubs, or live-in domestic workers. It has been argued that it is the market or availability in trafficked women that creates the demand, not the customers (Aronowitz and Koning, 2014).

Demand for (trafficked) sex workers is generated by three distinct groups. The first group comprises *customers or clients* of trafficked persons that generates *primary demand*. The second and third groups are the *employers* (owners or managers of brothels or massage parlors, or producers of pornographic films) and *third parties* involved in the trafficking process (recruiters, travel or employment agents, transporters). These two groups expect to generate revenues from human trafficking and create what is referred to as *derived demand*. With respect to the sex industry, the demand generated by customers is said to be the "most immediate and proximate cause," contributing to the expansion of the sex industry. Were it not for men's demand to purchase sex, pimps, recruiters, and traffickers would not generate a profit and "the prostitution market would go broke" (Raymond, 2004, 1160).

Demand is heavily influenced not only by price, cost, and revenue, but also by social and cultural contexts, attitudes, and practices within a country, and is more prevalent among certain occupational groups (soldiers, truck drivers) (Aronowitz and Koning, 2014). The exploitation of women in the booming billion-dollar commercial sex and entertainment industry is driven by "the unequal power relations that exist in patriarchal societies, power relations that sexualize women and objectify them for consumption" (Goward, 2003), which are more prevalent in certain societies and cultures than they are in others. According to Shelley, "[m]en frequenting prostitutes is deeply engrained in the culture of many Asian societies" (Shelley, 2010, 143).

According to Hughes (2005), two other components support the demand side of human trafficking. These are (1) the laws and policies toward exploited labor and prostitution in destination countries (Hughes, 2005, 8), and (2) the culture that condones or promotes (sexual) exploitation. Hughes argues that laws that legalize prostitution contribute to the demand for trafficked women. Others disagree, though. A culture that condones prostitution (measured by countries in which prostitution is legal, such as Germany and the Netherlands) does not condone sexual exploitation and human trafficking. Weitzer (2015b) also argues that there is no empirical support for the argument that countries with legalized prostitution have more cases of human trafficking.

The degree to which a culture condones the purchase of sex can perhaps be measured by the percentage of men in a society who purchase sex, and how this behavior is viewed. This figure varies widely between cultures and countries. A small-scale pilot study on the primary (customer) demand side of trafficking involved surveys and interviews with clients who had and men who had not purchased sex acts in Denmark, India, Italy, and Thailand. The study found significant differences between countries with regard to the extent and nature of the social acceptance of men to purchase sex. While, for instance, Danish men said they never experienced social pressure to buy sex, Thai men viewed purchasing sex acts as "part of a rite of passage, as well as a ritual to consolidate relationships with male friends" (Anderson and O'Connell Davidson, 2003,17).

One study (Månsson, 2004) found that visits to prostitutes by male clients in Europe ranged from a low of 7 percent in Great Britain, followed by Russia (10%), Norway (11%), Finland (13%), Sweden (13%), the Netherlands (14%), Switzerland (19%), to a high of 39 percent in Spain. A small-scale study of the percentage of men who purchase sex acts in Asian countries appears to be higher: 37 percent in Japan and 73 percent in Thailand reported having paid for a sexual contact (Anderson and O'Connell Davidson, 2003,17). Monto (1999; citing the National Health and Life Survey, 1992) found that 16 percent of men had ever purchased a sex act, but only 0.6 percent of men did so on a regular basis. Gleaning information from 21 studies conducted between 1994 and 2010, the organization Procon provides high and low estimates for the percentage of men who have paid for sex at least once in 15 different countries. Cambodia and Thailand rank highest with estimates of 80 and 75 percent respectively, followed by Italy (45%), Spain (39%), Japan (37%), the Netherlands (21.6%), the United States (20%), China (20.0%), Switzerland (19%), France (16%), Australia (15.6%), Sweden (13.6%), Finland (13%), Norway (12.9%), and the United Kingdom (8.8%) (Procon, 2011). It is clear from these studies that demand, prostitution, and trafficking markets must be studied within the specific context of a given country and—as laws and attitudes change—at a given time.

The study of human trafficking from a market (supply and demand) perspective must not ignore that which brings together the supply of persons and those demanding their services. Derived demand generated by managers of massage parlors and brothel owners is a linking pin between supply and primary (customer) demand. The presence of organized crime brings them together (Shelley, 2010). According to Kara (2009, 22), the level of complexity, sophistication, and coordination of organized crime groups across the globe is "astounding." International mafias from Albania, Romania, Moldova, and Nigeria collaborate with local Italian mafia groups to traffic victims to and from the country. Trafficking from the Mekong subregion by organized criminal groups facilitates the movement of victims into Thailand, from Bangladesh, Nepal, and Pakistan into Indian brothels (Kara, 2009).

Facilitators of Human Trafficking

Other factors, such as porous borders, corruption, policies at reception centers or work visa loopholes do not "cause," but facilitate human trafficking.

Porous borders between countries or visa-free travel between countries in particular regions (Schengen in the European Union, countries of the Commonwealth of Independent States, travel between the borders of Nepal and India) facilitates the movement of people without (legitimate) papers. Once entering the European Union, travel between the countries is, for the most part, unmonitored. Tribal affiliations between members of the Yoruba ethnic group, found in Southwestern and North Central Nigeria and South and Central Benin (in West Africa) are stronger than national ties. These tribal ties and porous borders contribute to cross-border trade and movement that could include human trafficking.

Operational policies also contribute to trafficking. Over a two-year period, Nigerian traffickers brought more than 140 Nigerian minors to the Netherlands under false pretenses and had the minors claim asylum upon entering the country.

Traffickers supplied the young women with false passports and instructions on how to apply for asylum upon landing at Schiphol airport. Dutch law prohibits asylum seekers from being deported until their case has been investigated. Unaccompanied minors were housed in an "open" reception center—they were free to come and go as they pleased—while awaiting a decision on their case. Shortly after their arrival, the young women disappeared into street prostitution in a number of European countries (Aronowitz, 2009). As a result of the traffickers' misuse of open reception centers to facilitate trafficking for sexual exploitation, a pilot project "Protected Reception of Unaccompanied Minor Aliens (UMA) at Risk," was introduced in 2008. This project was designed to protect minors who are considered to be at risk of disappearing and being trafficked. The program includes protected reception in "Warded Reception Centres" and the assignment of a guardian (Global Detention Project 2009, http://www.globaldetentionproject .org/countries/europe/netherlands/introduction.html).

Work visa practices in various countries, such as the U.S. H-2 Guest Worker Visa Program, Japan's Industrial Training Program and its Technical Internship Program, or the system of *kafala* in the Middle East, facilitate the entrance of foreign workers into the respective countries where their labor is often exploited under deplorable conditions (Aronowitz, 2015a; Slodkowski, 2014; Hepburn and Simon, 2013). Workers pay exorbitant recruitment and placement fees, and upon arrival in the host country, are often dependent upon their employer for work and housing while they are tied to a specific job. Documents are often confiscated, and in the case of the *kafala* system, workers must have an exit visa to leave the country—this being contingent upon the approval and support of the employer.

Conclusion

Trafficking can be studied from the perspectives of migration, globalization, gender inequality, criminal justice, human rights, and slavery, among others. These perspectives are not mutually exclusive. Even in the criminal justice/law enforcement model, there is room for a human rights–based approach, as victim-centered investigations are becoming the norm rather than the exception (Aronowitz, 2009, 2015b). The lens through which we view the trafficking problem will influence what we study and record and will determine which measures are taken to combat the problem. Whereas a criminal justice approach will emphasize the investigation of offenders and criminal organizations (to include illicit recruitment agencies), a human rights approach, or one focusing on gender inequality, will aim to protect and improve the rights of women in a society (in general) and trafficked (women) victims (in particular). Studying trafficking from the perspective of supply and demand requires one take a business or market approach to studying human trafficking.

References

Abdelkader, Galy Kadir, and Zangaou, Moussa. 2012. *Wahaya domestic and sexual slavery in Niger.* Anti-Slavery International and Association Timidria. http://www .antislavery.org/includes/documents/cm_docs/2012/w/ wahaya_report_eng.pdf. Accessed on July 22, 2015.

Abella, M. 1995. "Asian migrant and contract workers in the Middle East." In R. Cohen (Ed.), *The Cambridge survey of world migration* (pp. 418–423). Cambridge: Cambridge University Press.

Aghatise, Esohe. 2005. "Women trafficking from West Africa to Europe: Cultural dimensions and strategies." *Mozaic, Human Rights: A Gendered Approach.* http://www.koed.hu/ mozaik15/esohe.pdf

Allain, Jean, and Bales, Kevin. 2012. *Slavery and its definition.* Queen's University Belfast Law Research Paper No. 21–06. http://papers.ssrn.com/sol3/papers.cfm?abstract_id=2123155. Accessed on August 22, 2015.

Allred, Keith. 2005. "Human trafficking: Breaking the military link." *Partnership for Peace Consortium Quarterly Journal*, Winter, 63–72.

Allred, Keith. 2006. "Peacekeepers and prostitutes: How deployed forces fuel the demand for trafficked women and new hope for stopping it." *Armed Forces and Society*, *33*(1), 5–23.

Allred, Keith. 2009. "Human trafficking and peace keepers." In Conelius Friesendorf (Ed.), *Strategies against human trafficking: The role of the security sector* (pp. 299–328). Vienna, Austria: National Defense Academy.

Amnesty International. 2014, 30 September. "The death toll in the Mediterranean rises while Europe looks the other way". https://www.amnesty.org/en/latest/news/2014/09/death-toll-mediterranean-rises-while-europe-looks-other-way/

Anderson, B., and O'Connell Davidson, J. 2003. *Trafficking—A demand-led problem?* Stockholm: Save the Children.

Anti-Slavery International. 2003. *The migration-trafficking nexus. Combating trafficking through the protection of migrants' human rights.* http://www.antislavery.org/includes/documents/cm_docs/2009/t/the_migration_trafficking_nexus_2003.pdf

Anti-Slavery International. No date. "Bonded labour." http://www.antislavery.org/english/slavery_today/bonded_labour/default.aspx

Anti-Slavery International. No date. "Descent based slavery." http://www.antislavery.org/english/slavery_today/descent_based_slavery/slavery_in_mauritania/default.aspx

Aronowitz, Alexis A. 2001. "Smuggling and trafficking in human beings: The phenomenon, the markets that drive it and the organisations that promote it." *European Journal on Criminal Policy and Research, 9*(2), Summer, 163–195.

Aronowitz, Alexis A. 2004. *Coalitions against Trafficking in Human Beings in the Philippines—Research and Action Final Report*, United Nations Office on Drugs and Crime and United Nations Interregional Crime and Justice Research Institute. http://www.unodc.org/pdf/crime/human_trafficking/coalitions_trafficking.pdf

Aronowitz, Alexis A. 2006. *Measures to combat trafficking in human beings in Benin, Nigeria and Togo.* Vienna: United Nations Office on Drugs and Crime. http://www.unodc.org/documents/human-trafficking/ht_research_report_nigeria.pdf

Aronowitz, Alexis A. 2009. *Human trafficking, human misery: The global trade in human beings.* Westport, CT: Praeger.

Aronowitz, Alexis A. 2012. "Sex tourism and sex trade." In J. Ciment and C. Bates (Eds.), *Encyclopedia of global social issues* (pp. 838–845). Armonk: M.E. Sharpe Publishers.

Aronowitz, Alexis A. 2015a, April 17–21. "The social etiology of human trafficking: How poverty and cultural practices facilitate trafficking." Paper presented at the Pontifical Academy of Social Sciences, *Human trafficking: Issues beyond criminalization,* Casina Pio IV, Vatican City. http://www.endslavery.va/content/endslavery/en/publications/acta_20/aronowitz.html

Aronowitz, Alexis A. 2015b. "Victims of human trafficking: A complex issue." *Dossier of Analysis: Human Trafficking,* Centro de Estudios Internacionales—CEI Facultad de Ciencias Sociales Universidad de los Andes. http://cei.uniandes.edu.co/index.php/component/docman/cat_view/5-dossier?Itemid=

Aronowitz, Alexis A., and Koning, Anneke. 2014. "Understanding human trafficking as a market system: Addressing the demand side of trafficking for sexual exploitation." *Revue Internationale de Droit Penale, International Review of Penal Law,* 85, 669–696.

Aronowitz, Alexis A., and Peruffo, Monica. 2003. "Trafficking of human beings and related crimes in West Africa." In Colin Sumner (Ed.), *The Blackwell companion to criminology* (pp. 394–414). Malden, MA: Blackwell.

Asian Development Bank. 2003. *Combating trafficking of women and children in South Asia*. https://openaccess.adb .org/bitstream/handle/11540/254/combating-trafficking-south-asia-paper.pdf?sequence=1. Accessed on July 4, 2015.

Baldwin-Edwards, M. 2011. *Labour immigration and labour markets in the GCC countries: national patterns and trends*. LSE Global Governance, Number 15.

Bales, Kevin. 2004. *Disposable people: New slavery in the global economy*. Berkeley, CA: University of California Press.

Bales, Kevin. 2007. "What predicts human trafficking?" *International Journal of Comparative and Applied Criminal Justice, 31*(2), 269–279. http://lastradainternational.org/ lsidocs/bales_test_theory_0607.pdf

Bales, Kevin, and Robbins, Peter. 2001. " 'No one shall be held in slavery or servitude': A critical analysis of international slavery agreements and concepts of slavery." *Human Rights Review, 2*(2), 18–46.

Banks, Duren, and Kyckelhahn, Tracey. 2011, April. *Characteristics of suspected human trafficking incidents, 2008–2010*. U.S. Department of Justice. http://www.bjs .gov/content/pub/pdf/cshti0810.pdf. Accessed on July 18, 2015.

Bazzi-Veil, L. 2000. *The status of child trafficking for economic exploitation in West and Central Africa*. Abidjan, Côte d'Ivoire: UNICEF.

BBC. 2015a, August 21. "Macedonia migrants: Hundreds rush border." *BBC News*. http://www.bbc.com/news/world-europe-34014353. Accessed on August 21, 2015.

BBC. 2015b, August 28. "Migrant crisis: Libya boats sink off Zuwara carrying hundreds." *BBC News.* http://www .bbc.com/news/world-africa-34082304. Accessed on August 28, 2015.

Bedoya, Eduardo, Alvaro Bedoya, and Patrick Belser. 2009. "Debt bondage and ethnic discrimination in Latin America." In Beate Andrees and Patrick Belser (Eds.), *Forced labor: Coercion and exploitation in the private economy* (pp. 35–50). Boulder, CO: Lynne Rienner Publishers, Inc.

Berlin, Ira. 1998. *Many thousands gone: The first two centuries of slavery in North America.* Cambridge, MA: Harvard University Press.

Bielke, Audra. 2004, June. "Illegal migration in China and implications for governance." *The National Review, 14*(26). https://csis-prod.s3.amazonaws.com/s3fs-public/legacy_ files/files/media/csis/press/040630bielke_ni.pdf. Accessed on November 3, 2016.

Bolkovac, Kathryn, and Lynn, Cari. 2011. *The whistleblower.* New York: Palgrave MacMillan.

Box, Heide. No date. "Human trafficking and minorities: Vulnerability compounded by discrimination." *Topical Research Digest: Minority Rights.* http://www.du.edu/korbel/ hrhw/researchdigest/minority/Trafficking.pdf. Accessed on July 21, 2015.

Burke, Mary (Ed.). 2013. *Human trafficking: Interdisciplinary perspectives.* New York: Routledge.

Cameron, Sally, and Newman, Edward (Eds.). 2008. *Trafficking in humans: Social, cultural and political dimensions.* Tokyo: United Nations University.

Chuang, Janie A. 2014. "Exploitation creep and the unmaking of Human Trafficking Law." *American Journal of International Law, 108*(4), 609. American University, WCL Research

Paper No. 2014–49. http://iilj.org/courses/documents/ JChuangdraft.pdf

Council of Europe. 2007. *Trafficking in human beings: Internet recruitment.* https://ec.europa.eu/anti-trafficking/ sites/antitrafficking/files/trafficking_in_human_beings_ internet_recruitment_1.pdf

Davis, Kathleen. 2006. "Brides, bruises and the border: The trafficking of North Korean women into China." *SAIS Review*, XXVI(1), Winter–Spring, 131–141.

De Lange, A. 2009. "Trafficking for labor exploitation in West and Central Africa." In H. Hindman (Ed.), *The world of child labor: An historical and regional survey*. Armonk: M.E. Sharpe Publishers.

De Lind, van Wijngaarden, J.W., and Rani, B. 2011. "Male adolescent concubinage in Peshawar, Northwestern Pakistan." *Culture, Health and Sexuality, 13*(9), 1061–1072.

Doezema, Jo. 2000. "Loose women or lost women? The re-emergence of the myth of white slavery in contemporary discourses of trafficking in women." *Gender Issues, 18*(1), 23–50.

Dottridge, Mike, 2002, "Trafficking in children in West and Central Africa." *Gender and Development, 10*(1): 38–49.

EUROPOL. 2009. *Trafficking in human beings in the European Union: A EUROPOL perspective.* The Hague: EUROPOL.

EUROPOL. 2011. *Trafficking in human beings in the European Union.* The Hague: EUROPOL.

Fight Slavery Now. http://fightslaverynow.org/why-fight-there-are-27-million-reasons/otherformsoftrafficking/ chattel-slavery/

Gallagher, Anne. 2013. *Abuse of a position of vulnerability and other 'means' within the definition of trafficking in persons.* United Nations Office on Drugs and Crime.

https://www.unodc.org/documents/human-trafficking/
2012/UNODC_2012_Issue_Paper_-_Abuse_of_a_
Position_of_Vulnerability.pdf

Godoy, Emilio. 2007, August 13. *Rights-Mexico: 16,000
victims of child sexual exploitation.* UN Inter Press Service.
http://www.ipsnews.net/2007/08/rights-mexico-16000-
victims-of-child-sexual-exploitation/. Accessed on July 15,
2015.

Goward, P. 2003. *Stop the Traffic 2*, Australian Human
Rights Commission. Paper presented 23–24 October,
2003, Melbourne, Australia. http://www.hreoc.gov.au/sex_
discrimination/publication/traffic/speeches/goward.html

Hayase, Yasuko, and Liaw, Kao-Lee. 1997, September.
"Factors on polygamy in sub-Saharan Africa: Findings
based on the demographic and health surveys."
The Developing Economies XXXV(3), 293–327.

Heinrich, Mark. 2007, April 23. "U.N. anti-trafficking drive
hits culture barriers." *The Scotsman.*

Heller, Lauren, Robert Lawson, Ryan Murphy, and Claudia
Williamson. 2016, March. "Is human trafficking the dark
side of economic freedom?" *Defence and Peace Economics.*

Hepburn, Stephanie, and Simon, Rita. 2013. *Human
trafficking around the world: Hidden in plain sight.* New
York: Columbia University Press.

Heyzer, Noeleen. 2002. "Combating trafficking in women
and children: A gender and human rights framework."
Paper presented at the Conference, *The Human Rights
Challenge of Globalization: Asia-Pacific-U.S.*, Honolulu,
Hawaii, UNIFEM. http://www.childtrafficking.org/pdf/
user/unifem_gender_and_human_rights_framework.pdf.
Accessed on March 15, 2015.

Howard, Neil. 2011. "Is 'child placement' trafficking?
Questioning the validity of an accepted discourse."
Anthropology Today, 27(6), 3–7.

Hughes, Donna. 1998. *Use of the Internet for global sexual exploitation of women and children.* http://www.uri.edu/artsci/wms/hughes/pubtrfrep.htm. Accessed on August 17, 2015.

Hughes, Donna. 2004. "The role of 'marriage agencies' in the sexual exploitation and trafficking of women from the former Soviet Union." *International Review of Victimology, 11,* 49–71.

Hughes, Donna. 2005. "The demand for victims of sex trafficking." www.academia.edu/3415676/The_Demand_for_Victims_of_Sex_Trafficking

Human Terrain Team AF-6 (HTT). 2009. *Pashtun sexuality.* Unclassified Government Document, U.S. Army. https://publicintelligence.net/afghanistan-human-terrain-team-pashtun-homosexuality-report/. Accessed on February 15, 2015.

ILO (International Labour Organization). 2001, June. *World of Work Magazine, No. 39.* http://embargo.ilo.org/wcmsp5/groups/public/—dgreports/—dcomm/documents/publication/dwcms_080613.pdf. Accessed on March 1, 2015.

ILO. 2010. *ILO Convention on Forced Labour No. 29.* http://www.ilo.org/dyn/normlex/en/f?p=NORMLEXPUB:12100:0::NO::P12100_ILO_CODE:C029#A2

ILO. No date. *Labour migration.* http://www.ilo.org/global/topics/labour-migration/lang—en/index.htm. Accessed on July 18, 2015.

IOM. 2005. *Data and research on human trafficking: A global survey,* Geneva, 2005. http://publications.iom.int/system/files/pdf/global_survey.pdf

Johnston, Nicola. 2004. "Peace support operations." In *Inclusive security, sustainable peace: A toolkit for advocacy and action* (pp. 33–50). Hunt Alternatives Fund. https://www.inclusivesecurity.org/wp-content/uploads/2013/05/101864251-Toolkit-for-Advocacy-and-Action.pdf

Jones, Sam, and Shaheen, Kareem. 2015, July 9. "Syrian refugees: Four million people forced to flee as crisis deepens." *The Guardian.* http://www.theguardian.com/global-development/2015/jul/09/syria-refugees-4-million-people-flee-crisis-deepens. Accessed on August 17, 2015.

Kangaspunta, Kristiina. 2008. "A short history of trafficking in persons." *F3, Freedom from Fear,* Unicri, Torino, Italy, pp. 38–41. http://f3magazine.unicri.it/wp-content/uploads/F3_UNICRI_MAX-PLANCK_01.pdf

Kapiszewski, A. 2006, May 15–17. *Arab versus Asian migrant workers in the GCC countries.* United Nations Expert Group Meeting on International Migration and Development in the Arab Region, UN/POP/EGM/2006/02, United Nations Secretariat, Beirut.

Kara, Siddharth. 2009. *Sex trafficking: Inside the business of modern slavery.* New York: Columbia University Press.

Limanowska, B. 2003. *Trafficking in human beings in South Eastern Europe*, UNICEF, UNOHCHR, OSCE. http://www.ceecis.org/child_protection/PDF/Traff2003.pdf

Limanowska, B. 2005. *Trafficking in human beings in South Eastern Europe*, UNICEF, UNOHCHR, OSCE. http://www.unicef.org/ceecis/Trafficking.Report.2005.pdf

Londoño, E. 2012a, April 4. "Afghanistan's 'dancing boys' are invisible victims." *The Washington Post.* http://www.washingtonpost.com/world/asia_pacific/afganistans-dancing-boys-are-invisible-victims/2012/04/04/gIQAyreSwS_story.html

Londoño, E. 2012b, April 5. "Afghanistan's 'dancing boys': Behind the story." *The Washington Post.* http://www.washingtonpost.com/blogs/blogpost/post/afghanistans-dancing-boys-behind-the-story/2012/04/05/gIQAFXzJxS_blog.html

Månsson, S.A. 2004. "Men's practices in prostitution and their implications for social work." In S.A. Månsson and C. Proveyer (Eds.), *Social work in Cuba and Sweden: Achievements and prospects.* ENATW. http://www.aretusa .net/download/centro%20documentazione/03contributi/ c-05Men_practices.doc

Manzo, K. 2005. "Exploiting West Africa's children: Trafficking, slavery and uneven development." *Area, 37*(4), 393–401.

Martin, L., and Shaheen, M. 2014, March 29. "Crime or culture: The revival of slave boys in Afghanistan; a UK perspective." *Criminal Law and Justice Weekly, 178*, 193–195.

Mendelson, Sarah. 2005. *Barracks and brothels.* Washington, DC: Center for Strategic and International Studies. http:// www.csis.org/media/csis/pubs/0502_barracksbrothels.pdf

Monto, M.A. 1999. *Focusing on the clients of street prostitutes: A creative approach to reducing violence against women.* Submitted to the National Institute of Justice, October 30, 1999. www.ncjrs.org/pdffiles1/nij/grants/182860.pdf

Newman, Brooke. 2013. "Historical perspective: Slavery over the centuries." In Mary Burke (Ed.), *Human trafficking: Interdisciplinary perspectives* (pp. 24–48). New York: Routledge.

Okojie, C. 2003. *Programme of action against trafficking in minors and young women from Nigeria to Italy for the purpose of sexual exploitation, report of field survey in Edo State, Nigeria,* UNICRI. http://www.unicri.it/topics/ trafficking_exploitation/archive/women/nigeria_1/research/ rr_okojie_eng.pdf. Accessed on March 15, 2015.

Omelaniuk, Irena. 2005. "Trafficking in human beings." United Nations Expert Group Meeting on International Migration and Development. http://www.un.org/esa/ population/meetings/ittmigdev2005/P15_IOmelaniuk.pdf. Accessed on January 11, 2015.

Picarelli, John T. 2007. "Historical approaches to the trade in human beings." In Maggy Lee (Ed.), *Human trafficking* (pp. 26–48). London: Routledge.

Piscitelli, A. 2012. "Revisiting notions of sex trafficking and victims." *Vibrant, Virtual Braz. Anthr, 9*(1), 274–310. http://www.scielo.br/pdf/vb/v9n1/10.pdf

Procon. 2011, January 6. *Percentage of men (by country) who paid for sex at least once: The Johns Chart.* http://prostitution .procon.org/view.resource.php?resourceID=004119# Cambodia. Accessed on August 17, 2015.

Raymond, J. G. 2004. "Prostitution on demand: Legalizing the buyers as sexual consumers." *Violence Against Women: An International and Interdisciplinary Journal,* 10(10), 1156–1186. http://www.catwinternational.org/Content/ Images/Article/172/attachment.pdf. Accessed on November 4, 2016.

Reynolds, M. 2002, April 3. "Kandahar's lightly veiled homosexual habits." *LA Times.* http://articles.latimes .com/2002/apr/03/news/mn-35991

Rogers, Chris. 2008. "The shocking truth about the vice trade: Girls of 14 working as sex slaves." *The Daily Mail,* January 25, 2008. http://www.dailymail.co.uk/home/ moslive/article-510380/The-shocking-truth-vice-trade- Girls-14-working-sex-slaves.html. Accessed on August 17, 2015.

Salah, R. 2001, February 19–23. "Child trafficking in West and Central Africa: An overview." Paper presented at the First Pan African Conference on Human Trafficking, Wotclef, International Conference Centre, Abuja. http:// www.unicef.org/media/newsnotes/africchildtraffick.pdf. Accessed on January 20, 2015.

Schut, M., and Van Baarle, E. 2014. "Dansjongens: een artikel over de praktijk van bacha bazi." *Carré 1.* Radboud University, Nijmegen, The Netherlands, 32–37.

Shelley, Louise. 2003. Statement to the Subcommittee on European Affairs United States Senate Committee on Foreign Relations Hearing on "Combating Transnational Crime and Corruption in Europe." October 30, 2003.

Shelley, Louise. 2006. "The globalization of crime and terrorism." *The Challenges of Globalization,* eJournal, pp. 42–45.

Shelley, Louise. 2010. *Human trafficking: A global perspective.* Cambridge: Cambridge University Press.

Shelley, Louise. 2014. *Human smuggling and trafficking into Europe: A comparative perspective.* Washington, DC: Migration Policy Institute.

Siegel, Dina, and De Blank, S. 2010. "Women who traffic women: Women in human trafficking—Dutch cases." *Global Crime, 11*(4), 436–447.

Slodkowski, Antoni. 2014, June 12. "Interns abused as labor crisis grows." *The Japan Times.* http://www.japantimes .co.jp/news/2014/06/12/national/social-issues/interns-abused-labor-crisis-grows/#.VdRqfXnouWg. Accessed on June 14, 2015.

Smith-Spark, Laura, and Faith Karimi. 2015, August 28. "Austria: 71 refugees found in abandoned truck probably died of suffocation." *CNN.* http://edition.cnn.com/2015/08/28/europe/migrant-crisis/index.html. Accessed on August 28, 2015.

Terre des Hommes. 2014, September 12. *Document submitted by Terre des Hommes for the Day of General Discussion of the Committee on the Rights of the Child: "Digital media and children's rights."* https://www.tdh .ch/en/news/%E2%80%9Cdigital-media-and-childrens-rights%E2%80%9D. Accessed on August 14, 2015.

Tlou, Sheila. 2002. "Gender and HIV/AIDS." In Max Essex, Souleymane Mboup, Phyllis Kanki, Richard Marlink, and Sheila Tlou (Eds.), *AIDS in Africa.* New York: Kluwer.

Tomiuc, Eugen. 2003. "Interpol official discusses human
trafficking, internet pornography." *Global Security*. http://
www.globalsecurity.org/security/library/news/2003/05/
sec-030514-rfel-142137.htm

Trevizo, Perla. 2015. "Border deaths down as deadliest part of
the year begins." *Arizona Daily Star*. Tucson.com. http://
tucson.com/news/border-deaths-down-as-deadliest-part-
of-the-year-begins/article_eb602cfc-d719-578c-a90b-
41254ae88fc4.html

Truong, T. 2006. *Poverty, gender and human trafficking in
sub-Saharan Africa: Rethinking best practices in migration
management*. Paris: UNESCO.

UNDP (United Nations Development Program). 2007.
Human trafficking and HIV. UNDP Regional Centre in
Colombo. https://www.unodc.org/documents/hiv-aids/
publications/human_traffick_hiv_undp2007.pdf. Accessed
on June 14, 2015.

UNDP. No date. *Table 1: Human development index and
its components*. http://hdr.undp.org/en/content/table-1-
human-development-index-and-its-components. Accessed
on January 15, 2015.

UNHCR. 2015. *2015 UNHCR country operations profile—
Iraq*. http://www.unhcr.org/pages/49e486426.html.
Accessed on August 22, 2015.

UNHCR. No date. *Syria regional refugee response*. http://
data.unhcr.org/syrianrefugees/regional.php. Accessed on
August 22, 2015.

UNICEF. 2002. *Child trafficking in West Africa: Policy
responses*. Florence, Italy: Innocenti Research Centre.

UNICEF. 2003. *Trafficking in human beings, especially women
and children, in Africa*. Florence, Italy: Innocenti Research
Centre.

UNICRI (United Nations Interregional Crime and Justice
Research Institute). 2006. *Trafficking in human beings and*

peace-support operations, Turin, Italy. http://lastrada
international.org/lsidocs/407%20THB%20and%20
peace%20support%20operations%20-%20UNICRI
.pdf. Accessed on November 4, 2016.

UNICRI. No date. *Counter-trafficking: Peace support areas.*
http://www.unicri.it/topics/trafficking_exploitation/
archive/peacekeeping/

United Nations. 1999, November. "Secretary-General says
persistence of slavery, in an era of human rights progress,
demands action by global community." *Press Release SG/
SM/7242.* http://www.un.org/press/en/1999/19991130
.sgsm7242.doc.html

United Nations Department of Peacekeeping Operations.
2004. *Human trafficking resource package.* http://www
.unrol.org/files/DPKO,%20Human%20Trafficking%20
Resource%20Package,%202004.pdf. Accessed on August 17,
2015.

UNODC (United Nations Office on Drugs and Crime). 2004.
*United Nations convention against transnational organized
crime and the protocols thereto.* Vienna: UNODC. https://
www.unodc.org/documents/middleeastandnorthafrica/
organised-crime/UNITED_NATIONS_CONVENTION_
AGAINST_TRANSNATIONAL_ORGANIZED_CRIME_
AND_THE_PROTOCOLS_THERETO.pdf

UNODC. No date. "What are the root causes of trafficking?"
In *Toolkit to combat trafficking in persons* (pp. 423–425).
https://www.unodc.org/documents/human-trafficking/
Toolkit-files/08–58296_tool_9–2.pdf

Upadhyaya, Krishna Prasad. 2008. *Poverty, discrimination
and slavery: The reality of bonded labour in India, Nepal
and Pakistan.* Anti-Slavery International. http://www
.antislavery.org/includes/documents/cm_docs/2009/p/
povertydiscriminationslaveryfinal.pdf

U.S. Department of State. 2014. *Trafficking in Persons Report.* Washington, DC. http://www.state.gov/documents/organization/226845.pdf

U.S. Department of State. 2015. *Trafficking in Persons Report.* Washington, DC. http://www.state.gov/j/tip/rls/tiprpt/2015/index.htm

Van Dijk, R. 2001. "Voodoo on the doorstep: Young Nigerian prostitutes and magic; policing in the Netherlands." *Africa, 71*(4), 558–585.

Vandenburg, Martina. 2002, April 24. "The U.N. and the sex slave trade in Bosnia: Isolated case or larger problem in the U.N. system?" *Hearing before the Subcommittee on International Operations and Human Rights of the Committee on International Relations House of Representatives.* http://commdocs.house.gov/committees/intlrel/hfa78948.000/hfa78948_0f.htm

Verbeet, D. 2000. *Combating the trafficking in children for labour exploitation in West and Central Africa,* Draft, Working Document based on the studies of Benin, Burkina Faso, Cameroon, Côte d'Ivoire, Gabon, Ghana, Mali, Nigeria, Togo, International Labour Organization, Abidjan, Côte d'Ivoire.

Watson Institute. 2015, February. "Costs of war: Iraqi refugees." Watson Institute, Brown University. http://watson.brown.edu/costsofwar/costs/human/refugees/iraqi

Weiners, Brad. 2015, April 10. "Dying at Europe's doorstep." *Bloomberg Businessweek.* http://www.bloomberg.com/graphics/2015-migrant-rescue-in-the-mediterranean/

Weissbrodt, David. 2002. *Abolishing slavery and its contemporary forms.* Office of the United Nations High Commissioner for Human Rights. http://www.ohchr.org/Documents/Publications/slaveryen.pdf

Weitzer, Ronald. 2015a. "Human trafficking and contemporary slavery." *Annual Review of Sociology, 41*, 223–242.

Weitzer, Ronald. 2015b. "Researching prostitution and sex trafficking comparatively." *Sexuality Research and Social Policy, 12*(2), 81–91.

World Bank. No date. *Personal remittances, received (% of GDP)*. http://data.worldbank.org/indicator/BX.TRF .PWKR.DT.GD.ZS/countries?display=default. Accessed on July 21, 2015.

World Bank. 2016. *Taking on inequality*. Washington, DC. https://openknowledge.worldbank.org/bitstream/ handle/10986/25078/9781464809583.pdf. Accessed on November 5, 2016.

Yousafzai, Sami, Moreau, Ron, and Bourreau, Marie. 2008. "The opium brides of Afghanistan." *Newsweek, 151*(14), 38–40.

CAN YOU SEE HER?

It's time to open our eyes. Victims of domestic servitude, forced labor, and the sex trade have been invisible, until now.

RECOGNIZE
HUMAN TRAFFICKING

TO REPORT SUSPECTED TRAFFICKING CALL

1-866-DHS-2-ICE
1 866-347-2423

For victim support call 1-888-373-7888 | Text INFO or HELP to BeFree (233733)

BLUE CAMPAIGN
One Voice. One Mission. End Human Trafficking.
DHS.GOV/BLUECAMPAIGN

BC-DS6-

This chapter outlines the most controversial issues dealing with the topic of human trafficking. A number of misconceptions exist that clouds our understanding of the issue. These misconceptions may have a dramatic impact upon the victims of trafficking who go unnoticed because no one is looking for them—they do not fit the typical victim profile. From a justice perspective, this is equally as important. If traffickers do not fit the typical "criminal" profile, they may be allowed to operate and exploit victims for years. Trafficking in human beings is a "fluid" crime—patterns of recruitment, choice of victims, trafficking routes, and markets of exploitation can change. It is important for all those involved in the investigation of the crime, identification and rescue of victims, and the provision of services to be aware of shifting patterns in order to be able to effectively raise awareness, target vulnerable groups, respond to the victims' needs, and effectively investigate the crime.

A poster that is part of the Department of Homeland Security (DHS) Blue Campaign, which raises public awareness of human trafficking. Awareness campaigns are underway at airports from New York to Los Angeles, as DHS has posted messages on video monitors and airport shopping bags. Other industries, including hotels and trucking, are increasing efforts to detect trafficking as well. (Department of Homeland Security)

The Extent of the Problem: Counting and Identifying Victims of Trafficking

Trafficking is a global problem identified and discussed in numerous government, intergovernmental, and academic sources (some of these are Belser et al., 2005; ILO, 2005; Laczko and Gozdziak, 2005; UNODC, 2016; U.S. Department of State, 2016; Aronowitz, 2009a; Shelley, 2010; Hepburn and Simon, 2013). We constantly hear that trafficking in human beings is a growing problem, and according to the President of the UN General Assembly, "it ranks as the world's third most profitable crime after illicit drugs and arms trafficking" (UN News Center 2014). But how do we know this?

There are two main sources of data on human trafficking: *actual numbers* of identified victims and *estimates*. Globally, only 40,177 victims of trafficking have been identified by government authorities and reported to the United Nations for inclusion in the semiannual Global Report on Trafficking in Persons (2014). These numbers vary drastically from the estimate of 2.45 million people trafficked globally in 2005 (Belser et al., 2005) and nearly 21 million people exploited in forced labor (ILO, 2012) to 45.8 million people estimated enslaved in 167 countries by the Walk Free Foundation (2016). Academicians such as Weitzer (2011, 2012a, 2014; see also Chapter 2 of Aronowitz, 2009a) are critical of the numbers and estimates; the true number of victims of trafficking probably lies somewhere between these estimates and actual numbers. Whether victims are identified will depend upon whether there is adequate legislation (e.g., U.S. trafficking legislation does not include trafficking for the purpose of organ removal; in some countries, trafficking legislation only focuses on forced prostitution), awareness of the plight of victims, political will to address the problem, and resources, manpower, and expertise to investigate and uncover victims (Aronowitz, 2009a). Finding victims is only the first step to counting them.

The difficulty in counting victims is due, in part, to how we identify trafficked persons, and whether we recognize, and they accept their victim status.

Identifying Victims of Trafficking

The UN Declaration of Basic Principles of Justice for Victims of Crime and Abuse of Power defines victims as "persons who, individually or collectively, have suffered harm, including physical or mental injury, emotional suffering, economic loss or substantial impairment of their fundamental rights, through acts or omissions that are in violation of criminal laws operative within Member States, including those laws proscribing criminal abuse of power" (UN Office of the High Commissioner for Human Rights, 1985).

Studies in criminology and victimology identify "pure" or ideal victims. Criminologist Nils Christie (cited in Newburn, 2013) identified a number of attributes of "ideal" victims. "These are (among others), the fact that the ideal victim is likely to be female, and very young or old. The victim should be virtuous and blameless for what has happened to him or her. Furthermore, the victim should be able to elicit sympathy and victim status" (Aronowitz, 2015b). There are further expectations placed upon victims of human trafficking. The "iconic" victim, according to Srikantiah (2007), "should be 1) female and trafficked for sexual exploitation; 2) assessed to be good witnesses by law enforcement; 3) fully cooperative with law enforcement investigations; and 4) rescued from the traffickers rather than escaping" (Aronowitz, 2015b). Victims who do not meet these requirements may not be seen as trafficked victims, in particular, those who willingly accepted an offer to work in prostitution and were deceived about the conditions of work, or those foreign male workers who willingly left their countries of origin to work in the Middle East as manual laborers.

Another problem in the identification of victims and one encountered by law enforcement and social or victim protection advocates is that victims often refuse to "self-identify"—admit to being or viewing themselves as victims. Victims may simply refuse to cooperate with authorities out of fear for their safety or the security of their family members whom traffickers often threaten to harm if victims cooperate with authorities. Fear of harm is not the only reason why victims refuse to come forward. Despite having experienced traumatic harm (Zimmerman et al., 2006; Tsutsumi et al., 2008; Lugris, 2013), not all victims see themselves as such. They may blame themselves for their situation (Brunovskis and Surtees, 2008) or may identify with their exploiter/pimp. A study of cases of sex trafficking in the Amsterdam Red Light district found intimate relationships between traffickers and their victims characterized not only by a combination of control, intimidation, and violence, but also affection and attachment (Verhoeven et al., 2015). According to the Polaris Project (2013, 1), clinicians and psychologists refer to this as traumatic bonding. "This occurs where a person has dysfunctional attachment that occurs in the presence of danger, shame, or exploitation. These situations often include seduction, deception or betrayal and some form of danger or risk is always present."

There are other reasons besides the fear of reprisal or the emotional attachment to traffickers that cause victims to refuse to self-identify. Shame of having been exploited, particularly in forced prostitution, causes some victims to blame themselves and reject the label of "victim." For others, there is a different reason. In a study of women returning from East Asia to Colombia, Warren (2012, 110) found that many women prefer to "distance themselves from their past. Many of these women see themselves as people who made unfortunate job decisions that resulted in their having to work in exploitative and dangerous conditions with poor pay." The conditions of exploitation in the destination country (Japan) were similar to the exploitative conditions at home.

Forcing women to accept the victim label denies women self-determination and agency (Warren, 2012; Piscitelli, 2012).

Applying the victim label "rejects the idea that these workers may well have other understandings of their work, alternative definitions of how jobs far from home might serve their family's financial goals, and other positions in the organizations they decide to work for" (Warren, 2012, 108). The fact that sex work is stigmatized reinforces the belief that women are incapable of rationally choosing to work in the sex industry. Therefore, all women found working in the sex industry must be victims of human trafficking—when, in fact, they may not see themselves as such (Aronowitz, 2015b).

For these reasons, perhaps we should not rely upon victims to recognize or admit to their victim status. Regardless of how they view themselves, when specific indicators point to the possibility of a person being trafficked (for a detailed list and how this list was comprised, see ILO, 2009), they should be registered as "presumed victims." Persons in the Netherlands suspected to be victims of trafficking—whether or not they agree that they are victims—are registered as presumed victims. The European Statistical Agency, Eurostat, tasked with collecting statistical information provided by European countries, publishes annual statistics on human trafficking in the European Union. The organization suggests registering both "identified" as well as "presumed" victims of human trafficking. Identified victims are those persons "who have been formally identified by the relevant authorities as a victim of trafficking in human beings." Presumed victims are those persons who have met the criteria of a trafficked victim but have not been formally identified by the relevant authorities or who have declined to be formally or legally identified as a trafficked victim (Eurostat, 2014, 21).

The Victim Pyramid

In addition to the difficulty in finding victims, and their unwillingness to self-identify, how we count victims of trafficking may depend upon what point they are identified in the process of the trafficking chain or the Criminal Justice system. Organizational goals and objectives may also determine how victims are identified. Victims may access the services of NGOs and be counted by these organizations, but refuse to cooperate with law enforcement, and will thus not be counted in official statistics generated by this organization.

One can imagine a Victim Pyramid. At the very bottom are those that are trafficked and have yet to be identified—the "dark figure" of victims. An analogy can be drawn with victims of rape or domestic violence who have not yet come to the attention of service providers, hospitals, or the police. Moving up one level are those who have been identified as "presumed victims of trafficking" or "possible victims of trafficking" because they have been identified in situations tantamount to exploitation and trafficking but may not identify themselves as such. The next group of victims are those who are identified by service providers (NGOs, police, medical staff, social workers, labor inspectors) and who self-identify or admit that they are victims of trafficking. These individuals may, however, refuse to cooperate with police investigations or refuse the services of shelters. Moving up the pyramid, one finds victims who accept the support of NGOs and cooperate with police investigations, but refuse to testify at trial. A small group of these victims of trafficking testify at trial and are repatriated. An even smaller number of victims are given permission to remain in a country for a limited to an extended period of time, or permanently, under visa systems such as the B-8 regulation in the Netherlands (Netherlands Ministry of Security and Justice) or the T-visa (T Nonimmigrant Status visa) in the United States (U.S. Citizenship and Immigration Services). While the trafficking pyramid may not be drawn to scale (there may be more victims accepting assistance and cooperating with law enforcement than those who refuse aid in certain countries or in certain sectors), Figure 2.1 attempts to illustrate the complexity of identifying and quantifying victims of trafficking. NGOs would be more inclined to identify victims as anyone who is identified in an exploitative situation, whereas law enforcement or prosecutors view victims

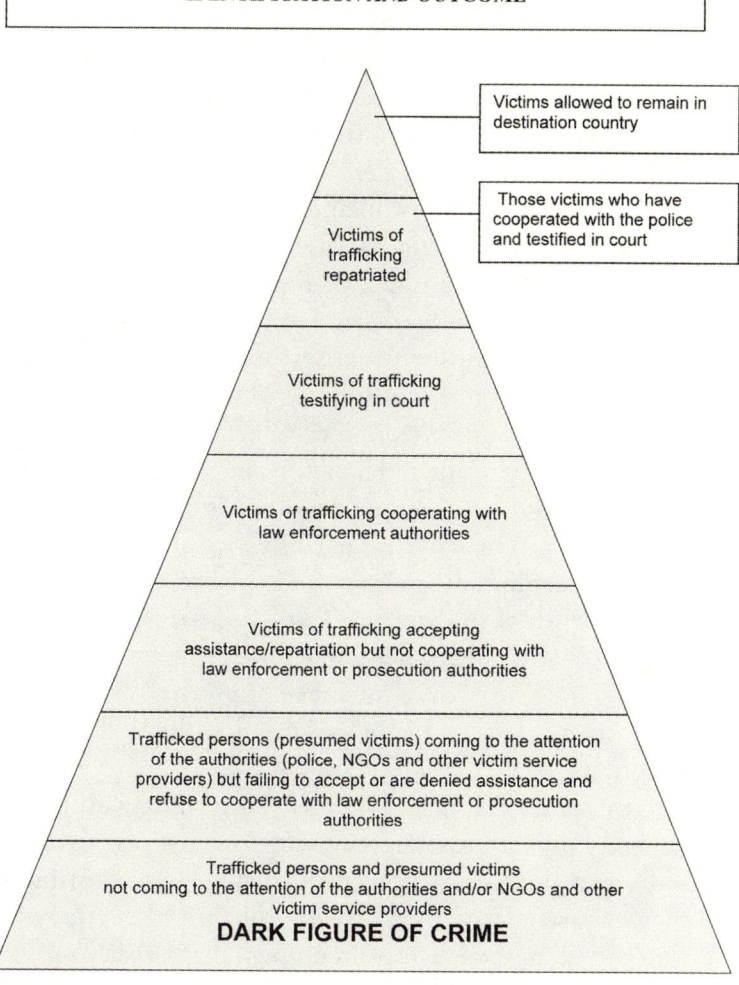

Figure 2.1   Victim Pyramid: Presumed and Trafficked Persons: Identification and Outcome.

Source: (Aronowitz, 2009b. *Guidelines for the Collection of Data on Trafficking in Human Beings, Including Comparable Indicators.* Vienna: International Organization for Migration and Federal Ministry of the Interior of Austria. Used by permission.)

as those who have been identified in a police investigation and cooperate in a criminal prosecution. It is easy to understand why different agencies may produce different numbers of victims of trafficking (Aronowitz, 2009b, 2014b).

Trafficking as a Process Rather than a Single Crime

Unlike most criminal offenses that are limited in time and space (a burglary, arson, assault, homicide), human trafficking is a process that can span weeks to years and occur in numerous cities or countries. This crime comprises a number of phases, beginning with the recruitment of victims. This can occur through a number of means, including force or deception. Individuals are deceived through false promises of work, or in the case of what has been identified as the "loverboy" modus operandi in the Netherlands and other countries, through a romantic relationship or promises of marriage. In the second phase, the transportation phase, victims may be brought within their own country from a rural area to a city, or in the case of international trafficking, victims may be brought across borders and through numerous countries into the destination country. Exploitation may occur while victims are in transit. They may be exploited in either forced labor or prostitution during the length of the journey. Trafficked persons may travel to their international destination with legitimate documents (by entering a country on a tourist or study visa), with fraudulent documents, or by being smuggled without documents across borders.

Up to this point, trafficked victims' journeys may differ. One 25-year-old Nigerian woman spent close to two years traveling by land across the African continent to enter Italy. During her ordeal, she was exposed to violence throughout her trip, while she watched some of her travel companions perish (Aronowitz, 2009a; allAfrica, 2006). In contrast, Filipino women who were trafficked to the Gulf States, Japan, and Korea (Aronowitz, 2003), traveled to their destination by air over a period of hours or days and remained in luxury hotels while in transit.

At the third phase, the exploitation phase, victims reach their destination and are placed in positions of forced labor. In addition to the exploitation, other crimes are perpetrated against victims. According to EUROPOL, some of these offenses are

Recruitment/Entry	Transportation	Exploitation	Victim Disposal	Criminal Proceeds
* *Fraudulent promises* * *Kidnapping* Document forgery Illegal adoption (for purpose of exploiting child) Corruption of government officials	* *Assault* * *Illegal deprivation of liberty* * *Rape* * *Forced Prostitution* Corruption of government officials Document forgery Abuse of immigration laws	* *Unlawful coercion* * *Threat* * *Extortion* * *Sex or Labour exploitation* * *Illegal deprivation of liberty* * *Theft of documents* * *Sexual Assault* * *Aggravated Assault (cruel and degrading treatment)* * *Forced participation in crimes (forced begging, transportation of drugs, organized theft)* * *Rape* * *Murder* * *Removal of organs* Corruption of government officials	* *Assault* * *Abandonment* * *Murder* * *Victim sold to another trafficker*	Money Laundering Tax Evasion Corruption of government officials

Offenses in italics preceded by an asterisk indicate that the offenses are perpetrated against the individual victim.

Figure 2.2   Human Trafficking as a Process.

Source: (Aronowitz, Alexis, Theuermann, Gerda, and Tyurykanova, Elena, 2010. *Analysing the Business Model of Trafficking in Human Beings to Better Prevent the Crime*. OSCE Office of the Special Representative and Coordinator for Combating Trafficking in Human Beings: Vienna, Austria, 19. Used by permission.)

instrumental criminal activities perpetrated in direct further-
ance of the trafficking activity (EUROPOL, 2000) such as
forced prostitution, violence against victims to maintain control over them, or corruption of government officials to facilitate the trafficking operation. Other offenses, such as money
laundering and tax evasion, are secondary and occur as a result
of the trafficking activity (Aronowitz, 2009a).

The fourth phase is the "victim disposal" phase. In this phase,
victims are discarded when they are no longer of any use to the
trafficker. This may occur when child victims become too old
to be exploited in forced begging, when victims become pregnant, too difficult to control, or too sick to work. Victims may
be allowed to leave, or in the worst case, they may be resold or
murdered.

The final phase in the trafficking process is the spending or
investment of criminal proceeds. It is included in the model
as the laundering of funds is an essential element in sizable
human trafficking schemes generating huge profits. "Following the money" should be an essential part of criminal investigations into trafficking. Furthermore, investigations into tax
fraud and money laundering may uncover human trafficking
operations as the source of the illicit funds (FATF, 2011;
Kleemans, 2015).

Figure 2.2 portrays the trafficking process. At each stage, the
crimes perpetrated against the victim and the state are identified. Crimes against individual victims are listed first and identified in italics.

Markets in Which Victims Are Trafficked

Much attention has been paid to the sexual exploitation of
young women and girls. Brothels near military bases have
existed for decades (Aronowitz, 2012) and the link between
prostitution and human trafficking (forced prostitution) has
been clearly documented (O'Connor and Healey, 2006). Since
the early 1990s and the fall of the Soviet Union and the Iron

Curtain, large numbers of Eastern and Central European women began showing up in brothels and on streets in Western European and U.S. cities (Hughes, 2000; Sulaimanova, 2006). This emphasis on sexual exploitation has resulted in a skewed understanding of human trafficking. Less visible, but no less abusive, is exploitation in other forms and sectors of trafficking.

Exploitation in the sex industry is viewed as more harmful to the victims; however, the harm to persons exploited in other industries should not be underestimated. Persons are trafficked into "the underpaid, exploitative '3D' jobs—dirty, degrading and dangerous unskilled work" (Jordan, no date). Individuals exploited in legitimate industries are subjected to horrific health and safety conditions, often deprived of food, sleep, and adequate medical care. Exploitation of persons in conventional markets also result in severe human rights abuses.

Markets into which people are trafficked can be divided into forced labor in (1) legitimate or "traditional" labor markets, (2) illicit and criminal markets (to include criminal activities), and (3) the category "other," into which cases of human trafficking involving child soldiers, forced marriage, and organ trafficking can be placed.

Traditional Markets

Exploitation takes place in legal or conventional industries. In countries where prostitution is legal (in most European countries and those in Central and South America, Canada, New Zealand, and parts of Australia), trafficking into prostitution would constitute exploitation in a legitimate sector. Other conventional or legitimate industries in which trafficking has been identified include agriculture, fishing, mining, manufacturing, sweatshops, domestic service, construction, and the hotel and restaurant sector (Cameron and Newman, 2008; Aronowitz, 2009a; ILO, 2013; UNODC, 2014; Human Rights Watch, 2014; U.S. Department of State, 2016). Exploitation in the domestic service industry should be considered separately. Domestic servants lack many of the legal protections provided to laborers in other markets. They are often isolated and can be enslaved for longer periods of time (a couple, both doctors, in the United States kept a Filipina domestic servant in their home as a virtual slave for nearly 20 years; see ICE, 2012). Trafficking for forced domestic service often involves women who have traveled internationally and who are isolated geographically and linguistically. The ILO estimated in 2010 that there were 53 million domestic workers worldwide, the majority of them women (ILO, "Who are domestic workers?"). Many of these serve as domestic servants in households in countries in the Middle East. They are subject to harsh treatment, abuse, low pay, violence, sexual intimidation, and rape (Vlieger, 2011). The case of a 49-year-old Sri Lankan woman, L. T. Ariyawathi, and others similar to her have been reported in the press. After having complained of an excessive workload, her Saudi employer and his wife hammered 24 hot nails into her hands, legs, and forehead (Aneez, 2010).

Illicit Markets

As prostitution is illegal in many countries, trafficking into prostitution or other forms of sexual exploitation constitutes work in the illicit sector. Sexual exploitation can also take place in the making of pornographic films. The (forced) prostitution industry is quite varied, with victims working in brothels, private homes, bars, massage parlors, clubs, on the streets, and as escorts (Weitzer, 2009, 2012b; Aronowitz, 2014a). The fact that persons working in prostitution have contact with clients increases the chance that they may be identified or come to the attention of police or service providers more quickly than victims in forced labor who may be more isolated.

Another form of trafficking in illicit markets is that of trafficking for forced begging and criminal activities (Anti-Slavery International, 2014; UNODC, 2014; U.S. Department of State, 2014). These activities include forced begging, cannabis cultivation, theft, pickpocketing, benefits fraud, shoplifting, drug trafficking, and terrorism. The U.S. Department of State (2014) reports that organized criminal groups in Mexico have forced migrants and children to work in the production and sale of drugs, and as assassins. In France (Paris and suburbs), Roma children were forced to commit burglaries. Children in Afghanistan and Pakistan have been used as suicide bombers. Those victims forced to beg or commit illegal activities are often arrested and charged with crimes rather than recognized as victims. The problem is particularly poignant in the case of forced begging in which children are often used (Anti-Slavery International, 2014).

Unusual Forms of Human Trafficking

The third category is that comprising other forms of exploitation to include human trafficking for forced armed combat (child soldiers), forced marriage of young girls or women, and trafficking of human beings for the purpose of organ removal.

The involvement of child soldiers in armed groups is still being documented. In May 2014, UNICEF reported that at least 6,000 children were recruited by armed groups in the Central African Republic. The UN Organization Stabilization Mission documented the recruitment of 996 children over a 20-month period in 2012–2013 in the Democratic Republic of the Congo. These child victims are both Congolese, as well as children from neighboring countries, as these armed groups operate cross-border within the entire Central African region (UNODC 2014 citing reports from UNICEF, the UN Organization Stabilization Mission in the DRC, and Report of the Secretary-General on the UN Organization Stabilization Mission in the Democratic Republic of the Congo).

The modus operandi used to recruit children into armed forces may depend upon the government or rebel force in which the child serves. While the Lord's Resistance Army in Uganda (Joseph Kony) was notorious for kidnapping and forcing children to join its rebel forces (Human Rights Watch,

1997), children in other rebel forces have voluntarily joined (Human Rights Watch, 2007; War Child, 2007). They do so for reasons of protection, revenge, socioeconomic motivations, and cultural and ideological beliefs (War Child, 2007).

Despite the fact that the majority of children working as combatants are males, female children are also found in militias. They, and also younger children, are used in support roles as porters, messengers, cooks, guards, suicide bombers, or sex slaves. The use of children in armed forces, while also perpetrated by governments (U.S. Department of State, 2014), is of particular concern when the children are used in rebel forces. In 2012, children fighting in rebel forces were identified in Afghanistan, Burma, Central African Republic, Chad, Colombia, Democratic Republic of Congo (DRC), India, Iraq, Philippines, Somalia, South Sudan, Sudan, Thailand, and Yemen (Human Rights Watch, 2012). Additionally, the governments of Burma, Central African Republic, Democratic Republic of the Congo, Rwanda, Somalia, South Sudan, Sudan, Syria, and Yemen have been implicated in the use of child soldiers (U.S. Department of State, 2014).

Disturbing reports of new forms of trafficking and exploitation of young girls have surfaced recently. According to relatives of the 234 girls kidnapped in Chibok, Nigeria, in April 2014, mass wedding ceremonies occurred and the girls were sold for as little as US$12 to Boko Haram's Islamist militants to be used as wives (McCoy, 2014). Similar atrocities have been linked to ISIS, which is reported to have kidnapped and trafficked Yazidi women and children and sold them for as little as US$25 or kept them as slaves (Shelley, 2014; Batha, 2015). These examples are not just of forced marriage, but are tantamount to slavery.

Organ trafficking, or the act of trafficking human beings for the purpose of organ removal—usually a kidney—is a global problem (Organization for Security and Cooperation in Europe [OSCE] Office of the Special Representative and Coordinator for Combating Trafficking in Human Beings, 2013) and follows patterns similar to more traditional forms of trafficking. There are traditional donor and recipient countries (Aronowitz and Isitman, 2013). Donors are usually young and poor; recipients are wealthy and older. Urban legends exist of victims awakening in a bathtub filled with ice and a huge scar where they used to have a kidney. This scenario belies the fact that many donors consent to sell an organ (Yie, 2010). Deception occurs when donors are not informed of medical risks, nor are they given adequate postoperative care. Victims may not be paid the agreed-upon sum or given any compensation for their organ. Other cases involve deception in which body parts are removed without the permission—or in some cases even the knowledge—of the donor. A patient undergoing an operation to have an ovarian cyst removed was surprised to find that the hospital removed her kidney without informing her or her doctor (Schepper-Hughes, 2001). In Argentina, the director of an asylum for mentally ill persons exploited his patients by providing corneas, kidneys, and blood to area hospitals (Schepper-Hughes, 2003).

Organ trafficking differs from other forms of trafficking in that the crime cannot occur without the complicity of medical personnel. Unlike trafficking for criminal activities or practices in illicit markets (forced prostitution), in which the trafficker or trafficking organization may comprise only criminals or persons involved in criminal activities, the practice of organ trafficking requires highly skilled medical personnel to carry out the procedure in clinics or hospitals. The demand is generated not by the desire for inexpensive products or services—as is the case with domestic service, prostitution, and products produced through forced labor—but the need for a life-saving operation.

The market in which human trafficking takes place will vary between and within countries and may be influenced by such things as the need for seasonal workers in agriculture, the presence of large construction projects in a given city (for large sporting events), or an influx of tourists creating a demand for (child) sex tourism in a specific holiday location. This ever-changing pattern requires risk analysis at the local level, a topic discussed in more detail later in this chapter.

The Victims

While trafficking cuts across age and gender, the demographic variables of victims is largely determined by the market in which victims are found and the region of the world in which data are collected. In many parts of the world, women and children are most often the victims of human trafficking, particularly with respect to sexual exploitation and domestic service. In other sectors, such as fishing or construction, men are the victims of exploitation. Trafficking is not just a problem of poor countries; persons are trafficked even within affluent societies (see U.S. Department of State, 2016, and previous reports; World Bank, 2009). Most experts agree that it is not poverty but vulnerability that places persons at risk of being trafficked. The U.S. Department of Health and Human Services (HHS) identifies common characteristics that make persons vulnerable to trafficking. "They often come from countries or communities with high rates of crime, poverty, and corruption; lack opportunities for education; lack family support (e.g., orphaned, runaway/thrown-away, homeless, family members collaborating with traffickers); and/or have a history of physical and/or sexual abuse" (Clawson and Dutch, 2008). To more fully understand what puts certain people at risk of trafficking, one must understand the risk factors to which they are exposed.

Risk Factors for Trafficking

According to the World Bank (2009, 11), the following serve as risk factors for human trafficking:

- Poverty
- Gender
- Age

- Limited economic and educational opportunity
- Poor governance
- Lack of rule of law
- Political conflict and war
- Violence
- Social exclusion
- Social and cultural structures (power, hierarchy, and social order)
- Marginalization and discrimination based on ethnicity, race, disability, and religion
- Community's tradition of movement (migration) and other social practices
- Climate change and natural disaster
- Individual's drug and alcohol addiction and mental health

The factors identified by the World Bank comprise individual factors (e.g., individual's drug and alcohol addiction, gender, and age), structural or recurring external factors (e.g., poverty, poor governance, and lack of rule of law), and intermittent factors (e.g., climate change and natural disaster—an example of this occurred during the tsunami in Banda Aceh, Indonesia, in December 2004. During the crisis, children were separated from their parents and before protective mechanisms could be put in place, human traffickers began moving in to take children).

It is often not one but a combination of risk factors that, when combined, make individuals more likely to become victims of trafficking. The International Labour Organization— International Programme on the Elimination of Child Labour (ILO-IPEC) has identified risk factors for the trafficking of children and adolescents into commercial sexual exploitation. Vulnerability or risk factors can be broken down into family-related risk factors, child-specific risk factors, socioeconomic risk factors, and environmental risk factors. A child may score high (or low) on a combination of these factors. This may explain why children in a particular village may be at risk due to the existence, for example, of child sex tourism, but why some children ("high" on family-related or child-specific risk factors) become trafficked victims while others do not, or even why one child in a particular family is more at risk than another. Table 2.1 identifies individual variables within each category.

Table 2.1   Vulnerability Factors of Children and Adolescents to Commercial Sexual Exploitation

Child-specific risk factors
- Absence of legal identity or documentation, lack of citizenship
- Need to earn money to survive
- Homelessness, living on the street
- Expulsion or exclusion from school
- Child pregnancy and maternity
- Consumerism
- Low self-esteem
- History of drug or alcohol abuse
- Cultural obligation to help support the family
- Negative peer pressure
- Being a victim of domestic violence and/or sexual abuse
- Being a victim of other forms of child labor
- Having been trafficked for other forms of child labor

Family-related risk factors
- Poverty
- Social exclusion, including being from an ethnic minority
- Weakening of family and community networks
- Absence of parental figures
- History of sexual abuse within families
- Witnessing or being victims of domestic violence
- HIV/AIDS infection within the family
- Practices of prostitution among family members
- Gender inequalities and discrimination
- Low education levels of caregivers and low value attached to education
- Prejudice against homosexuality

Socioeconomic-related risk factors

- High population density
- Working or living in or near risk environments: streets or slums; concentration of night entertainment (bars, discos, brothels)
- High poverty and unemployment levels
- Movement of people
- Access to highways, ports, or borders

Environmental-related risk factors

- Existence of child labor
- Tolerance of prostitution at community or national level
- Existence of sex tourism
- Consumerism
- Irresponsible exercise of sexuality, especially male sexuality
- Perpetrator preferences for young children and adolescents
- Perpetrator preferences for young children in the context of HIV/AIDS
- Proximity to military camps, large public works, mining camps
- Proximity to armed conflict zones
- Impunity caused by weak laws and law enforcement
- Corruption, organized crime

Source: ILO-IPEC, Commercial Sexual Exploitation of Children and Adolescents (no date, p. 3).

Male Victims

Due to the emphasis on trafficking for sexual exploitation, much less is known about adult male victims of trafficking than about female and child victims (although the ILO and International Trade Union Confederation have done much to profile the abuses and exploitation of workers worldwide; Surtees, 2008). Almost nothing is known about the sexual exploitation of adult men, although the U.S. Department of State (2016) profiles a case involving Hungarian men who came to the United States to work as escorts, only to find themselves trafficked into prostitution and having to work 18–20 hours a day without pay. Slowly, countries are becoming more adept at investigating cases of labor exploitation. What we find is that adult males are (over)represented as victims of exploitation in often legitimate labor markets—the mining, fishing, construction, and manufacturing industries. This pattern varies across countries and geographical regions. Mexican and Guatemalan men have been found in forced labor in Florida's citrus industry (Free the Slaves, 2004). In Western Europe, male victims have been found trafficked into forced labor in restaurants and sweat shops. In Italy, trafficked victims forced to work in the manufacturing industry have been linked to international fashion houses that make use of underpaid labor (Savona et al., 2003). Internal trafficking is prevalent in Brazil, and Brazilian men are exploited in rural areas, often in logging, mining, agriculture, charcoal production camps, on cattle ranches, and sugarcane plantations (U.S. Department of State, 2014). Victims are exploited in the fishing industry in countries that rely heavily upon the trade, such as Thailand (Bollinger and McQuay, 2012).

With regard to the gender of victims of sexual exploitation, the majority of those identified are female (UNODC, 2014). However, the trafficking of young boys into sexual exploitation is a pattern that has been identified in numerous countries, particularly those attracting child sex tourists (in countries such as the Dominican Republic, Mexico, Sri Lanka, or Thailand). In Afghanistan and Pakistan, boys are forced to partake in the cultural practice of *bacha bazi* (where boys dressed as girls dance at private parties and weddings solely attended by men), and afterwards are often offered to the highest bidder (U.S. Department of State, 2016; Aronowitz, 2015a; Martin and Shaheen, 2014; see also the PBS documentary *The Dancing Boys of Afghanistan*). Sexual exploitation of boys is reported in the Czech Republic, the Gambia, and Ghana (U.S. Department of State, 2016).

Young foreign men from Africa, Asia, and South America, some of them minors, were brought into the Netherlands and forced into prostitution (Van der Zee, 2013). The National

Rapporteur on Trafficking in Human Beings and Sexual Violence against Children in the Netherlands reports that men in forced prostitution are the invisible victims, who because of shame and the lack of awareness of the problem rarely come to the attention of first responders and police (see also Human Trafficking Search, 2014).

Child Victims

Children are particularly susceptible to trafficking due their innocence, powerlessness, and inability to protect themselves. Compared to adults, children can be made to work longer hours with less food, are easier to manipulate, and less willing or able to claim their rights (ILO-IPEC, 2002). When removed from their social networks and families, victims become isolated and this increases their vulnerability to exploitation.

Child trafficking patterns vary by region (UNODC, 2014; 2016). In East Asia and the Pacific, the majority of children trafficked often end up in prostitution, although some are exploited in agricultural and industrial work. In West Africa, young children are forced to wash cars, beg, work as domestic servants, petty traders or hawkers, bus conductors, on farms, or in rock quarries (Aronowitz, 2006). In Nigeria, for example, young boys from the age of five or six may be entrusted by their families to serve a religious leader, or *marabout*. In addition to performing various household tasks, the child is often, as part of the learning process, forced to beg (U.S. Department of State, 2016; this same pattern was confirmed by participants from West and Central Africa at a training program in regional cooperation, peace, and stability for diplomats from West Africa and the Sahel at the Clingendael Institute in The Hague, May 28, 2015). In Europe, children are trafficked for sexual and labor exploitation. Girls as young as 13, mainly from Eastern Europe and Asia, are trafficked as "mail-order brides" and are then forced to become involved in pornography or prostitution (UNICEF, *Factsheet: Child Trafficking*). In China, children are often abducted and trafficked into forced labor and begging (U.S. Department of State, 2016). This pattern differs in the Americas and the Caribbean, where child trafficking is driven by child sex tourism. In South Asia, children are sold into bondage to settle debts (UNICEF, http://www .unicef.org/sowc06/profiles/trafficking.php). This pattern has also been observed in Afghanistan (U.S. Department of State, 2014). In the Gulf States, children under the age of five from South Asia and Africa have been forced, in the past, to become camel jockeys, while in other parts of the world, young boys are kidnapped, sold by parents, or willingly join militias to serve as child soldiers.

Children trafficked into labor exploitation or forced begging are not necessarily safe from sexual assaults or sexual exploitation. Children hired to work as domestic servants in families report being sexually abused by their owners. Children used for forced begging are often moved into prostitution when they become too old to beg. Children trafficked into one form of labor (such as work in factories or as domestic servants) may be sold into another form of labor (forced prostitution).

Other Vulnerable Victims

A position of vulnerability is often exploited by traffickers. Cases have been documented of recruitment among vulnerable groups, to include the mentally or physically impaired, homeless or drug addicts, or runaway children. In the countries of the former Soviet Union, disabled people have been forced into street begging (Baskakova et al., 2005), while the exploitation of disabled persons was documented in Austria, Colombia, Iraq, the Republic of Korea, and Romania (U.S. Department of State, 2016). Operation Golf uncovered Roma children (a highly marginalized ethnic minority group) who were trafficked into a large-scale begging and crime ring in the United Kingdom (ECPATUK, 2010), and in Florida, law enforcement officials uncovered a case of domestic trafficking involving U.S. men recruited from shelters for the homeless, as well as men who might be suffering from mental illness or who were addicted to drugs and subsequently forced to work in the agricultural sector (OSCE, 2006). The U.S. Department of State (2014, 132) reports that in China, "traffickers are increasingly subjecting deaf and mute individuals to forced labor" and "persons with developmental disabilities for forced begging and forced labor."

The Impact of Human Trafficking: Harm to the Victims

The trauma experienced by victims varies from one individual to the other and may be influenced by the nature of the exploitation, the length of time a victim is exploited, the age of the victim upon being trafficked, and the degree of violence and manipulation to which the victim is exposed (Aronowitz, 2009a).

Victims of both sexual exploitation and forced labor suffer severe human rights abuses (Bales, 2005; Feingold, 2005). A leading authority on slavery has stated that "Victims of forced labor have been tortured, raped, assaulted, and murdered. They have been held in absolute control by their captors and stripped of their dignity. Some have been subjected to forced abortion, dangerous working conditions, poor nutrition, and humiliation. Some have died during their enslavement. Others have been physically or psychologically scarred for life. Once freed, many will suffer from a host of health-related problems, including repetitive stress injury, chronic back pain, visual and respiratory illnesses, sexually transmitted diseases, and depression" (Bales, 2005, 52). Stories abound of the harm done to victims of sexual exploitation. A closer study of media reports on labor exploitation in the Gulf States, and in particular Qatar, exposes abominable living conditions and hundreds of deaths of foreign workers in building the 2022 World Cup stadiums in Qatar (Gibson, 2014).

Researchers in the United Kingdom studied the physical and psychological health consequences of 207 women and adolescent victims of sex trafficking from 14 countries in the European Union. They measured the impact of a number of problems at three different times. The first measurement took place within the first two weeks after a woman entered a post-trafficking assistance program. The second interview occurred between 28 and 56 days after entry into care, while the third interview was usually conducted after a period of three months (Zimmerman et al., 2006). The researchers found a number of physical, neurological, gastrointestinal, sexual and reproductive, and other health problems associated with the trafficking experience. The most common problems were headaches, fatigue, dizzy spells, back pain, stomach or abdominal pain, and difficulty remembering things. Other symptoms were weight loss and loss of appetite, vaginal infections, chest pain, vision problems, and rashes (Zimmerman et al., 2006).

With respect to mental health problems, women reported symptoms of depression (lack of interest in things, hopeless about the future, feelings of worthlessness, loneliness, and suicidal thoughts), anxiety (fearful, tense, terrified, restless, scared, and nervous), and hostility (urges to hurt someone or destroy property, frequent arguments, easily irritated, and outbursts of temper; Zimmerman et al., 2006). The percentages of women reporting these symptoms at each of the three interview stages can be found in the Table 2.2. What is clear from these data is that the most critical time for victims is the two weeks after they have been placed in care programs. A smaller percentage of the population reports exhibiting these symptoms at later interviews.

Women also reported symptoms that are characteristic of posttraumatic stress disorder (PTSD). More than half of the victims (56%) reported having enough symptoms to be suggestive of PTSD at the initial interview. The proportion of women with these symptoms decreased to 12 percent during

Table 2.2   Prevalence of Women Reporting Depression, Anxiety, and Hostility Symptoms

	Women Reporting Any Symptoms (%)		
Depression Symptoms	**Interview 1**	**Interview 2**	**Interview 3**
No interest in things	73	56	41
Hopelessness about the future	76	72	59
Worthlessness feelings	78	68	52
Loneliness	88	79	72
Depression/very sad	95	90	75
Suicidal thoughts	38	9	6
Anxiety Symptoms			
Fearful	85	71	43
Tense or keyed up	84	68	37
Terror/panic spells	61	33	8
Restlessness	67	51	19
Scared suddenly without reason	75	61	24
Nervousness or shakiness inside	91	81	51
Hostility Symptoms			
Urges to beat, injure, or hurt someone	36	8	8
Urges to break or smash things	29	8	8
Frequent arguments	57	12	8
Annoyed/irritated easily	83	27	19
Temper outbursts that cannot be controlled	67	12	10

Source: Zimmerman et al., 2006; Table 5, p. 18.

the second interview and to 6 percent by the third interview (Zimmerman et al., 2006). The data can be found in Table 2.3.

The previous study examined women trafficked into sexual exploitation (slightly more than 92% of the sample), or women who had been sexually abused while they served as domestic workers. The question remains—what impact does exploitation have on victims of labor trafficking? Researchers in Nepal studied the effects upon the mental health of survivors of human

Table 2.3   Prevalence of PTSD-Associated Symptoms over Time

PTSD-Associated Symptoms	Women Ranking Symptoms as Severe (%)		
	Interview 1	Interview 2	Interview 3
Recurrent thoughts/memories of terrifying events	75	35	16
Feeling as though event is happening again	52	18	8
Recurrent nightmares	54	16	13
Feeling detached/withdrawn	60	26	14
Unable to feel emotions	44	10	2
Jumpy, easily startled	67	20	16
Difficulty concentrating	52	15	8
Trouble sleeping	67	35	24
Feeling on guard	64	20	6
Feeling irritable, having outbursts of anger	53	19	16
Avoiding activities that remind of traumatic or hurtful event	61	11	13
Inability to remember part of most traumatic or hurtful event	36	6	3
Less interest in daily activities	46	10	6
Feeling as if you do not have a future	65	36	10
Avoiding thoughts or feelings associated with the traumatic events	58	17	23
Sudden emotional or physical reaction when reminded of the most hurtful or traumatic events	65	16	14

Source: Zimmerman et al., 2006; Table 6, p. 20.

trafficking for sexual and labor (nonsexual) exploitation. Both groups were diagnosed with anxiety, depression, and PTSD. There were no statistically significant differences between victims trafficked for sex (97.7%) or nonsexual exploitation (87.5%) on measures of anxiety. There were, however, statistically significant differences between the groups on measures of depression and PTSD. All victims of sexual exploitation scored above the cutoff point for depression, whereas only 80.8 percent of the non–sex workers scored above the cutoff point for depression. The numbers were lower for PTSD (29.5% of the sex worker group as opposed to 7.5% of the non–sex worker group).

Although measures on mental health problems were higher in those exposed to sexual exploitation than the non–sex workers group, the findings indicate that victims of labor trafficking also suffer emotional harm. Additionally, almost 30 percent of the victims of sex trafficking tested positive for HIV, while none of the victims of labor trafficking tested positive (although 80% of the sample was not tested). Other differences were found between the two groups of survivors. Victims of nonsexual (labor) exploitation were trafficked at a younger age and were exploited for a longer period of time (Tsutsumi et al., 2008).

Victims of sexual exploitation face stigmatization from their families and the community. This hampers efforts to repatriate them and reintegrate them into their home communities (this problem is also faced by child soldiers who have often committed atrocities against residents in their communities). The Nigerian Immigration Service and workers from NGOs in Nigeria reported that the women trafficked into prostitution in Italy, and who are subsequently arrested and deported from Italy, are "crazed" when they return home. "They are angry and belligerent due to the trauma experienced both by the traffickers and police and immigration officials who arrest and deport them with little more than the clothes they were wearing at the time of arrest. After having spent weeks to months working in prostitution, the women are not even allowed to take the few possessions and clothes that they had been able to accumulate" (Aronowitz, 2009a, 47; Information provided to the author during trafficking assessments to Nigeria in November 2000 and 2003.).

The International Organization for Migration, which often comes into contact with trafficking victims who need assistance in resettling in their home countries, reports that victims "who do escape have been so brutalized that they experience life-long psychological trauma, and, according to psychologists, only 30 percent fully recover to live a normal life" (Counter trafficking.org). It should be noted that the victims with whom IOM comes into contact are not representative of all victims of trafficking. Many do not desire or accept assistance, and these individuals' experiences and how they deal with them may differ from victims who accept assistance.

Why Victims Do Not Identify Themselves as Victims

The "typical" victim does not exist and not all victims suffer from severe physical and mental health problems as a result of their trafficking experience. One important quality that differentiates victims is the way in which they cope with their situation. While some victims recognize their victimization and are willing to seek assistance, others refuse to relate to the term of trafficking victim or identify with the victim role and thus refuse assistance. In a study of trafficked women exploited in various sectors of the sex industry (from massage parlors to strip clubs) in Canada, even women brought to Canada under false pretenses, subjected to debt bondage and forced to work in slavery-like conditions, did not consider themselves trafficked victims (McDonald and Timoshkina, 2007). The same pattern occurred in the Netherlands. In the largest case involving trafficking for sexual exploitation in a number of cities in the Netherlands, the police identified 55 suspects and 120 prostitutes working for the trafficking network. Seventy-eight of the women were identified as possible or presumed victims of forced prostitution. Only 10 women filed an official complaint with the police against the group—some of these wanted to withdraw their statements at a later point in time during the investigation (KLPD—Dienst Nationale Recherche). One woman whom police believed to be a victim in the case responded to accusations that she was forced into prostitution and subjected to exploitation and violence with the following comment, "This scenario appears to be more like a Hollywood film than reality" (Navis, 2008, 8).

In addition to fear, traumatic bonding, and romantic relationships that some victims form with their traffickers, some victims simply refuse to self-identify or accept assistance because they are able to rely upon family support in their countries of origin. Others, having failed in their first attempt to go abroad, are determined to "go abroad again" (Brunovskis and Surtees, 2007), a euphemism for returning to prostitution, but the victims often believe that once they have "learned the ropes" they can work as freelance sex workers the second time around. During a visit to a shelter in Tirana, Albania, the author met with a number of young girls who had been repatriated from different countries in the European Union. All appeared to be under the age of 20 and had been forced to work in prostitution for a number of years. One young woman sat with a baby on her lap. When asked what she had planned for her future, she replied that she wanted to return to Amsterdam and continue working in prostitution—the next time on her own.

From Victim to Survivor

In the trafficking discourse, the terms "victim" and "survivor" may be used interchangeably. Both refer to individuals who were trafficked and exploited. They differ in terms of the context in which they are used. The term "victim," often used by criminal justice system practitioners, refers to a person who has suffered harm as the result of a crime. Victims of crimes are entitled to certain legal standing and rights within the criminal justice system. In contrast, the term "survivor" is widely preferred and used by service providers to empower individuals and "to recognize the strength and courage it takes to overcome victimization" (Office of Victims of Crime).

The Office for Victims of Crime (part of the U.S. Department of Justice) suggests that task forces consult and partner with survivors in their community. A National Survivor

Network was established in 2011 in an effort to support connections between survivors of trafficking and strengthen their position. Members of the network come from 24 countries, residing in over 32 states in the United States. Members identify key pieces of federal legislation that they believe are most important to the prevention of human trafficking and the protection of victims and play an influential role as advocates (National Survivor Network).

Traffickers: Who They Are and Why They Become Involved in the Crime of Human Trafficking

Rational choice theory argues that criminals, as reasoning beings, chose a path after weighing the costs, benefits, and risks of their acts. In the case of traffickers, considerations would be the need for economic gain weighed against the risk of arrest and prosecution, and the severity of the punishment. Rational choice theory has not only been popular in explaining predatory economic crimes, such as burglary or robbery, but can also be used to understand human trafficking. Rational choice theory is both offence and offender specific and differentiates between crime as an event and criminality as a personal trait (Siegel, 2004; Cornish and Clarke, 1987). The theory is, therefore, capable of explaining both the involvement of professional criminals in trafficking enterprises as well as otherwise 'law-abiding' citizens who exploit and enslave a domestic worker (Klopott, 2009; at least 42 allegations of diplomats engaged in the trafficking and exploitation of their domestic servants have been documented in the United States since 2000). Regarding *offense-specific* acts, the offender, in this case the trafficker, reacts to the characteristics of a particular offence. Every criminal act has certain risks and rewards. In trafficking, the reward is the almost endless supply of potential victims, high demand for their services, large profits, and low risk of being caught and prosecuted. *Offender-specific* implies that the individual considers whether or not he or she possesses the "prerequisites to commit a successful criminal act, including the proper skills, motives, needs and fears" (Siegel, 2004,109). These two characteristics are interactive and form a process known as *choice structuring*.

Criminals involved in drug dealing and burglary have been shown to rationally choose (1) the *type of crime* in which to become involved as well as their target and the time and place of the crime. In the case of trafficking, traffickers make rational choices to increase profit by moving victims from rural to urban areas within a country or from transitional or developing nations to industrialized nations. They set up brothels near military bases or traffic women to construction sites to service the male victims of trafficking who have been brought there (the Mexican Cadena family created a market for sexual services among illegal migrant workers in Florida and then supplied the men with often underage women from Mexico).

Criminals have also been known to (2) *select the target* of crime. Traffickers are quick to identify vulnerable victims— families facing economic crises, daughters with sick parents or siblings, or naïve women or those with low self-esteem. They prey on runaway children or those who are victims of child abuse, in which parents are alcoholic or administrators of orphanages (Shelley, 2010). Traffickers may target runaway or street children knowing that no one will miss them and notify the authorities. A common pattern found in some Western European countries is the recruitment of women already working in prostitution in their home countries for forced prostitution in the destination country. This deliberate choice of women already working in prostitution before being trafficked, is "a strategic way for traffickers to mitigate some of the resistance of unwilling victims" (Surtees, 2008, 51).

Rational choice theory also considers criminals' (3) choice of *time and place of the crime and target locations*. The concept of time may be relevant in trafficking for forced commercial sexual exploitation when large sporting events occur or in seizing orphaned, separated, or displaced children after a natural disaster. It may prove to be more relevant for trafficking in labor exploitation when the need for seasonal workers in agriculture at particular times of the year may generate a demand for cheap labor, which can easily be filled with trafficked victims. Place is also important with respect to moving *prostituted* women (or trafficked persons) to less visible places (from brothels to private apartments) that are more difficult for authorities to monitor.

Whether or not an individual decides to become involved in the crime of trafficking, and the degree to which one is willing and able, depends upon "[t]heir previous learning and experience—the values and norms around them, their moral code, their personal and vicarious experience with crime, their view of themselves and the degree to which they are able to plan and exercise foresight" (Aronowitz et al., 2010, 30). Previous learning experiences may be influenced by such things as age, gender, experiences in the family, morals, values, and individual traits (Cornish and Clarke, 1987).

The longer traffickers perpetrate the crime and go unpunished, the more professional they become at their activities, which may expand to trafficking larger numbers of victims, the use of forged documents, or the corruption of border control or law enforcement officials. This newly accrued "expertise" helps to increase profits while reducing risks. Traffickers may become more dependent upon their easily made criminal earnings and their involvement in crime—and perhaps the need to cooperate in buying and selling victims, procuring forged documents, renting apartments to use as brothels—forces them or facilitates their orientation towards criminal peer groups.

Rational choice may explain which practical considerations and actions are necessary for an individual to consider his or her involvement in crime. Another perspective, neutralization theory, examines the justifications used by otherwise law-abiding people to validate their actions. Neutralization theory puts forth a number of arguments, but the most relevant to the crime of human trafficking are *denial of the victim, denial of injury,* and *denial of responsibility.* With respect to denial of the victim, traffickers may deny that victims are harmed because they may have been working as prostitutes in their home country or may have willingly agreed to sell an organ (having been deceived in terms of the extent of the exploitation). Denial of injury occurs when traffickers may argue that a domestic servant (despite exploitation) is living in a beautiful home and earning more money than he or she would have at home in their country of origin. Denial of responsibility is used to place blame for a criminal act outside of the responsibility of the actor, who argues that poor upbringing, a difficult life, or unemployment was responsible for involvement in crime (Sykes and Matza, 1957).

A two-year European Union Study of human traffickers and their motivations, *Trafficking as a Criminal Enterprise* (TRACE), examined 160 court files and collected data on 334 human traffickers from Bulgaria, Cyprus, the Netherlands, and Romania (with information supplemented from Poland and the United Kingdom). The results of the study found that traffickers—those who were caught and prosecuted—were predominantly male (82%), had low levels of education, were unemployed with high debts or receive social benefits, and many had a criminal record and came from families with criminal records. Some were diagnosed with psychological health problems (according to experts, personality disorder and narcissistic personality) and they lack empathy and remorse. Many view women as a commodity. They show a high need for sensation and action. Criminals indicate a number of motives and incentives for becoming involved in human trafficking. Among these are the desire to improve one's social life, to become better integrated into a group, prestige and power, or the desire to feel "macho," excitement, to achieve success, the desire to maintain friendships within a group of people who were involved in illegal activities, or to be accepted in a relationship (one trafficker was in love with fellow traffickers; TRACE, 2016). These motivations may explain why individuals initially become involved in trafficking activities. Their psychological makeup (narcissistic personality disorder, lack of empathy, and guilt feelings) may explain how traffickers can continue to exploit victims without caring about them.

A word of caution should be made about the traffickers included in this study. They were the individuals who were caught. Many traffickers are not caught and tried in court, and often in large-scale trafficking operations, the head of the organization or the "brains behind the operation" may elude arrest and prosecution. This sample, therefore, may be biased.

Use of Violence and Threats to Control Victims

Violence or threats of violence are often used to intimidate or punish noncompliant victims. The degree to which traffickers exercise control over their victims has been well documented in victims' accounts. Seizure of documents, threats of beatings, or to harm the victim's family in the country of origin have been reported to police and NGOs. In one case in the United Kingdom, a trafficker threatened to use a young Czech mother's children in pornographic videos if she did not cooperate and work for him as a prostitute (Russel, 2008). Violence is used routinely to "keep victims in line" or prevent future transgressions. Violence is also used as punishment for rule-violating behavior. Women who have tried to escape, communicate with customers, or cooperate with police are often severely beaten. The Director of the United States Office to Monitor and Combat Trafficking in Persons told of a meeting in a shelter in Thailand with a young Burmese woman. The woman was forced to work in a shrimp farming and processing factory, which resembled a prison camp. When she tried to escape but was caught by prison guards, she was beaten for trying to flee, tied to a pole in the middle of the courtyard, and refused food or water.

As another form of punishment, to stigmatize her, Aye Aye's hair was shaved off (Lagon, 2007). Numerous studies report that between a quarter to more than half of trafficked women seeking assistance from organizations working with migrants or those repatriated have been severely beaten and/or raped by their pimps and traffickers (Farr, 2005).

Another instance in which violence is used by traffickers is as a warning to keep other trafficked victims "in line." Punishment is extreme and occurs publicly. Two such examples involve a murder in Istanbul, Turkey, of two Ukrainian women who were thrown to their deaths from a balcony while six of their Russian friends watched. In another incident in Serbia, a woman who refused to work as a prostitute was beheaded in public (Spector 1998).

A large-scale and highly sophisticated trafficking-prostitution ring run by two Turkish-German brothers (Hasan and Saban Baran) in the Netherlands—the Sneep case—was described as one of the most brutal. Women who spoke to police were beaten with baseball bats and then submerged in cold water to prevent or reduce the visibility of bruises. They were forced to undergo abortions and breast implants. A number of victims were also tattooed with the name or initials of one of the two brothers. The message: the girls were not for sale (Dongen, van, 2007a, 2007b).

While seizure of documents and beatings are common methods to exert control, other forms are more psychological, nuanced, and less visible. The Baran brothers, in addition to beating and constantly supervising the women they forced into prostitution, played games with them in order to ensure their compliance. Women were complimented, made jealous, belittled, and abused (Dongen, van, Menno, 2007a, 2007b). This same pattern is found in the practices of "loverboys" (a modus operandi) in the Netherlands in which slightly older men (usually of foreign descent) target often insecure or emotionally dependent younger (Dutch) women. After a period of courtship, the young woman is often told that she could help her "boyfriend" out of financial problems if she would have sex for money and turn the earnings over to the boyfriend. This creation of emotional dependence facilitates the long-term exploitation of young women who may not even realize that they are being exploited (Bovenkerk and Pronk, 2007; National Rapporteur on Trafficking in Human Beings and Sexual Violence Against Children, 2005). In a case that shocked the Netherlands, a 16-year-old girl, over a period of 10 days, was suspected of having been forced into prostitution with between 50 and 80 clients, while her 21-year-old "boyfriend" remained in the hotel room bathroom "to protect her." Two of the clients under investigation committed suicide. The young girl told authorities that she was not forced into having sex (Back 2015; Klompenhouwer 2015). The Deputy Director at the Washington-based Polaris Project describes the same pattern in the United States. Runaway girls are targeted by pimps and showered with a mixture of affection and violence, gifts and degradation. The girl may be required to tattoo her pimp's name on her thigh as a sign of ownership. In exchange, she may be given jewelry or clothing as presents. It is the emotional bond and fear that keeps the victim tied to the trafficker (Kristof, 2008).

The situation may be changing in some countries. According to organizations working with or conducting research on trafficked victims, trafficking is increasing, but fewer victims are coming to the attention of these or other official agencies. The pattern of exploitation and abuse is changing. There is a decreased use of physical abuse and overt violence, and psychological abuse and manipulation is increasing (Surtees, 2007). Exploitation is becoming more subtle and control over victims is more relaxed. Victims are being given small payments and are even being moved into their own apartments, in an attempt on the part of traffickers to buy the victim's silence and ensure that victims to do not denounce the traffickers (Leman and Janssens, 2008). This diffuses the sharp line drawn between trafficked victims and freelance sex workers and makes it difficult for law enforcement and agencies providing assistance to identify who is a trafficked victim entitled to help and who is (an undocumented migrant and) a freelance sex worker (and possibly subject to deportation).

From Victim to Victimizer: How Victims Become Traffickers

In perhaps no other crime category does one see former victims becoming perpetrators. With respect to human trafficking, this phenomenon has been documented in the case of organ donors becoming organ brokers—the key person linking future donors with hospitals willing to perform the illegal transplant (Bienstock, 2013), as well as with trafficked women forced into prostitution who later become part of the same criminal organization (Hughes, 2000; Siegel and de Blank, 2010), as is the case of Nigerian victims who become madams.

It is not always clear if the trafficked persons moving up the trafficking chain do so willingly, whether they are coerced into recruiting other victims or whether they do so to have their debt removed. Women may be sent back to their countries of origin to recruit friends under the watchful eye and threat of the organization that trafficked them. They may knowingly recruit women as a way to buy their freedom or may have willingly become part of the trafficking organization (Surtees, 2008). The United Nations has a name for it: "happy trafficking," although there is nothing happy about it. It has been described as a sort of human pyramid scheme in which a few of the trafficked victims are released, sometimes accompanied by financial incentives, to return to their home countries and recruit other victims. The term "happy" refers to the illusion that the new recruiters create by pretending that they have had a wonderful experience in a legitimate job abroad. This manipulative method reduces the risk to organizers by putting women in visible positions as recruiters and at the same time increases profits, turning victims into "proxy recruiters" and eventually traffickers (Tomiuc, 2008).

Child victims of labor exploitation are often completely unaware of the fact that they have been exploited. NGOs working with children in West Africa have reported that in spite of being exploited at hard labor under deplorable conditions for years at time, children are given their promised bicycle at the end of their term and are allowed to return home, proud of the fact that they are the only ones with a bicycle in their village. Some of these children return to their village and recruit other children to work abroad (Aronowitz, 2009a).

Trafficking Organizations

There is no such thing as a "typical trafficker" or trafficking organization. Traffickers and their organizations vary and can be placed on a continuum from individual, solo operators or pairs of offenders to small groups of criminals working together in a network, to sophisticated, international organizations moving large numbers of victims across continents (Schloenhardt, 1999). The individual or solo trafficker is responsible for the entire range of services from recruitment to transportation and exploitation (Monzini, 2001). These persons often exploit one or more victims who they recruit through false promises of work or marriage. Examples of individual traffickers are the so-called loverboys who court their victim and then force her into prostitution. Pairs of traffickers may work in a similar fashion. Foreign diplomats have been linked to the exploitation of their domestic servants (ACLU). In a study of 46 trafficking cases in the State of Texas, researchers found that approximately 22 percent (n=10) were identified as "Mom and Pop" cases of exploitation in domestic servitude. Their victims were primarily foreign born; the traffickers were often a highly educated married couple from the same country of origin as the victim (Busch-Armendariz et al., 2009). From the same study, and also in the category of individual trafficker, is the "Minor Pimp," an adult male involved in domestic sex trafficking, often of minors. These cases also comprised almost 22 percent of the cases studied (Busch-Armendariz et al., 2009).

The second type of trafficking organization is often labeled a "network" and characterized by small groups of organized criminals. They may be involved in domestic trafficking within a country's borders or small-scale international trafficking, usually from nearby countries. These "loose confederations of organized criminal entrepreneurs or enterprises" exhibit some degree of sophistication and specialization (Aronowitz, 2009a, 67).

At the end of the continuum are the highly structured, criminal organizations controlling the entire trafficking process (from recruitment, transportation, exploitation) and providing the full set of services (to include documentation forgery and/or corruption of police officials, and safe houses [where necessary]) from start to finish. Each sector has a delineated task from the recruitment to the exploitation phase (Monzini, 2001). These complex organizations have been characterized as decentralized, horizontal, and flexible, allowing cooperation with other criminal groups and a rapid response to changes in law enforcement activity and legislation, as well as fluctuations in market supply and demand (Aronowitz, 2009a).

Trafficking organizations have been described as learning organizations due to their ability to rapidly change and adapt to their environment to avoid detection and increase profits (Leman and Janssens, 2008). An example of this is seen in European countries (Belgium and the Netherlands) among some trafficking groups. Traffickers are using less physical violence and more subtle psychological coercion. Victims are being given more freedom and small wages. Traffickers have found that this increased freedom buys the women's silence and ensures their allegiance to the traffickers.

Due to the highly sophisticated organization, members may be located in origin, transit, and destination countries providing services along the route (Aronowitz, 2009a). Larger organizations may be divided into smaller subunits that employ criminal specialists, who provide expertise and particular services (e.g., forged documents) that might otherwise be beyond the capability of the criminal organization itself. This enables the organization to rapidly adjust to new market opportunities (Adamoli et al., 1998; Schloenhardt, 1999). Furthermore, large international trafficking networks are involved in other cross-border criminal activities (Schloenhardt, 1999).

Research between 2000 and 2003 by the Bureau of the Dutch National Rapporteur on Trafficking in Human Beings on 167 prosecution case files identified three organizational forms. Slightly more than a quarter (28%) of the cases involved individual traffickers or solo operators—generally "one-man businesses" who may be helped by an assistant in a marginal role. Approximately 25 percent of the cases involved isolated criminal groups of between two and five members who were responsible for all the activities involved in forced sexual exploitation. In almost half of the cases (47%), criminal networks (of six or more persons) were involved. These were described as an undefined criminal infrastructure, in which members are bound together and in which membership and clear clusters are based on geographical proximity, family relationships, friendships, trade relations, and related activities (National Rapporteur on Trafficking in Human Beings, 2005).

A more recent study of 155 cases in the UNODC case law database, found that 14 percent of the cases involved individual perpetrators. An additional 19 percent involved traffickers working in pairs. The majority of cases (53%) involved 3–5 perpetrators. Twelve percent of the cases involved 6–9 perpetrators, and only 2 percent involved large-scale trafficking operations with more than 10 perpetrators (Aronowitz, forthcoming).

Roles within Trafficking Organizations

In simple trafficking processes involving the local recruitment of a single victim by a single trafficker, the trafficker assumes the role of recruiter, transporter, and exploiter. In more sophisticated operations moving large numbers of victims over numerous countries for long periods of time, many individuals may be involved and they may assume different roles, providing specific services. In studying migrant smuggling organizations, Schloenhardt (1999) identified many of the roles often found in trafficking organizations, as well. These are (Aronowitz, 2001, 175):

- Investors: Those who put forward funding for the operation and oversee the entire operation. These people are unlikely to be known by the everyday employees of the operation, as they are sheltered by an organizational pyramid structure that protects their anonymity.
- Recruiters: They seek out potential migrants and secure their financial commitment. These people may be members of the culture and the community from which migrants are drawn.
- Transporters: They assist the migrants in leaving their country of origin, either by land, sea, or air.
- Corrupt public officials or protectors: They may assist in obtaining travel documents, or accept bribes to enable migrants to enter/exit illegally.
- Informers: They gather information on matters such as border surveillance, immigration and transit procedures, asylum systems, law enforcement activities.
- Guides and crew members: They are responsible for moving illegal migrants from one transit point to the other or helping the migrants to enter the destination country.
- Enforcers: They are primarily responsible for policing staff and migrants, and for maintaining order.
- Debt collectors: They are in the destination country to collect fees.
- Money launderers: They launder the proceeds of crime, disguising their origin through a series of transactions or investing them in legitimate businesses.
- Supporting personnel and specialists: They may include local people at transit points who might provide accommodation and other assistance.

It is important in the investigation of trafficking operations for all members of the organization to be arrested and the entire operation dismantled. Failure to do this may allow for the replacement of individuals or their roles and the continuance of the exploitation of victims.

Measures to End Trafficking

Due to the multifaceted nature of human trafficking, the different markets in which individuals are exploited, the varying patterns of trafficking around the world, as well as individual victim needs, an interdisciplinary approach by numerous organizations is the only way to prevent and combat this insidious crime. It appears from the large number of estimates of people enslaved in forced labor (ILO, 20012; Walk Free Foundation, 2016) and the small number of victims rescued and identified by governmental and nongovernmental organizations (UNODC, 2014; 2016, and U.S. Department of State, 2016) that much still needs to be done.

Based upon the principle that "human trafficking is a crime of such magnitude and atrocity that it cannot be dealt with successfully by any government alone," the UN Global Initiative to Fight Human Trafficking (UN.GIFT) was launched to promote and strengthen international, multi-stakeholder cooperation and strategies that build upon national efforts (UN.GIFT). Efforts include increasing knowledge, providing technical assistance, cooperation and coordination between stakeholders, focusing on rights-based approaches, building the capacity of state and nonstate stakeholders, and fostering partnerships for joint action (UN.GIFT). The basis for all measures to effectively prevent and suppress human trafficking can be found in the UN Protocol to Prevent, Suppress and Punish Trafficking in Persons, Especially Women and Children, Supplementing the United Nations Convention Against Transnational Organized Crime (2000).

Many governments, intergovernmental organizations, and national and local nongovernmental organizations (NGOs;

many of which are profiled in Chapter 4) are involved in the fight against human trafficking.

Traditionally, the measures to fight human trafficking have included the four Ps: Prevention, (Victim) Protection, Prosecution (of offenders, to include law enforcement initiatives), and Partnerships. All four are necessary for a comprehensive and successful approach to eradicating human trafficking.

Prevention

Prevention measures can be both short term and long term. Those required under the UN Trafficking Protocol address the need for research, information, and mass media campaigns (short term) and social and economic initiatives (long term) to prevent and combat trafficking in persons.

Awareness Raising

Awareness-raising programs are necessary in source countries to warn the general population, or more specifically, those at risk of being trafficked, of the dangers and harm of human trafficking. Such programs have included lectures and films at schools, television spots, flyers, and newspaper ads. They are often in countries of origin and aimed at individuals considering migrating. An example of this is MTV's EXIT project, a series of awareness-raising commercials and documentaries aimed at ending exploitation and human trafficking (MTV). YouTube is filled with documentaries on human trafficking, ranging from forced commercial sexual exploitation (National Geographic's *21st Century Sex Slaves*) to forced labor involving children on cocoa plantations (*The Dark Side of Chocolate*) and organ trafficking (*Organs across Borders—World*). Numerous organizations, in particular IOM, raise awareness of the dangers of human trafficking to migrants traveling abroad for work. Winrock International has teamed up with government and nongovernment partners to conduct pre-migration trafficking awareness as part of their counter-trafficking program (http://www.winrock.org/sites/default/files/publications/attach ments/Leaflet%20English%20new.pdf). Such pre-migration awareness raising is supported by the governments of many countries with high outbound migration (such as the Philippines and Nepal). Awareness raising also focuses on publicity campaigns to alert residents who may see signs of trafficking in their surroundings and ensure that they know which agencies or organizations to contact in such cases.

In addition to raising awareness among persons considering migrating—potential victims of trafficking—others who could benefit from these campaigns are third parties who may come into contact with trafficked persons. Service providers (such as taxi and limousine drivers or hotel personnel) may come into contact with prostitutes and may (unknowingly) be facilitating human trafficking. Hotels and the transportation industry should be informed and raise awareness among personnel such as concierges and bus drivers. Awareness-raising campaigns may prompt these parties to (anonymously) report information on persons whom they suspect to be trafficked, or might be at risk—such as runaway children.

Awareness-raising campaigns are also aimed specifically at customers of prostitutes in an effort to reduce primary demand and encourage clients to report suspected cases of trafficking.

National Hotlines

National hotlines—many of which are available 24 hours a day, 7 days a week—have been launched in many origin and destination countries (examples are Unseen's hotline in the United Kingdom or the National Human Trafficking Resource Center hotline in the United States). These hotlines are often combined with awareness-raising campaigns, as in the Netherlands where the organization "M" (*Meld Misdaad Anoniem* or Report Crime Anonymously, similar to CrimeStoppers in other countries) ran a campaign to raise awareness among clients of prostitutes to look for signs of exploitation and possible victims of trafficking and to report this to the police. Between June 2012 and

December 2013 (following a successful campaign in 2006), "M" launched another awareness-raising campaign. Police conducted investigations as a result of approximately 250 tips. This resulted in the arrest of 28 individuals and the dismantling of a trafficking network with 4 suspects from Lithuania and Albania. In the first six months of 2015, 125 tips over human trafficking were reported to "M" (Meld Misdaad Anoniem, https://www.meldmisdaadanoniem.nl/blog/2015/09/10/halfjaarcijfers-anonieme-melders-waardevol-bij-aanpak-brand-stichting-en-mensenhandel/).

More Permanent Prevention Measures

Many prevention measures are aimed not only at preventing human trafficking but also at preventing other harms—such as homelessness, domestic violence, runaway children, drug dependency, and mental health problems—problems that put people at risk of trafficking. These measures must be aimed at the target group (those with multiple risk factors are the most susceptible to being trafficked). Risk assessment must be conducted at the local level to identify what factors promote trafficking in a particular community—whether it is a lack of job or educational opportunities, discrimination against women, or an ethnic minority identity (trafficking of Rohingya minorities into Thailand or Roma children to the United Kingdom and France) or life experience (child victims of domestic violence or runaway children). Programs must be developed to provide opportunities to and protect those at risk, particularly children.

Since many of those trafficked are from poorer countries or are the most disadvantaged and marginalized in a society, it is important to promote income-generating activities and opportunities. Educational opportunities and job training skills are important, but in addition to skills, individuals must be provided with the tools to ply their trade. Strengthening social protection systems for high-risk children can prevent their victimization. In parts of Southeastern Europe, multidisciplinary teams comprising professionals such as social and health workers and law enforcement officials help identify high-risk children and implement measures to protect them (UN.GIFT, 2008).

In countries where victims are likely to be trafficked, it is essential that governments regulate the labor market and areas into which victims may be trafficked. This demands shifting the emphasis from sex trafficking and looking beyond the traditional brothels, nightclubs, karaoke bars, and massage parlors into more traditional labor exploitation markets such as the construction, agricultural, fishing, and hotel and restaurant industries.

Victim Assistance and Protection

Article 6 of the UN Trafficking Protocol spells out what measures should be taken to ensure the protection of victims. These include implementing measures to provide for the physical, psychological, and social recovery of victims of trafficking in persons, through the provision of housing, counselling, legal support, medical, psychological and material assistance, educational, training, and employment opportunities. This should be done in cooperation with NGOs and other relevant organizations (UN Trafficking Protocol, 2000). Victim assistance must be offered not only in the host or destination country to victims who have been identified, but also in the country of origin when victims are repatriated.

The U.S. Office for Victims of Crime, of the U.S. Department of Justice (https://www.ovcttac.gov/taskforceguide/eguide/2-forming-a-task-force/) has identified numerous needs of victims of human trafficking. These include:

- Case management
- Child-specific (dependent) assistance
- Civil legal award
- Clothing
- Crime victims' rights and benefits
- Criminal justice assistance

- Crisis intervention
- Cultural community/support
- Dental care (emergency and long term)
- Disability assistance
- Education/GED classes
- English as a Second Language (ESL) classes
- Financial literacy
- Family contact/reunification
- Food
- Housing
- Identification documents
- Illiteracy or limited literacy assistance
- Job preparation and placement
- Legal representation (immigration, criminal, civil)
- Medical care (emergency and long term)
- Mental health care (emergency and long term)
- Public assistance benefits
- Religious and spiritual assistance
- Repatriation assistance
- Safety and safety planning
- Housing (emergency, transitional, permanent)
- Sexual assault trauma services
- Substance abuse services
- Translation and interpretation
- Transportation
- Victim advocacy

In the Host Country

Victims may suffer severe trauma upon escaping or being rescued, and it is important to provide them with a safe environment to recover. Victims should be provided a "reflection period" of minimum one month and preferably three months (the Expert Group on Reflection Period and Residence Permit for Victims of Trafficking in Human Beings of the European Union recommends a period of not less than three months) in which to heal, consider their options, and if they so desire, cooperate with law enforcement officers in building a case against their traffickers. During this time, victims (some prefer the word "survivors") should be provided with shelter, medical, psychological, economic, and legal support. The period of reflection is to allow the victim to begin the healing process and should not be contingent upon their cooperation with criminal justice authorities.

A National Referral Mechanism (NRM) or similar construction is necessary to protect victims of trafficking. The OSCE defines an NRM as "a co-operative framework through which state actors fulfil their obligations to protect and promote the human rights of trafficked persons, coordinating their efforts in a strategic partnership with civil society. The basic aims of an NRM are to ensure that the human rights of trafficked persons are respected and to provide an effective way to refer victims of trafficking to services. In addition, NRMs can work to help improve national policy and procedures on a broad range of victim-related issues such as residence and repatriation regulations, victim compensation, and witness protection. NRMs can establish national plans of action and can set benchmarks to assess whether goals are being met" (OSCE, 2004, 15). In essence, the NRM is a roadmap to ensure the protection of victims. One such example is the NRM established in the United Kingdom in 2009 (for more on which partners are involved and how the NRM operates, see their website at http://www.nationalcrimeagency.gov.uk/about-us/what-we-do/specialist-capabilities/uk-human-trafficking-centre/natio nal-referral-mechanism).

Persons who have been forced into committing criminal activities (prostitution, begging, pickpocketing, burglary, transporting drugs) are often not recognized as victims, and end up in the criminal justice system as suspects. Those in the country illegally are often viewed as undocumented migrants, arrested, detained, and deported, or prosecuted and incarcerated. The United Nations (Working Group on Trafficking in Persons, 2010) urges the nonpunishment and nonprosecution of persons who may have committed offenses while there were trafficked victims. If crimes have been perpetrated under duress or force, Member States (of the United Nations) are urged to establish the principle of nonliability of the illegal acts committed by trafficked victims. This is very often referred to as the "Principle of Nonpunishment." There are two provisions. The *duress-based* provision (a trafficked person is compelled to commit the offense) applies to those who are coerced into working for the criminal organization such as recruiting new victims, working as drivers, money collectors, or guards. The second, the *causation-based* provisions would apply to victims who are in the country illegally, those forced to work in prostitution (in countries where prostitution is illegal), or forced to beg, steal, or commit other offenses. Trafficked persons should not be viewed as criminals, rather "they should be viewed through the lens of a human rights-based approach—and protected" (Aronowitz, 2015b).

Risk analysis should be conducted to determine whether it is safe to repatriate the trafficked victim to his or her home country or community. If this is not possible, governments should consider granting asylum or special status to the victim. In the United States, a foreign victim of trafficking may be allowed to remain under the T-visa program (U.S. Citizenship and Immigration Services). Many countries in the European Union have also introduced a reflection period and means to allow trafficked victims to remain in the country. The ability to remain in the destination country is often tied to the victim's willingness to cooperate with officials in the investigation and prosecution of the perpetrators. From a human rights perspective, the requirement to cooperate with authorities should *not* be a requirement to obtain a residency permit (Rijken, 2009).

In extreme cases where it is impossible to provide residency in the destination country or repatriate the person to the country of origin, other measures must be found to protect victims (and their families). One of the trafficked Albanian women in an IOM shelter had a price tag placed on her life for testifying against her trafficker. The author was told by an OSCE representative working on her case that the OSCE was in negotiations with a third country to grant the young woman asylum (meeting with the OSCE representative in Tirana, Albania, February 2003).

Upon Returning Home

Victim assistance in the country of origin is challenging. Coordination between service providers in the destination and origin countries is essential to ensure that there is continuity in the care "package" provided to the victim. Most assistance strategies are aimed at safely returning and reintegrating the trafficked victim into his or her home country or community. This is no easy task as victims may not wish to return home. Their decision may be influenced by the shame and social stigma of having worked in prostitution, fear of reprisals from the traffickers, rejection by family members, or lack of adequate medical and psychosocial services in the villages from which they came. With young children, the situation may be complicated by the fact that the child might have initially left to escape a home filled with sexual or physical violence, or it was a parent who gave the child away, or sold the child into slavery. Returning a child to its parental home might not be a safe and sustainable option (Buet et al., 2012).

Effective reintegration programs—similar to those in the destination country—must address housing, mental and physical health issues, trauma and substance abuse treatment, education, and employment. To succeed, a reintegration program must be tailored to the specific needs of the individual, who should be allowed to exercise agency in also making decisions regarding the program.

Programs in the country of origin may not always be sufficiently funded and resourced to provide the full range of economic, cultural, social, or psychosocial services needed by the victim. In many countries of origin, there are limited training and employment opportunities. Resources are limited and long-term follow-up to ensure the success of any assistance and reintegration program is almost nonexistent.

Victims of trafficking are highly susceptible to being re-trafficked. The IOM examined cases of persons who had been trafficked at least a second time after having been provided assistance. The organization found that persons who are particularly young are at high risk of being re-trafficked. Furthermore, those at greatest risk are "formerly trafficked persons who are members of ethnic minority groups and, as a result, are subject to discrimination in the country of origin; where there are significant gender inequalities in the country of origin; where victims of trafficking originate from countries where conflicts are ongoing or recent; or where trafficked persons are also refugees or displaced persons" (IOM, 2010, 12). Persons attempting to migrate again are also at high risk due to the limited possibilities to migrate legally. According to the Immigration Law Practitioners' Association in the United Kingdom, "The question is not whether re-trafficking takes place, but how fast?" (information on *The Hearth* reported in ILPA, 2006).

Law Enforcement and Prosecution

It is necessary to increase arrests and successful prosecutions if the criminal justice system hopes to increase the risks and reduce the rewards of human trafficking. It is challenging, and according to global conviction statistics, countries have not been particularly successful (more data will be provided in Chapter 5).

Law Enforcement Investigations and Arrests

Law enforcement's job is made particularly difficult due to the fact that victims may refuse to cooperate with investigations.

Law enforcement must begin relying upon other means to secure evidence against the traffickers, such as wiretaps, but even this is becoming more difficult as criminals dispose of or rotate telephones and numbers. A successful investigation demands a coordinated approach between local, regional, and international partners and often involves months of investigative work. With 35 detectives from the national police, 3 from the Social Intelligence and Investigative Service, 4 detectives involved in the investigation of the network's financial structure, the military police, assistance from the regional police departments, cooperation with the German police, and 26,000 telephone taps later, the police were able to arrest the members of the trafficking network in the Netherlands in the Sneep case (Aronowitz, 2009a; Dongen, van, 2007a, 2007b).

Above all, law enforcement and the criminal justice system must take a victim-centered approach, in which the victim's safety, well-being, and wishes are taken into consideration at all steps of the investigation and subsequent trial or immigration hearings. The U.S. Office for Victims of Crime (U.S. Justice Department) suggests that "[a]ll professionals involved in human trafficking cases must advocate for the victim. Avoid activities that can ostracize a victim, those that mirror the behavior of a trafficker, however unintentionally, by limiting or not offering a victim choices in the recovery process" (https://www.ovcttac.gov/taskforceguide/eguide/1-understanding-human-trafficking/13-victim-centered-approach/).

Law Enforcement Training

To strengthen the law enforcement response to trafficking, a number of (international) organizations have developed training manuals or modules. The UNODC has developed a "Toolkit to Combat Trafficking in Persons," providing practical help to governments, policy makers, police, NGOs, and others, through "best practices" (UNODC, *Toolkit*, 2006). The UN Development Program, together with the International Centre for Migration Policy Development, has developed comprehensive training scheme targeting specific groups, using their "Law Enforcement Manual for Combating Trafficking in Human Beings" (UNDP, *Anti-trafficking Manual*, no date). The OSCE, spanning 57 countries from North America and Europe to Central Asia, provides law enforcement assessment needs and training. The Government of India, in conjunction with UNODC, published a "Compendium on Best Practices on Anti-Human Trafficking by Law Enforcement Agencies" outlining best approaches on investigating and prosecuting traffickers, protecting victims, and preventing trafficking (UNODC, 2007).

The training need for patrol officers—those working the streets and the first to come into contact with victims of trafficking—is exemplified in the following story, told by Acting Deputy Attorney General Sally Yates at a U.S. Department of Justice event marking National Slavery and Human Trafficking Prevention month. A local sheriff's deputy in Greene County, Georgia, who had recently received training on signs of human trafficking, stopped a 29-year-old motorist for speeding. His passenger was a 17-year-old girl. Noticing telltale signs of trafficking, and rather than ticketing the driver and allowing him to leave, the officer questioned the two occupants of the vehicle separately and was told by the girl that she had been forced into prostitution by the pimp since the age of 14. She was rescued and her pimp received an 11-year prison sentence (http://www.justice.gov/opa/speech/acting-deputy-attorney-general-sally-quillian-yates-delivers-remarks-justice-department).

In February 2011, the Anti-Trafficking Coordination Team (ACTeam) Initiative was launched in six U.S. cities (Atlanta, El Paso, Kansas City, Los Angeles, Memphis, and Miami) with the aim of streamlining rapidly expanding interagency human trafficking enforcement efforts. The ACTeam Initiative focuses on investigating and prosecuting forced labor, international sex trafficking, and sex trafficking of adults by force, fraud, or coercion. ACTeams participated in an intensive, interactive Advanced Human Trafficking Training Program at the Federal

Law Enforcement Training Center, receiving cutting-edge anti-trafficking expertise. The training produced results. From the data in Table 2.4, it is clear that cases filed, defendants charged, and convicted increased dramatically in districts in which ACTeam training occurred, compared to districts in cities or statistics nationwide where no such training occurred.

What Will Guarantee Law Enforcement's Success and Ensure a Victim-Centered Approach?

Law enforcement officers must be taught where to look and how to identify victims of trafficking, particularly in areas outside the commercial sex industry. It is essential that law enforcement takes a human rights approach in dealing with trafficked victims. Until victims feel safe, they will not cooperate with government officials. It is important that during the interviewing phase, victims understand that they are victims who will be protected and not criminals who will be arrested, prosecuted, or deported. When potential victims have been uncovered during trafficking police raids in the United Kingdom, the police can use an MP3 player with prerecorded voice files in the language of the potential victim. This prerecorded message explains to the victim exactly what is happening and what the victims can expect from the police in terms of their rights (information presented at the UN.GIFT workshop "Technology and Human Trafficking," Vienna, February 14, 2008; see also http://www.ibixtranslate.com/).

Table 2.4   Performance Measures on Human Trafficking Comparing ACTeam Districts, Non-ACTeam Districts to Nationwide Results

	ACTeam Districts	Non-ACTeam Districts	Nationwide
Cases filed	119%	18%	35%
Defendants charged	114%	12%	28%
Defendants convicted	86%	14%	26%

Source: Anti-Trafficking Coordination Team (ACTeam) Initiative Fact Sheet (http://www.justice.gov/opa/file/623176/download).

Interpreters must be present during interviews so that victims clearly understand what is happening, and throughout the entire process, the safety and rights of victims must be guaranteed. An NGO victim liaison contact person may be useful in supporting the victim throughout the investigation and trial (UN.GIFT Workshop, 2008).

Prosecutions

To increase successful prosecutions, we must ensure that the victim's rights are protected and their needs are met during (investigation and) trial, and that expertise in prosecuting cases of human trafficking is developed within the prosecutor's offices. In addition to providing a victim or community-based advocate who accompanies and supports the victim throughout the investigation, trial, and assistance process, the victim may require legal representation in court. Their privacy and identity must be protected, and if necessary, victims should be allowed to testify behind screens, via video link or in a courtroom after the public has been removed (UNODC, *Toolkit*; https://www.unodc.org/documents/human-trafficking/Tool kit-files/08–58296_tool_5–18.pdf).

The need for expertise in prosecuting cases of human trafficking has become evident. Trafficked victims do not make good witnesses. Due to trauma, fear, and self-blame, many change their stories or withdraw their charges. It is essential that prosecutors (and judges) understand the needs and behavior of the victim. A number of countries have established special prosecutors to deal with cases of human trafficking.

"In the U.S. in 2007, the Civil Rights Division created the Human Trafficking Prosecution Unit (HTPU) within the Criminal Section to consolidate the expertise of some of the nation's top human trafficking prosecutors. HTPU prosecutors work closely with Assistant United States Attorneys (AUSAs) and law enforcement agencies to streamline fast-moving trafficking investigations, ensure consistent application of trafficking statutes, and identify multijurisdictional trafficking networks. Early notification of any case with potential human trafficking angles allows the HTPU to provide victim assistance resources, legal guidance, and coordination between districts prosecuting overlapping criminal networks on a timely basis" (U.S. Department of Justice, HTPU; http://www.justice.gov/crt/about/crm/htpu.php). The investment in building expertise has paid off. Between 2010 and 2015, the Civil Rights Division's HTPU, in conjunction with U.S. Attorneys nationwide, has prosecuted record numbers of labor trafficking, international sex trafficking, and adult sex trafficking cases—56 percent more than in the previous five years.

We still have a long way to go. Global statistics on prosecutions and convictions for human trafficking are disappointing. Statistics provided in the U.S. Department of State's annual *Trafficking in Persons Report* shows a relatively limited number of prosecutions and convictions (see Table 2.5), many of which are probably attributed to a handful of countries.

Table 2.5   Global Law Enforcement Data

Year	Victims Identified	Prosecutions	Convictions
2006	–	5,808	3,160
2007	–	5,682 (490)	3,427 (326)
2008	30,961	5,212 (312)	2,983 (104)
2009	49,105	5,606 (432)	4,166 (335)
2010	33,113	6,017 (607)	3,619 (237)
2011	42,291 (15,205)	7,909 (456)	3,969 (278)
2012	46,570 (17,368)	7,705 (1,153)	4,746 (518)
2013	44,758 (10,603)	9,460 (1,199)	5,776 (470)
2014	44,462 (11,438)	10,051 (418)	4,443 (216)
2015	77,823 (14,262)	18,930 (857)	6,609 (456)

Source: U.S. Department of State, *Trafficking in Persons Report 2015 and 2016*.

Note: These statistics are estimates only, given the lack of uniformity in national reporting structures. The numbers in parentheses are those of labor trafficking prosecutions, convictions, and victims identified.

Partnerships

No single agency is capable of addressing the problem of human trafficking. International cooperation is necessary in the case of international trafficking involving destination and source (and sometimes a number of transit) countries. "The multi-disciplinary approach to anti-trafficking work is based on the principle that effective strategies require systematic and coordinated services from a wide variety of professionals" (Reed, 2013). Birkenthal (2011–2012) identifies a role for agencies at different levels. Intergovernmental agencies should coordinate international activities, state governments should pass legislation to protect victims, prevent trafficking, and punish offenders, while NGOs should provide grassroots aid to victims.

The Public Sector

The need for coordination and cooperation between government agencies is evident in international human trafficking cases. Even within a country, cooperation between numerous agencies is necessary to address this multifaceted problem. At the national level, the U.S. President's Interagency Task Force to Monitor and Combat Trafficking in Persons involves 17 agencies: Department of State (DOS), Department of Defense (DOD), Department of Justice (DOJ), Department of the Interior (DOI), Department of Agriculture (USDA), Department of Labor (DOL), Department of Health and Human Services (HHS), Department of Transportation (DOT), Department of Education (ED), Department of Homeland Security (DHS), Domestic Policy Council (DPC), National Security Staff (NSS), Office of Management and Budget (OMB), Office of the Director of National Intelligence (ODNI), Federal Bureau of Investigation (FBI), U.S. Agency for International Development (USAID), and the U.S. Equal Employment Opportunity Commission (EEOC); (http://www.state.gov/j/tip/response/usg/).

Another example can be found in the Netherlands. In that country, the Barrier Model, a conceptual framework to construct barriers to traffickers trying to bring persons into the Netherlands, has been implemented. Its strength lies in identifying illicit actors and activities at each phase of the trafficking process—entrance, housing, identity, work, and finance—and the "numerous stakeholders that are in a position to collaborate in constructing structural barriers to make it more difficult for human beings to be trafficked into the Netherlands" (for more on the Barrier Model, see Aronowitz et al., 2010, 75–77). Partners include the Military Police, Immigration and Border Control, the municipal government, housing corporations, the fire department, the Fiscal Information and Investigation Service, the Social Information and Investigation Service, banks, money exchange offices, and the Chamber of Commerce.

Cooperation between government officials and civil society is imperative. Article 9 of the UN Trafficking Protocol, dealing with prevention, cooperation, and other measures, calls for government cooperation with NGOs, other relevant organizations, and other elements of civil society in the formulation of policies, programs, and other measures. Civil society is an unmissable element in government programs and policies as trafficked persons, who mistrust government officials, are more likely to cooperate with NGOs. Additionally, insight that NGOs have obtained on victim identification and needs has been translated into training for police and prosecutors. The Indian NGO Network Impulse partnered with the Northeastern Police Academy to develop material and implement training courses for police officers in eight states in Northeast India. Staff from the NGO traveled to the police academies to conduct the training for hundreds of officers. The trafficking prevention handbook has become part of the compulsory training curriculum for all police officers in the region (https://www.changemakers.com/stopviolence/entries/training-law-enforcement-north-east-india-combat-human). Other actions initiated by NGOs, together with the police, have proven successful. The NGO Action Pour Les Enfants (APLE) provided information to police in Cambodia that led to the arrest of 21 child-sex offenders, monitoring the activities of local police and judicial officials, and facilitating the involvement of foreign police (U.S. Department of State, 2007). The Ethiopian NGO, Forum for Street Children, has collaborated with international NGOs and local and regional law enforcement to help establish Child Protection Units within police stations in the capitol and nine towns throughout the country. The NGO provides training to the police, and has rescued and repatriated over 1,000 children with their families (U.S. Department of State, 2008). The human rights organization International Justice Mission (IJM) works to free young women from forced prostitution and assist local authorities in building cases against traffickers in Africa, Latin America, Southeast Asia, and South Asia. IJM has helped train police in the Philippines and IJM lawyers in all countries where the organization is active, work to secure conviction and sentencing of traffickers, and ensure that victims get access to aftercare services. The work of the organization has assisted in the freedom for hundreds of girls and women trafficked into the commercial sex trade (Haugen 2015; see also IJM's website for more information at https://www.ijm.org/).

The Private Sector

According to the U.S. Department of Labor (2014), 74 countries from Afghanistan to Zambia have been identified using child or forced labor in the production of goods. In 21 of these countries, both child labor and forced labor has been identified in the production of goods and harvesting of crops. Many of the products ranging from cotton, corn, sugarcane, bricks, rice, beans, cocoa, coffee, tobacco, and shrimp are products that we consume (for a complete list of the countries and products produced using forced or child labor, see the Department of Labor's complete report at http://www.dol.gov/ilab/reports/pdf/TVPRA_Report2014.pdf). The private sector cannot escape its responsibility in preventing human trafficking, and has either conformed to the pressure of NGOs or has, in some cases, taken the lead itself in finding solutions. Better supply chain management of goods, to ensure that they are not produced with child or slave labor, could eradicate trafficking in certain industries.

Members of international companies have pooled their power, resources, and knowledge in the Global Business Coalition Against Human Trafficking—a coalition of leading international companies that have taken steps to eradicate all forms of human trafficking in their company supply chains or the service industry. Businesses should be encouraged to become partners or utilize the expertise established by the Global Business Coalition Against Trafficking; the coalition is working on a Supply Chain Toolkit to educate their employees and other businesses, and provide information concerning case studies and best practices. Member organizations include Carlson, Cision, Coca-Cola, Delta, Ford, Hilton, LexisNexis, ManpowerGroup, Microsoft, NXP, and Travelport. Through education and training, exchange of best practices, awareness raising, and monitoring of supply chains, the organization hopes to contribute to the eradication of global exploitation and human trafficking (see more at http://www.gbcat.org/assets/gbcatbrochure.pdf). As an example, Carlson, the company that owns Radisson and other hotels around the world, has updated its supplier contracts with anti-trafficking language and outlines expectations of its suppliers. Additionally, the company trained its employees and requires all 80,000 of its employees to participate in a responsible business training program to help them recognize and respond to child trafficking at its hotels (Gage, 2014).

Other initiatives have also proven successful. Thousands of children were working as slaves on cocoa farms in Côte d'Ivoire, which produces over a third of the world's cocoa crop. In order to ensure that chocolate is "child-slave-free," major players in the food industry in October 2007 initiated a program for a more sustainable "cocoa supply chain" aimed at improving environmental and social practices. A draft farm-level certification code, developed by local stakeholders (government departments, NGOs, and farmers), was tested in pilot projects in Côte d'Ivoire. Independent certifiers have been trained and the program, which has also been launched in Ghana, is expected to expand to other West African nations. Fair trade, Rainforest Alliance, and UTZ certification organizations prohibit child labor and guarantee that farmers in Ghana and Côte d'Ivoire receive fair pay for their cocoa (Nieburg, 2012). The British Biscuit, Cake, Chocolate and Confectionery Association, which opposes the use of trafficked persons in the production of cacao, reports that U.K. manufacturers were spending about US$12 million annually to develop monitoring and certification schemes (BBC, April 6, 2007). Even local companies can make a change. Bettys & Taylors of Harrogate (the United Kingdom), a traditional family business specializing in coffees and teas, has also trained their buyers as social auditors, visiting farms that grow tea and coffee purchased by the company, to ensure that workers throughout their supply chain are fairly treated.

The financial sector can also be instrumental in the fight against trafficking and exploitation. Investigators at the International Centre for Missing and Exploited Children (ICMEC) identified 70,000 customers using their credit cards and paying US$29.95 per month to access graphic images of small children being sexually assaulted. Determined to eradicate the problem, the ICMEC teamed up with the U.S. National Center for Missing and Exploited Children, 30 major online companies, and financial institutions to form the Financial Coalition against Child Pornography. The coalition was launched on March 15, 2006, with the aim of shutting down the payment accounts being used by traders and purchasers of child pornography, and thus terminating the operations. Members of the coalition cover 90 percent of the credit card industry (BBC, 2006).

Another successful initiative in helping corporations to identify potential cases of human trafficking involved the collaboration between the Manhattan District Attorney's Office, the Thomson Reuters Foundation, and financial institutions. By looking for irregularities and red flags in financial transactions, the collaborators hoped to identify early signs of human trafficking operations. The Bank of America, Barclays, Citigroup, JPMorgan Chase & Co., TD Bank, Wells Fargo, American Express, Western Union, the Human Trafficking Pro Bono Legal Center, the Polaris Project, and the deputy chief of the fraud section for the criminal division of the Justice Department (Theodore S. Greenberg) participated in the effort. "The U.S. Financial Crimes Enforcement Network (FinCEN), in dialogue with other U.S. agencies, private industry, NGOs, academia, and law enforcement, launched a similar initiative to identify financial red flags and provide guidance to financial institutions on how to detect and properly report suspected human trafficking. FinCEN's goal is to supplement and aid law enforcement investigations by supporting the effective detection and reporting of human trafficking financing through Suspicious Activity Reports. Through these efforts, financial institutions are developing the ability to identify suspicious financial activity that may help identify human traffickers" (U.S. Department of State, 2014).

Religious Institutions

Faith-based groups and institutions can be instrumental in addressing the issue and raising awareness of human trafficking, pressuring governments to pass and enforce laws against human trafficking, and to protect and assist trafficked victims. In some communities, religious institutions are one of the most influential social institutions. The Religious in Europe Networking Against Trafficking and Exploitation (RENATE), the U.S. Catholic Sisters Against Human Trafficking (USCSAHT), and the Australian Catholic Religious Against Trafficking in Humans (ACRATH) are just a few of the religious organizations that have joined the fight against trafficking to rescue and restore victims (see their websites at http://www .sistersagainsttrafficking.org/; http://www.renate-europe.net/; http://acrath.org.au/). Pope Francis has recently joined the dialogue on human trafficking and modern-day slavery, calling it "a crime against humanity" (Pontifical Academy of Social Sciences; http://www.pass.va/content/scienzesociali/en/ events/2014–18/humantrafficking.html). In December 2014, the Pope and other religious leaders from the Anglican, Buddhist, Catholic, Hindu, Jewish, Orthodox, and Islamic faiths signed a declaration pledging to work together to help end modern slavery in the world by 2020 (http://www.pass.va/ content/scienzesociali/en/events/2014–18/jointdeclaration .html; U.S. Department of State, 2015, 10)

Other concrete initiatives have been launched in countries around the world. In Moldova, the IOM launched the Inter-Denominational Coalition for the Prevention of Trafficking in Human Beings, involving religious institutions representing the majority of faiths in the country. More than 650 religious leaders, including monks, have participated. Seminars offered to religious leaders teach them how to become active in prevention activities within their communities, alerting them to the risks of trafficking, and encouraging "a tolerant attitude towards victims among lay and religious communities"—not always a simple task when many of the child and women victims have been forced to work in prostitution. Once victims have been returned to Moldova, priests have been instrumental in granting protection and assistance and assisting in victims' reintegration back into society (IOM, 2007).

The Church of Bangladesh, through its social development program and commitment by its parishioners, is actively involved in raising awareness among vulnerable people and in the community at large on the dangers of trafficking. At the same time, it provides support to former trafficked women (Mackay, 2006). The Catholic Diocesan Development and Welfare Society in India established a Catholic rehabilitation center,

Bal Vikas Ashram, for child slave victims in Uttar Pradesh, India. In Rome, Sister Eugenia Bonetti coordinates the work of 250 religious nuns from 70 different world congregations. Her full-time work involves helping young trafficked women forced into prostitution regain their independence. Across countries in South America and the Caribbean (Bolivia, Colombia, Peru, and the Dominican Republic), India, and Japan, the "Sisters of Adoration, Slaves of the Blessed Sacrament and of Charity" operate missions to provide support to victims of sex trafficking (Kralis, 2006).

Measures to Reduce Primary Demand

Article 9(5) of the Protocol to Prevent, Suppress and Punish Trafficking in Persons, especially Women and Children, calls upon state parties to "adopt or strengthen legislative or other measures, such as educational, social or cultural measures, including through bilateral and multilateral cooperation, to discourage the demand that fosters all forms of exploitation of persons, especially women and children, that leads to trafficking" (UNODC, 2000, 5). Article 19 of the Council of Europe Convention on Action Against Trafficking in Human Beings requires parties to the convention to consider the criminalization of knowingly using the services of a trafficking victim. One of the considerations for including this provision in the convention was "the desire to discourage the demand for exploitable people that drives trafficking in human beings" (Council of Europe, 2005, 36).

Chapter 1 briefly touched upon the different types of demand and the social and cultural contexts that promote and support this demand. This section examines different interventions that law enforcement agencies, governments, and community organizations can employ or have already employed to tackle demand for the services of trafficked victims. Demand reduction is frequently aimed at reducing the demand among clients for prostitution, rather than *forced* prostitution. Demand reduction can be accomplished through repressive, legislative, educational, cultural, and social measures. These approaches are based primarily on the assumption that at least a proportion of the men who purchase the services of prostitutes are amenable to educational programs, "treatment," or deterrence (Wilcox et al., 2009). Demand reduction for other goods (e.g., food, clothing, carpets) and services (health care, domestic service, construction) often focuses on awareness raising among consumers and emphasis upon purchasing products or using services provided by companies monitoring their supply chain.

The following sections examine measures that have been taken to reduce demand for commercial sexual services.

Repressive Measures

Worldwide, police have taken repressive measures to penalize male buyers—often the arrest of male clients for the solicitation of prostitution (these actions may be facilitated by the use of undercover female agents). An extensive study by the U.S. Department of Justice in 2007 found that arrest of male buyers reduced the likelihood of future prostitution arrest by approximately 70 percent (Brewer et al., 2007). Despite these results, the general deterrent effect of arrest of prostitution clients for soliciting is questionable. Only a very small proportion of men visiting prostitutes is arrested (Brewer et al., 2007). An unexpected outcome is that several studies have found that the likelihood of arrest heightens excitement and encourages men motivated by risk to visit prostitutes (Monto, 1999).

Other, more repressive measures include blocking off streets with cement barriers to prevent men from stopping and soliciting prostitutes on certain streets, city ordinances to prevent men from cruising to look for street prostitutes, seizing and impounding the vehicles of men who solicit women in prostitution, issuing driving bans to habitual buyers, and checking identity cards (Aronowitz and Koning, 2014). It can be expected that these measures have a larger specific deterrent effect on men purchasing commercial sex acts, particularly if family members or spouses are made aware of the offense. Little to no empirical evidence exits, however, to determine the effectiveness of such programs.

Legislative Measures

To protect women working in (or trafficked into) prostitution, a number of countries have legalized the sale but criminalized the purchase of commercial sex (Sweden, Finland, and Iceland). Women (or men) cannot be arrested for "selling sex" but the buyer can be punished for its purchase. The rationale behind the approach is that when buyers risk punishment, the consumer demand for buying prostitutes will decrease (Aronowitz and Koning, 2014). What has become known as the Swedish model, under the Swedish Penal Code, chapter 6, section 11, "A person who . . . obtains a casual sexual relation in exchange for payment shall be sentenced for the purchase of a sexual service to a fine or imprisonment for at most six months" (Ministry of Industry, Employment and Communications, 2005, 1). While the number of street prostitutes has decreased significantly, the statistics on trafficked women appear to have remained fairly constant (Ekberg, 2004).

To combat human trafficking in the form of child sex tourism, a number of countries have passed extraterritorial legislation allowing for the prosecution of their citizens who travel abroad and engage in sexual relations with children. The U.S. Federal Law Regarding Child Sex Tourism, 18 USC 2423, punishes anyone who "travels with intent to engage in illicit sexual conduct" or those who "engage in illicit sexual conduct in foreign places." This also covers interstate travel within the United States (http://www.justice.gov/usam/criminal-resource-manual-2002-transportation-minors-18-usc-2423). Under the U.K. Sexual Offences Act, 2003, article 72, persons can be prosecuted for a sexual crime that is viewed as a criminal offence in both countries (http://www.legislation.gov.uk/ukpga/2003/42/pdfs/ukpga_20030042_en.pdf). Similarly,

Australia has passed the Crimes (Child Sex Tourism) Amendment Act 1994, No. 105, 1994, punishing its citizens for having sexual relations with a child under the age of 16 outside of the territory (Aronowitz, 2009a). As of June 2008, more than 40 countries had some form of extraterritorial legislation (ECPAT, 2008).

Awareness-Raising Campaigns

Awareness-raising campaigns have been aimed at (potential) clients of prostitutes, warning them that sex workers may be victims of trafficking. A particularly powerful campaign of CrimeStoppers in the United Kingdom warned men that trafficked women are forced to sell sex, and forced sex (with an unwilling partner) is rape. The message: "Walk in a punter (customer), walk out a rapist." A similar poster campaign in Indonesia was aimed at men visiting Indonesia's Batam Island sex area: "How Would You Feel if Someone Did This to Your Daughter?" (Aronowitz and Koning, 2014).

Social and Cultural Measures

Educational programs have targeted men who have been arrested for (solicitation) prostitution. Programs such as the First Offender Prostitution Program in the United States (commonly referred to as "john schools") were designed to reduce the demand for commercial sex by educating "customers" about the negative consequences of prostitution. Men arrested for soliciting prostitutes were given the option of being prosecuted or paying a fee and attending a one-day class (Aronowitz and Koning, 2014).

Studies on the effectiveness of these john school programs show diverse results. An evaluation of the program in San Francisco found that "it has been effective in substantially reducing recidivism among men arrested for soliciting prostitutes" (Shively et al., 2008, 4); The San Francisco First Offender

Prostitution Program showed that of the 2,200 men who attended the one-day educational program between 1997 and 2001, only 18 (0.008%) were rearrested for prostitution (Yen, 2008). Other programs have not been as promising. Comparison of men attending a john school workshop in Portland, Oregon, with a group of men who did not attend the workshop showed no statistically significant differences between the groups (Monto and Garcia, 2001); however, it should be noted that the recidivism rates in both groups were very low. This supports the hypothesis of Brewer and colleagues (2007) that post-arrest interventions, such as john schools, may have a limited impact given the strong deterrent effect of arrest.

A more long-term strategy focusing on the reduction in the overall demand for prostitution requires "long term awareness raising and educational work to bring about a fundamental re-visioning of sexuality, age, gender relations and prostitution. Such campaigns would need to target young people in particular" (Anderson and O'Connell Davidson, 2004, 9). This demand reduction strategy must take the shape of a social marketing campaign aimed at raising awareness and educating boys and young men (Lederer, 2009). Projects in Canada, the United States, France, the Philippines, and Indonesia have attempted to challenge and change the sexual attitudes and practices of men and boys in recognizing their role as buyers of women in prostitution, and educate these consumers to the harm of prostitution and trafficking. An example of this is the campaign featuring role models such as Ashton Kutcher, Bradley Cooper, Jamie Foxx, Sean Penn, Justin Timberlake, and Isaiah Mustafa, among others, raising awareness with the message: "Real Men Don't Buy Girls."

Demand Reduction among Military Personnel

Accusations of misconduct have been levied at peacekeepers and support personnel from the UN, the OSCE, and NATO. To address the problem, the UN Department of PeaceKeeping Operations (DPKO) has developed training materials to prevent trafficking and provide protection to victims of sexual abuse by UN peacekeeping personnel. The United Nations has appointed special Anti-Trafficking Focal Points or established special investigative units and has encouraged personnel to report violations, systematically monitoring complaints (UNDPKO Statistics, no publication date). Other international entities such as NATO (North Atlantic Treaty Organization) and the OSCE have adopted policies condemning trafficking and have implemented measures to ensure that members participating in missions are not involved in the abuse. NATO requires its members to take a variety of actions to reduce human trafficking, including the following: provisions that prohibit contractors from engaging in or facilitating human trafficking; training all personnel taking part in NATO-led operations; committing to evaluate implementation of their efforts; and ratification of the UN Trafficking Protocol (U.S. Department of State, 2016; Aronowitz, 2009a; Allred, 2006).

In 2004, the U.S. Department of Defense implemented a zero-tolerance policy regarding sex trafficking and activities—such as prostitution—that may contribute to trafficking. Since the end of 2006, patronizing a prostitute is a criminal charge under the Uniform Code of Military Justice. An anti-trafficking program was developed by U.S. Forces in Korea, focusing on awareness, victim identification, demand reduction, and cooperation with local authorities. Considered a model approach, it now serves as the basis for NATO's training modules (U.S. Department of State 2007). Anti-trafficking training, available online (U.S. Department of Defense, no publication date), is now mandatory for all U.S. service members and military police; they are receiving specialized training to assist them in recognizing and identifying possible trafficking situations and victims, especially overseas (U.S. Department of State, 2007). Forty-five other countries provide anti-trafficking, sexual exploitation, or human rights training to personnel being sent to peace support operations. Training is provided either by the government or in conjunction with international organizations such as IOM (Aronowitz, 2009a).

Raising Costs and Risks, Reducing Profit: Hitting Traffickers Where It Hurts

A number of measures must be taken to increase the risks and costs and reduce the profit to human traffickers. From a business model, these concepts are intricately related, as measures that increase the risk and cost of human trafficking should at the same time reduce the profits. Trafficking for sexual exploitation can be combated by reducing the demand for *exploitative* sex. Demand reduction will, in turn, affect the market's profitability. Costs will rise and profit will be reduced if heavy fines and seizure of assets are imposed on convicted traffickers (Aronowitz et al., 2010).

Measures to reduce profits and increase costs and risks include, but are not limited to, measures to educate the public, protecting migrants by verifying job applications and securing their passports, increasing funding and training for stakeholders (criminal justice, municipal, and civil society) to identify high-risk victims, situations and markets susceptible to trafficking, and creating local multidisciplinary groups to monitor vulnerable sectors. Criminal justice (reform) measures include adopting comprehensive legislation, training and reforming police, prosecutorial and judicial systems to eradicate corruption, improving passport controls, creating mixed national and international investigation teams, introducing periodic risk assessments and proactive controls, increasing the likelihood of arrest and prosecution—also for enablers (those that assist in trafficking while they may not be part of the trafficking organization) and customers—and increasing penalties, conducting financial investigations, and providing for administrative controls to allow for the closure of businesses that knowingly use trafficked labor. All these measures and the impact that they would have on the trafficking business are outlined in Table 2.6 (Aronowitz et al., 2010).

Table 2.6   Measures to Raise Costs and Risks and Reduce Profits in Human Trafficking

Measures	Effect	Upon Whom
Public education efforts to warn vulnerable people about how traffickers operate	Lowers the recruitment yield per dollar and raises recruiters' total costs	Recruiter
Public education directed at unwitting enablers such as customers of commercial prostitution and companies that subcontract with other companies that deal in slave labor; a system could be devised to ensure that no slave labor was involved in the production or supply chain of products	Lowers profit	Owners and traffickers
Reform police, judicial, and other official systems to make them less corruptible and eradicate corruption	Raises the costs and risks	Traffickers and owners of illicit business operations
Insistence or encouragement by "sending" countries that their vulnerable citizens are protected when they go abroad	Raises the risk of discovery and/or forces traffickers to adopt higher cost ways around their current recruitment approaches	Traffickers
Monitor websites and communications where the trafficking victims are advertised	Raises risk of being discovered	Traffickers
Develop a system of "job checking," in which labor services in cooperation with NGOs in sending or receiving countries would vet job offers made by companies or individuals in their home countries allowing an applicant in a source country to verify that a job offer is legitimate	Raises the costs of recruitment as well as the risk of discovery	Traffickers or owners of mala fide businesses
Increased funding and training for police, border guards, labor inspectorates, and other stakeholders in identifying markets, situations, and places in which trafficking occurs	Raises risk, increases costs	Traffickers
Better passport, visa, and border controls to identify persons who are possible victims	Raises risk	Traffickers/transporters

(continued)

Table 2.6 (*continued*)

Measures	Effect	Upon Whom
Introduce mixed national and international joint investigation teams to increase likelihood of arrest and overcome corruption	Raises risk, increases costs	Traffickers and transporters
Proactive controls of businesses in high risk markets	Raises risk	Owners
Periodic risk assessments in vulnerable markets	Raises risk	Traffickers
Support the creation of local multidisciplinary or referral groups to monitor vulnerable sectors, identify and "rescue" victims of trafficking	Raises risk, lowers profits	Traffickers and owners
Adoption of legislation prohibiting and providing adequate punishment for all forms of human trafficking	Raises risk of punishment	Traffickers
Increase likelihood of arrest and successful prosecution and punishment of traffickers and enablers; this could also include customers (solicitation for prostitution) of prostitution or corporate producers, sellers, and distributors of slave labor products	Lowers profit, raises risk and costs	Traffickers and owners
Increase success of prosecution and sentences for convicted traffickers	Raises risk, raises costs	Traffickers
Conduct financial investigation and seize all assets purchased with proceeds from human trafficking (provide remuneration or compensation to victims)	Lowers profits	Traffickers
Provide for administrative approaches to controlling trafficking through withdrawal or refusal to issue licenses to businesses suspected or convicted of using slave labor	Raises risk and cost, lowers profit	Traffickers, owners

Source: Aronowitz et al., 2010, 71. Information in this table was taken in part from Pennington et al., 2008, 131.

Effecting Permanent Change

Many of the projects established to prevent trafficking (awareness raising) or assist victims (shelters) provide limited protection to persons at risk and trafficked victims. In order to truly
eradicate the problem of trafficking, governments, donors,
civil society, faith-based organizations, and private industry
must invest in long-term sustainable strategies. This requires
changes in economic and social policies and cultural and historical practices to address structural factors that serve as root
causes of migration and exploitation. According to La Strada
International, "As long as women cannot live their lives free
from the threat of violence and discrimination and do not have
equal opportunities in the labor market, they will choose to
take on unregulated work opportunities to support themselves
and their families, abroad and at home" (http://lastradainter
national.org/lsidocs/Newsletter_8_08.pdf). This applies not
only to women, but also to the most disadvantaged and marginalized in a society.

By reducing the endless supply of exploitable victims, it may
also be possible to affect the demand. Failing to address demand reduction addresses only half the problem. A more permanent solution is to ensure that slave labor is not involved in
the supply chain of goods purchased and to reward companies
that uphold their corporate social responsibility, while drawing
attention to others that do not.

Long-term sustainable strategies must address structural factors and include the eradication of poverty and corruption and
the provision of education, job, and career opportunities for
the most vulnerable populations in the society. At the same
time, governments and society must ensure gender equality
and focus on the reduction of discrimination and violence in
the family aimed at women and children.

Long-term prevention measures must be combined with
effective law enforcement and justice responses while at the
same time taking a victim-centered and human rights–based

approach to the trafficking problem. As important as it is to wipe out criminal networks, it is just as important to ensure that victims are adequately protected and provided medical and psychosocial support and the skills to rebuild their lives. Only a merging of these various approaches will guarantee a humane and effective campaign to eradicate human trafficking (Aronowitz, 2009a).

What Can You Do to Help Fight Human Trafficking?

Individuals often feel powerless to make a difference in the fight against human trafficking. Nothing could be further from the truth. Slavery expert Kevin Bales (2005) has identified a three-step plan to ending modern day slavery.

Learn

Educate yourself about human trafficking and modern-day slavery. Read as much as you can, and visit the websites of organizations dealing with trafficking. Discuss the problem with others. Learn about products produced through forced or child labor—and our role in creating demand for such goods.

Become familiar with the signs of trafficking. It is possible that you have, or may in the future, come into contact with a trafficked person, cooking your meal in a Chinese restaurant, cleaning your room in a hotel, or taking care of your neighbor's children. If you are aware of the red flags and the national hotline number to report such possible cases of trafficking, you may be responsible for the rescue of a victim.

Join

Bales (2005) suggests that persons interested in antislavery and anti-trafficking movements join forces with organizations currently involved in the fight to eradicate this harm. It is possible, however, to join forces with others who are involved in eradicating human trafficking.

Act

Encourage others to learn about human trafficking. This can be done by hosting lectures or movies on human trafficking in schools, clubs, or at religious institutions. Identify companies that do and do not monitor the supply chain of the products they are producing. Reward companies that participate in anti-trafficking programs and encourage companies, including your own or the ones from which you purchase goods and services, to take steps to investigate and eliminate slavery and human trafficking in their supply chains and to publish the information for consumer awareness.

Petitions often circulate on the Internet. Add your name to an anti-trafficking petition. Other actions that are easy to undertake are things such as writing a letter to a local newspaper, or to local or state representatives. You can donate money or time to organizations addressing these issues.

Above all, avoid complacency. There is still much to be done. For more concrete suggestions on what can be done to help fight slavery and human trafficking, visit the website of the U.S. Department of State (15 Ways You Can Help Fight Human Trafficking at http://www.state.gov/j/tip/id/help/).

References

ACLU. No date. "Modern enslavement of migrant domestic workers by foreign diplomats in the United States." *Domestic Workers.* https://www.aclu.org/other/domestic-workers?redirect=domestic-workers

Adamoli, Sabrina, Di Nicola, Andrea, Savona, Ernesto, and Zoffi, Paola. 1998. *Organized crime around the world.* European Institute for Crime Prevention and Control (HEUNI), Helsinki. http://www.heuni.fi/material/attachments/heuni/reports/6KdD32kXX/Hreport_31.pdf

Aghatise, Esohe. 2005. "Women trafficking from West Africa to Europe: Cultural dimensions and strategies." *Mozaic,* 2005, 2011–2015.

All Africa. 2006, December 13. "Nigeria: Human trafficking—A tale of sorrow, tears and death." http://allafrica.com/stories/200612130687.html

Allred, Keith. 2006. "Peacekeepers and prostitutes: How deployed forces fuel the demand for trafficked women and new hope for stopping it." *Armed Forces and Society*, *33*(1), 5–23.

Amnesty International. 2014, September. *Lives adrift: Refugees and migrants in peril in the central Mediterranean.* http://www.amnesty.org/en/documents/EUR05/006/2014/en/

Anderson, B. and J. O'Connell Davidson. 2004. *Trafficking—A demand led problem? Part I: Review of evidence and debates*, Save the Children, Stockholm, Sweden.

Aneez, Shihar. 2010, August 26. "Saudi couple 'hammer 24 nails' into Sri Lanka maid." *Reuters.* http://www.reuters.com/article/2010/08/26/us-srilanka-maid-idUSTRE67P17420100826

Anti-Slavery International. 2014. *Trafficking for forced criminal activities and begging in Europe: Explanatory study and good practice examples.* London, UK. http://www.antislavery.org/includes/documents/cm_docs/2014/t/trafficking_for_forced_criminal_activities_and_begging_in_europe.pdf

Aronowitz, Alexis A. 2001. "Smuggling and trafficking in human beings: The phenomenon, the markets that drive it and the organisations that promote it." *European Journal on Criminal Policy and Research*, *9*(2), Summer, 163–195. http://mensenhandelao1112.wdfiles.com/local-files/artikels/Artikel%20A.%20A.%20Aronowitz.pdf

Aronowitz, Alexis A. 2003. *Coalitions against trafficking in human beings in the Philippines: Research and action final report.* Vienna and Turin: United Nations Office on Drugs and Crime and United Nations Interregional Crime and

Justice Research Institute. http://www.unodc.org/pdf/ crime/human_trafficking/coalitions_trafficking.pdf

Aronowitz, Alexis A. 2006. *Measures to combat trafficking in human beings in Benin, Nigeria and Togo.* Vienna: United Nations Office on Drugs and Crime. http://www.unodc .org/documents/human-trafficking/ht_research_report_ nigeria.pdf

Aronowitz, Alexis A. 2009a. *Human trafficking, human misery: The global trade in human beings.* Westport, CT: Praeger.

Aronowitz, Alexis A. 2009b. *Guidelines for the collection of data on trafficking in human beings, including comparable indicators.* Vienna, Austria: Austrian Federal Ministry of the Interior and the International Organization for Migration. http://www.emn.at/modules/typetool/pnincludes/uploads/ IOM_Vienna_AT_MoI_Guidelines%20for%20the%20 Collection%20of%20Data%20on%20THB.pdf

Aronowitz, Alexis A. 2012. "Sex tourism and sex trade." In J. Ciment and C. Bates (Eds.), *Encyclopedia of global social issues* (pp. 838–845). Armonk: M.E. Sharpe Publisher.

Aronowitz, Alexis A. 2014a. "To punish or not to punish: What works in the regulation of the prostitution market?" In Nina Persak and Gert Vermeulen (Eds.), *Reframing prostitution: From discourse to descriptio, from moralisation to normalisation* (pp. 223–252). Antwerp, Belgium: Maklu.

Aronowitz, Alexis A. 2014b. "Future possibilities for the utilization of EU statistics on human trafficking." In Jan van Dijk, Leontien van der Knaap, Marcelo Aebi, and Claudia Campistol (Eds.), *Counting what counts: Tools for the validation and utilization of EU statistics on human trafficking* (pp. 115–153). The Netherlands: Tilburg University.

Aronowitz, Alexis A. 2015a. "The social etiology of human trafficking: How poverty and cultural practices facilitate trafficking." Paper presented at the Pontifical Academy of Social Sciences, *Human Trafficking: Issues beyond Criminalization,* Casina Pio IV, Vatican City, April 17–21. http://www.endslavery.va/content/endslavery/en/publications/acta_20/aronowitz.html

Aronowitz, Alexis A. 2015b. "Human trafficking victims of human trafficking: A complex issue." *Dossier of Analysis.* International Study Center, Universidad de los Andes. http://cei.uniandes.edu.co/index.php/component/docman/cat_view/5-dossier?Itemid=

Aronowitz, Alexis A., and Isitman, Elif. 2013. "Trafficking of human beings for the purpose of organ removal: Are (International) legal instruments effective measures to eradicate the practice?" *Groningen Journal of International Law,* 1(2), 73–90. https://groningenjil.files.wordpress.com/2014/01/03-aronowitz-isitman.pdf

Aronowitz, Alexis A., and Koning, Anneke. 2014. "Understanding human trafficking as a market system: Addressing the demand side of trafficking for sexual exploitation." Revue Internationale de Droit Penale, *International Review of Penal Law,* 85, 669–696.

Aronowitz, Alexis A., Theuermann, Gerda, and Tyurykanova, Elena. 2010. *Analysing the business model of trafficking in human beings to better prevent the crime.* Vienna, Austria: OSCE Office of the Special Representative and Coordinator for Combating Trafficking in Human Beings.

Back, Maarten. 2015, April 22. "23 mannen bekennen in Valkenburgse zedenzaak." *Nrc.nl.* http://www.nrc.nl/nieuws/2015/04/22/23-mannen-bekennen-in-valkenburgse-zedenzaak/

Bales, Kevin. 2005. *Understanding global slavery.* Berkeley and Los Angeles: University of California Press.

Baskakova, Marina, Tiurukanova, Elena and Abdurazakova, Dono. 2005. "Human trafficking in the CIS." *Development and Transition,* (2), 3–6.

Batha, Emma. 2015, February 17. "Iraqi women trafficked into sexual slavery—Rights group." *Reuters*. http://www .reuters.com/article/2015/02/17/us-iraq-trafficking-women-idUSKBN0LL1U220150217

BBC News. 2006, 16 March. "Selling child porn targeted." http://news.bbc.co.uk/2/hi/technology/4812962.stm

Belser, Patrick, de Cock, Michaëlle, and Mehran, Farhad. 2005. *ILO minimum estimate of forced labour in the world*. Geneva, Switzerland: International Labour Organization. http://www.ilo.org/wcmsp5/groups/ public/-ed_norm/-declaration/documents/publication/ wcms_081913.pdf

Bienstock, Rik Esther. 2013. *Tales from the organ trade*. http:// www.talesfromtheorgantrade.com/

Birkenthal, Sara. (2011–2012). "Human trafficking: A human rights abuse with global dimensions." *Interdisciplinary Journal of Human Rights Law, 6,* 27.

Bollinger, Kate, and McQuay, Kim. 2012, February 8. "Human trafficking rampant in Thailand's deep-sea fishing industry." *Weekly Insight and Analysis in Asia*. Asia Foundation. http://asiafoundation.org/in-asia/2012/02/08/ human-trafficking-rampant-in-thailands-deep-sea-fishing-industry/

Bovenkerk, Frank and Pronk, G.J. 2007. "Over de bestrijding van loverboy methoden." *Mensenhandel, Justitiële Verkeningen*, (7), 82–95.

Brewer, D.P., Potterat, J.J., Muth, S.Q., Roberts, J.M., Dudek, J.A., and Woodhouse, D.E. 2007. *Clients of prostitute women: Deterrence, prevalence, characteristics and violence*. Washington DC: National Institute of Justice.

Brunovskis, Anette, and Surtees, Rebecca. 2007. *Leaving the past behind? When victims of trafficking decline assistance*. Fafo: Norway. http://fafoarkiv.no/pub/rapp/20258-20262/ 20258.pdf

Brunovskis, Anette, and Surtees, Rebecca. 2008. "Agency or illness—The conceptualization of trafficking: Victims' choices and behaviors in the assistance system." *Gender, Technology and Development, 12*(1), 53–76.

Buet, Laura, Bashford, Peter, and Basnyat, Muna. 2012. *Looking towards tomorrow: A study on the reintegration of trafficked survivors.* Asha Nepal, Shakti Samuha and Terre des hommes Foundation. http://www.asha-nepal.org/dbfiles/pages/116/reintegration_study.pdf

Busch-Armendariz, Noël, Nsonwu, Maura, Heffron, Laurie, Garza, Jacqueline, and Hernandez, Mayra. 2009. *Understanding human trafficking: Development of typologies of traffickers.* Austin: University of Texas. http://digital commons.unl.edu/cgi/viewcontent.cgi?article=1008&context=humtraffconf

Cameron, Sally, and Newman, Edward. 2008. "Trafficking in humans: Structural factors." In S. Cameron and E. Newman (Eds.), *Trafficking in humans: Social, cultural and political dimensions* (pp. 21–57). Tokyo, Japan: United Nations University Press.

Clawson, Heather, and Dutch, Nicole. 2008. *Identifying victims of human trafficking: Inherent challenges and promising strategies from the field.* U.S. Department of Health and Human Services. http://aspe.hhs.gov/hsp/07/humantrafficking/IdentVict/ib.pdf

Cornish, D., and Clarke, R. 1987. "Understanding crime displacement: An application of rational choice theory." *Criminology, 25,* 933–948.

Council of Europe. 2005. *Explanatory Report to the Council of Europe Convention on Action Against Trafficking in Human Beings.* https://rm.coe.int/CoERMPublic CommonSearchServices/DisplayDCTMContent?docu mentId=09000016800d3812

Countertrafficking.org. *Frequently asked questions.* http://www.countertrafficking.org/faq.html

"The dancing boys of Afghanistan." *Frontline/PBS*. http://
www.pbs.org/wgbh/pages/frontline/dancingboys/

"The dark side of chocolate." https://www.youtube.com/
watch?v=BeJy3dA4Ahk

Dongen, van, Menno. 2007a, February 13. "Pooierbroeders
konden jaren hun gang gaan." *De Volkskrant, 3.*

Dongen, van, Menno. 2007b, May 12. "Een geraffineerd
spel." *De Volkskrant, 26.*

ECPAT. 2008. *Extraterritorial laws: Why they are not working
and how they can be strengthened.* Bangkok. http://
resources.ecpat.net/worldcongressIII/PDF/Journals/
EXTRATERRITORIAL_LAWS.pdf

ECPATUK. 2010. "Child trafficking for forced criminality."
Discussion Paper. http://www.ecpat.org.uk/sites/default/
files/child_trafficking_for_forced_criminality.pdf

Ekberg, G. 2004. "The Swedish law that prohibits the
purchase of sexual services." *Violence against Women,
10*(10), 1187–1218.

European Commission. 2013. *The EU rights of victims of
trafficking in human beings.* Luxembourg. http://ec.europa
.eu/dgs/home-affairs/e-library/docs/thb_victims_rights/
thb_victims_rights_en.pdf

EUROPOL. 2000. *EUROPOL situation report THB 1999.*
The Hague, The Netherlands: EUROPOL.

Eurostat. 2014. *Trafficking in human beings.* http://
ec.europa.eu/dgs/home-affairs/what-is-new/news/news/
docs/20141017_working_paper_on_statistics_on_
trafficking_in_human_beings_en.pdf

Farr, Kathryn. 2005. *Sex trafficking: The global market in
women and children.* New York: Worth Publishers.

Feingold, David. 2005, September–October. "Human
trafficking." *Foreign Policy* No. 150, 26–30, 32.

Financial Action Task Force (FATF). 2011, July. *Money
laundering risks arising from trafficking in human beings and*

smuggling of migrants. Paris, France. http://www.fatf-gafi
.org/media/fatf/documents/reports/trafficking%20in%20
human%20beings%20and%20smuggling%20of%20
migrants.pdf

Fraser, Christian. 2005, January 11. "Protecting Aceh's
children." *BBC News.* http://news.bbc.co.uk/2/hi/asia-
pacific/4164107.stm

Gage, Patrick. 2014, November 15–16. "Hotels against
trafficking: Hospitality's role in fighting slavery."
Conference presentation at *Young People against Prostitution
and Human Trafficking: The Greatest Violence against
Human Beings,* Vatican City. http://www.endslavery.va/
content/endslavery/en/publications/youth_symposium_
2014/hotels.html

Gallagher, Anne. 2013. *Abuse of a position of vulnerability
and other "means" within the definition of trafficking in
persons.* Vienna: United Nations Office on Drugs and
Crime. https://www.unodc.org/documents/human-
trafficking/2012/UNODC_2012_Issue_Paper_-_Abuse_
of_a_Position_of_Vulnerability.pdf

Gibson, O., and Pattisson, P. 2014, December 23. "Death
toll among Qatar's 2022 World Cup workers revealed."
The Guardian. http://www.theguardian.com/world/2014/
dec/23/qatar-nepal-workers-world-cup-2022-death-
toll-doha

Haugen, Gary. 2015. "Lessons from two decades of casework:
How to restore survivors and communities to safety and
strength." Conference paper presented at the Pontifical
Academy of the Social Sciences, Vatican City, April
17–21. http://www.endslavery.va/content/endslavery/en/
publications/acta_20/haugen.html

Hepburn, Stephanie, and Simon, Rita J. 2013. *Human
trafficking around the world: Hidden in plain sight.* New
York: Columbia University Press.

Hughes, Donna. 2000. "The 'Natasha' trade: The transnational shadow market of trafficking in women." *Journal of International Affairs, 53*(2), Spring, 625–651.

Human Rights Watch. 1997. *The scars of death: Children abducted by the Lord's resistance army in Uganda.* http://www.hrw.org/legacy/reports97/uganda/

Human Rights Watch. 2007. *Early to war, child soldiers in the Chad conflict, 19*(9[A]). http://hrw.org/reports/2007/chad0707/chad0707webwcover.pdf

Human Rights Watch. 2012, March 12. *Child soldiers Worldwide.* https://www.hrw.org/news/2012/03/12/child-soldiers-worldwide

Human Rights Watch. 2014. *"I already bought you" abuse and exploitation of female migrant domestic workers in the United Arab Emirates.* United States. https://www.hrw.org/sites/default/files/reports/uae1014_forUpload.pdf

Human Trafficking Search. 2014. *Invisible men: Male victims of sex trafficking.* http://humantraffickingsearch.net/wp/invisible-men-male-victims-of-sex-trafficking/

ICE (Immigration and Customs Enforcement). 2012, June 15. "Wisconsin couple who kept modern-day slave for 19 years deported to the Philippines." *ICE Newsroom.* http://www.ice.gov/news/releases/wisconsin-couple-who-kept-modern-day-slave-19-years-deported-philippines

ILO (International Labour Organization). 2009. *Operational indicators of trafficking in human beings.* Geneva, Switzerland: International Labour Organization. http://www.ilo.org/wcmsp5/groups/public/@ed_norm/@declaration/documents/publication/wcms_105023.pdf.

ILO. 2010. *Operational indicators of trafficking in human beings; 2009.* Geneva, Switzerland: International Labour Organization. http://www.ilo.org/wcmsp5/groups/public/—ed_norm/—declaration/documents/publication/wcms_105023.pdf

ILO. 2012. *ILO global estimate of forced labour. Results and methodology.* Geneva, Switzerland: International Labour Organization. http://www.ilo.org/wcmsp5/groups/public/—ed_norm/—declaration/documents/publication/wcms_182004.pdf

ILO. 2013. *Caught at sea, forced labour and trafficking in fisheries.* Geneva, Switzerland: International Labour Organization. http://www.ilo.org/wcmsp5/groups/public/—ed_norm/—declaration/documents/publication/wcms_214472.pdf

ILO. No date. *Who are domestic workers?* http://www.ilo.org/global/docs/WCMS_209773/lang—en/index.htm

ILO-IPEC. 2002, October. "Combating child labour and HIV/AIDS in sub-Saharan Africa". News Update: Archive.

ILPA (Immigration Law Practitioners' Association). 2006, April 5. *ILPA response to tackling human trafficking—Consultation on proposals for a UK action plan.* http://www.ilpa.org.uk/resources.php/13138/tackling-human-trafficking-consultation-on-proposals-for-a-uk-action-plan-ilpa-response-and-annex-of

IOM (International Organization for Migration). 2007. "Efforts to engage clergy in counter trafficking reaches new high." http://www.iom.int/news/efforts-engage-clergy-counter-trafficking-reaches-new-high

IOM. 2010. *The causes and consequences of re-trafficking: Evidence from the IOM human trafficking database.* Geneva, Switzerland. http://publications.iom.int/bookstore/free/causes_of_retrafficking.pdf

Jordan, Ann. No date. *Trafficking and globalization.* Center for American Progress. https://www.americanprogress.org/wp-content/uploads/kf/TerrorinShadows-Jordan.pdf. Accessed on August 28, 2015.

Kleemans, Edward K. 2015. "Follow the money: Introduction to the special issue 'Financial Aspects of Organized

Crime'." *European Journal of Criminal Policy Research, 21*, 213–216.

Klompenhouwer, Laura. 2015, July 2. "Twee jaar cel voor hoofdverdachte in Valkenburgse zedenzaak." *Nrc.nl.* http://www.nrc.nl/nieuws/2015/07/02/twee-jaar-cel-voor-hoofdverdachte-in-valkenburgse-zedenzaak/

Klopott, F. 2009, November 20. "State department adds restrictions to diplomats bringing servants into the U.S." *Washington Examiner.* http://www.washingtonexaminer .com/state-department-adds-restrictions-to-diplomats-bringing-servants-into-the-u.s./article/20247

KLPD—Dienst Nationale Recherche (National Dutch Police—National Detectives). 2008. *Schone Schijn: De signalering van mensenhandel in de vergunde Prostitutiesector.* Rotterdam: Korps Landelijke Politiediensten.

Kralis, Barbara. 2006, August 4. "Catholic Church fights human trafficking & slavery." *Renew America.* http:// www.renewamerica.us/columns/kralis/060804

Kristof, Nicholas. 2008, March 16. "The pimps' slaves." *The New York Times.* http://www.nytimes.com/2008/03/16/ opinion/16kristof.html?_r=3&th&emc=th&oref=slogin& oref=slogin&oref=slogin

Kryszko, B., and Raymond, J. 2006. "Good practices: Targeting the demand for prostitution and trafficking." *Coalition Against Trafficking in Women.* http://action.web .ca/home/catw/readingroom.shtml?x=71327&AA_EX_Sess ion=794bc5fab1e5f8a943336c60bd545b5b

Laczko, Frank, and Gozdziak, Elzbieta (Eds.). 2005. *Data and research on human trafficking: A global survey.* Geneva, Switzerland: International Organization for Migration.

Lagon, Mark. 2007, July 9. *Remarks at swearing-in ceremony.* U.S. Department of State. http://2001–2009.state.gov/g/tip/ rls/rm/07/88003.htm

Lederer, L.J. 2009. "Addressing demand: Examining new practices." *Global Centurion*, October 26, 2009. http://www.facebook.com/notes/global-centurion/addressing-demand-examining-new-practices-by-laura-j-lederer-jd/180204359877

Leman, Johan, and Janssens, Stef. 2008. "The Albanian and post-Soviet business of trafficking women for prostitution: Structural developments and financial modus operandi." *European Journal of Criminology,* 5(4), 433.

Lugris, Veronica. 2013. "Human trafficking and post-traumatic stress disorder." In Mary C. Burke (Ed.), *Human trafficking: Interdisciplinary perspectives* (pp. 231–241). London: Routledge.

Lynch, Dennis. 2014, August 30. "ISIS sells 300 Yazidi women as brides to fighters in recent weeks." *International Business Times.* http://www.ibtimes.com/isis-sells-300-yazidi-women-brides-fighters-recent-weeks-1674452

Mackay, Maria. 2006, December 20. "Church of Bangladesh raises thousands for anti-trafficking work." *Christian Today*, http://www.christiantoday.co.uk/article/church.of.bangladesh.raises.thousands.for.antitrafficking.work/8795.htm

Martin, Louis, and Shaheen, Miriam. 2014, March 29. "Crime or culture: The revival of slave boys in Afghanistan; a UK perspective." *Criminal Law and Justice Weekly, 178,* 193–195.

McCoy, Terrence. 2014, April 30. "Hundreds of kidnapped Nigerian school girls reportedly sold as brides to militants for $12, relatives say." *Washington Post.* http://www.washingtonpost.com/news/morning-mix/wp/2014/04/30/hundreds-of-kidnapped-nigerian-school-girls-reportedly-sold-as-brides-to-militants-for-12-relatives-say/

McDonald, Lynn, and Natalya Timoshkina. 2007, Fall. "The working life of women trafficked from the Eastern bloc." *International Journal of Comparative and Applied Criminal Justice,* 31(2), 234–244.

Ministry of Industry, Employment and Communications (Regeringskansliet). 2005, April. *Prostitution and trafficking in human beings.* Stockholm, Sweden. http://www.nordic baltic-assistwomen.net/IMG/pdf/Sweden_Factsheet_on_ Prostitution_and_Trafficking-2.pdf

Monto, M.A. 1999, October 30. *Focusing on the clients of street prostitutes: A creative approach to reducing violence against women.* Submitted to the National Institute of Justice.

Monto, M.A., and Garcia, S. 2001. "Recidivism among the customers of female street prostitutes: Do intervention programs help?" *Western Criminology Review,* 3(2), 1–10.

Monzini, Paola. 2001, September 6–8. *Trafficking in women and girls and the involvement of organized crime, with reference to the situation in Central and Eastern Europe.* UNICRI.

MTV. *Project EXIT.* http://mtvexit.org/

National Geographic. *21st century sex slaves.* https://www .youtube.com/watch?v=ajbQVwbWRg0

National Rapporteur on Trafficking in Human Beings and Sexual Violence Against Children. 2005. *Trafficking in human beings.* Third Report. The Hague, The Netherlands. https://www.nationaalrapporteur.nl/binaries/rapportage-3-(eng)-tcm64-83607_tcm23-34847.pdf

National Survivor Network. http://nationalsurvivornetwork.org/

Navis, Jan Willem. 2008, May 29. "Spong: Rechtbank partijdig." *Spits,* 8.

Netherlands Ministry of Security and Justice. No date. *Residency regulation human trafficking.* https://ind.nl/EN/

organisation/themes/human-trafficking/residency-regulation-human-trafficking

Newburn, Tim. 2013. *Criminology*. Cullomption, Devon: Willan Publishing.

Nieburg, Oliver. 2012. "Cocoa certification: Pros, cons and costs." *Confectionary News.com*.

Nils, Christie. 1986. "The ideal victim." In F.A. Fattah (Ed.), *From crime policy to victim policy*. New York: St. Martin Press, cited in Tim Newburn. 2013. *Criminology*. Willan Publishing.

O'Connor, Monica, and Healy, Grainne. 2006. *The links between prostitution and sex trafficking: A briefing handbook*. Coalition Against Trafficking in Women. http://www.catwinternational.org/Content/Images/Article/175/attachment.pdf

Office for Victims of Crime. *Victim-centered approach*. Training and Technical Assistance Center. https://www.ovcttac.gov/taskforceguide/eguide/1-understanding-human-trafficking/13-victim-centered-approach/

Organs across Borders—World. https://www.youtube.com/watch?v=g6L6PMzan0w

OSCE. 2004. *National referral mechanisms—Joining efforts to protect the rights of trafficked persons: A practical handbook*. Vienna, Austria. http://www.osce.org/odihr/13967

OSCE Office for Democratic Institutions and Human Rights (ODIHR). 2004. *National referral mechanisms*. Warsaw, Poland. http://www.osce.org/odihr/13967?download=true

OSCE Office of the Special Representative and Coordinator for Combating Trafficking in Human Beings. 2006. *Human trafficking for labour exploitation, forced and bonded labour: Identification, prevention and prosecution*. Vienna. http://www.osce.org/cthb/31923?download=true

OSCE Office of the Special Representative and Coordinator for Combating Trafficking in Human Beings. 2013.

Trafficking in human beings for the purpose of organ removal in the OSCE region: Analysis and findings. Occasional Paper Series no. 6.

Pennington, Julia, Ball, A. Dwayne, Hampton, Ronald, and Soulakova, Julia. 2009. "The cross-national market in human beings." *Journal of Macromarketing, 29*(2), 119–134.

Piscitelli, A. 2012. "Revisiting notions of sex trafficking and victims." *Vibrant, Virtual Brazilian Anthropology* [online], *9*(1), 274–310.

Polaris Project. 2013. *Human trafficking legislative brief: Sex trafficking of minors.* https://www.polarisproject.org/what-we-do/policy-advocacy/prosecuting-traffickers/895-sex-trafficking-of-minors

Reed, Judy Hale. 2013. "Addressing the problem: Community-based responses and coordination." In Mary Burke (Ed.), *Human trafficking: Interdisciplinary perspectives* (pp. 256–277). Routledge: London.

Rijken, Conny. 2009. "A human rights based approach to trafficking in human beings." *Security and Human Rights, 20*(3), 212–222.

Russel, Andy. 2008, June 11. "'Callous' human trafficker jailed." *Manchester Evening News.* http://www.manchestereveningnews.co.uk/news/s/1053507_callous_human_traffickers_jailed. Accessed on September 10, 2016.

Savona, E. U., Belli, R., Curtol, F., Decarli, S., and Di Nicola, A. 2004. *Trafficking in Persons and Smuggling of Migrants into Italy.* Roma: Ministero della Sanità, 274 pp.

Scheper-Hughes, Nancy. 2001. "Commodity Fetishisms in Organ Trafficking." *Body and Science, 7*(2–3), 31–62.

Scheper-Hughes, Nancy. 2003, May 10. "Keeping an eye on the global traffic in human organs." *The Lancet, 361*, 1645–1648.

Schloenhardt, Andreas. 1999. "Organized crime and the business of migrant trafficking." *Crime, Law and Social Change, 32*, 203–233.

Shelley, Louise. 2010. *Human trafficking: A global perspective.* New York: Cambridge University Press.

Shelley, Louise. 2014, December 26. "ISIS, Boko Haram, and the growing role of human trafficking in 21st century terrorism." *The Daily Beast.* http://www.thedailybeast.com/articles/2014/12/26/isis-boko-haram-and-the-growing-role-of-human-trafficking-in-21st-century-terrorism.html

Shively, M., Jalbert, S., Kling, R., Rhodes, W., Finn, R., Flyage, C., Tierney, L., Hunt, D., Squires, D., Dyos, C., and Wheeler, K. 2008. *Final Report on the Evaluation of the First Offender Prostitution Program*, National Institute of Justice, U.S. Department of Justice. http://www.ncjrs.gov/pdffiles1/nij/grants/221894.pdf

Siegel, Dina, and De Blank, Sylvia. 2010, November. "Women who traffic women: the role of women in human trafficking networks—Dutch cases." *Global Crime, 11*(4), 436–447.

Siegel, Larry. 2004. *Criminology: Theories, patterns and typologies* (8th ed.). Belmont: Wadsworth.

Skogseth, Geir. 2006. *Trafficking in women—Fact-finding trip to Nigeria (Abuja, Lagos and Benin City).* Oslo, Norway: Landinfo. http://www.landinfo.no/asset/224/1/224_1.pdf. Accessed on September 7, 2016.

Spector, Michael. 1998, January 11. "Traffickers' new cargo: Naive slavic women." *The New York Times*, reprinted on Brama. http://www.brama.com/issues/nytart.html. Accessed on September 8, 2016.

Srikantiah, J. 2007. "Perfect victims and real survivors: The iconic victim in domestic human trafficking law." *Boston University Law Review, 87*, 157–211.

Sulaimanova, Saltanat. 2006. "Trafficking in women from the Former Soviet Union for the purposes of sexual exploitation." In Karen Beeks and Delila Amir (Eds.), *Trafficking and the global sex industry* (pp. 61–76). Lanham, MD: Lexington Books.

Surtees, Rebecca. 2007, October 31. "Trafficking victims in SEE—What we know, what we need to know." *Mensenhandel: achtergrond en aanpak*, Conference, Vrije Universiteit Amsterdam.

Surtees, Rebecca. 2008a. "Traffickers and trafficking in Southern and Eastern Europe: Considering the other side of human trafficking." *European Journal of Criminology*, 5(1), 39–68.

Surtees, Rebecca. 2008b. *Trafficking of men—A trend less considered; the case of Belarus and Ukraine*. Geneva, Switzerland: International Organization for Migration. http://publications.iom.int/system/files/pdf/mrs_36.pdf

Sykes, Gresham, and Matza, David. 1957, December. "Techniques of neutralization: A theory of delinquency." *American Sociological Review*, 22(6), 664–670.

Tomiuc, Eugen. 2008, February 20. "World: UN, campaigners highlight grim reality of 'Happy Trafficking'." *Radio Free Europe Radio Liberty*. http://www.rferl.org/content/article/1347744.html. Accessed on September 9, 2016.

TRACE (Trafficking as a Criminal Enterprise). 2015, June 10. "Trace workshop." *The Findings*. http://www.slideshare.net/trace_eu/trace-workshop-10-june-2015

TRACE Project Consortium. 2016. *Tracing human trafficking*. http://trace-project.eu/wp-content/uploads/2016/05/TRACE.pdf

Trevizo, Perla. 2015, June 2. "Border deaths down as deadliest part of the year begins." *Tucson.com*. http://tucson.com/news/border-deaths-down-as-deadliest-part-of-the-year-begins/article_eb602cfc-d719-578c-a90b-41254ae88fc4.html

Tsutsumi, Atsuro, Izutsu, Takashi, Poudyal, Amod K., Kato, Seika and Marui, Eiji. 2008. "Mental health of female survivors of human trafficking in Nepal." *Social Science & Medicine, 66*, 1841–1847.

UN.GIFT (United Nations Global Initiative to Fight Human Trafficking). http://www.ungift.org/knowledgehub/en/about/

UN.GIFT. 2008. *An introduction to human trafficking: Vulnerability, impact and action.* Vienna: United Nations Office on Drugs and Crime. http://www.unodc.org/documents/human-trafficking/An_Introduction_to_Human_Trafficking_-_Background_Paper.pdf

UNICEF. 2005. *Excluded and invisible. The state of the world's children 2006.* New York: UNICEF. http://www.unicef.org/sowc06/pdfs/sowc06_fullreport.pdf

UNICRI. http://www.unodc.org/pdf/crime/human_trafficking/coalitions_trafficking.pdf

United Nations. 2000. *Protocol to prevent, suppress and punish trafficking in persons, especially women and children, supplementing the United Nations convention against transnational organized crime.* http://www.uncjin.org/Documents/Conventions/dcatoc/final_documents_2/convention_%20traff_eng.pdf. Accessed on January 1, 2016.

United Nations Office of the High Commissioner for Human Rights. 1985. *Declaration of basic principles of justice for victims of crime and abuse of power.* Adopted by General Assembly resolution 40/34 of 29 November 1985. http://www.ohchr.org/EN/ProfessionalInterest/Pages/VictimsOfCrimeAndAbuseOfPower.aspx

United States Congress. *S.178—Justice for Victims of Trafficking Act of 2015.* Public Law No. 114–22. https://www.congress.gov/bill/114th-congress/senate-bill/178

UN News Centre. 2014, July 14. "Human trafficking has no place in modern world, General Assembly President says." http://www.un.org/apps/news/story.asp?NewsID=48271#.VZqdeGcw-t4

UNODC (United Nations Office on Drugs and Crime). 2006. *Toolkit to combat trafficking in persons.* Vienna, Austria. http://www.unodc.org/pdf/Trafficking_toolkit_ Oct06.pdf

UNODC. 2007. *Compendium on best practices on anti- human trafficking by law enforcement agencies.* https:// www.unodc.org/documents/human-trafficking/India_ Training_material/Compendium_of_Best_Practices_by_ Law_Enforcement_Agencies.pdf

UNODC. 2010. Working group on trafficking in persons. Second meeting, 27–29 January, Vienna, Austria. https:// www.unodc.org/unodc/en/human-trafficking/2010/ expert-panelists-address-working-group-on-human- trafficking.html

UNODC. 2013. *Abuse of a position of vulnerability and other "means" within the definition of trafficking in persons.* http://www.unodc.org/documents/human-trafficking/2012/ UNODC_2012_Issue_Paper_-_Abuse_of_a_Position_of_ Vulnerability.pdf

UNODC. 2014. *Global report on trafficking in persons.* https://www.unodc.org/documents/data-and-analysis/ glotip/GLOTIP_2014_full_report.pdf.

UNODC. 2016. *Global report on trafficking in persons.* http:// www.unodc.org/documents/data-and-analysis/glotip/2016_ Global_Report_on_Trafficking_in_Persons.pdf.

USAID. 2008, 2 May. "Clergy joins fight against human trafficking."

U.S. Citizenship and Immigration Services. No date. *Victims of human trafficking: T nonimmigrant status.* http://www .uscis.gov/humanitarian/victims-human-trafficking-other- crimes/victims-human-trafficking-t-nonimmigrant-status

U.S. Department of Defense. No date. *T.I.P. Awareness Training.* http://ctip.defense.gov/Training.aspx.

U.S. Department of Labor. 2014. *List of goods produced by child labor or forced labor.* Washington, DC. http://www.dol.gov/ilab/reports/pdf/TVPRA_Report2014.pdf

U.S. Department of State. 2007. *Trafficking in persons report 2007.* Washington, DC.

U.S. Department of State. 2008. *Trafficking in persons report 2008.* Washington, DC.

U.S. Department of State. 2014. *The intersection between environmental degradation and human trafficking.* Washington, DC: Office to Monitor and Combat Trafficking in Persons. http://www.state.gov/documents/organization/228266.pdf

U.S. Department of State. 2015. *Trafficking in persons report 2015.* Washington, DC. http://www.state.gov/documents/organization/245365.pdf

U.S. Department of State. 2016. *Trafficking in persons report 2016.* Washington, DC. http://www.state.gov/documents/organization/258876.pdf

Van der Zee, Renate. 2013, August 17. "Jongenshandel. Ik wist niet wie ik kon vertrouwen." *Vrij Nederland.* http://www.fier.nl/upload/f7193e57-2ccb-4698-bca1-cf4d405e3a97.pdf

Verhoeven, Maite, van Gestel, Barbra, de Jong, Deborah, and Kleemans, Edward. 2015, April. "Relationships between suspects and victims of sex trafficking. Exploitation of prostitutes and domestic violence parallels in Dutch trafficking cases." *European Journal of Criminal Policy Research, 21*(1), 49–64.

Vlieger, A. 2011. *Domestic workers in Saudi Arabia and the Emirates: A socio-legal study on conflicts.* Amsterdam, The Netherlands: University of Amsterdam.

Walk Free Foundation. 2016. *Global slavery index.* http://www.globalslaveryindex.org/

War Child. 2007, March. *Child soldiers: The shadow of their existence.* http://www.warchildholland.org/sites/default/files/bijlagen/node_492/6-2013/report_child_soldiers_english1.pdf

Warren, K. 2012. "Troubling the victim/trafficker dichotomy in efforts to combat human trafficking: The unintended consequences of moralizing labor migration." *Indiana Journal of Global Legal Studies, 19*(1), Winter, 105–120.

Weitzer, Ronald. 2009. "Sociology of sex work." *Annual Review of Sociology,* 35, 213–234.

Weitzer, Ronald. 2011, August 24. "Myths about human trafficking." *The World Post.* http://www.huffingtonpost.com/ronald-weitzer/human-trafficking-myths_b_935366.html

Weitzer, Ronald. 2012a. "'Sex Trafficking and the Sex Industry' the need for evidence-based theory and legislation." *The Journal of Criminal Law & Criminology,* 101(4), 1337–1370.

Weitzer, Ronald. 2012b. *Legalizing prostitution: From illicit vice to lawful business.* New York: New York University Press.

Weitzer, Ronald. 2014. "New directions in research on human trafficking." *The Annals of the American Academy of Political and Social Science,* 653, 6–24.

Wieners, Brad. 2015, April 10. "Dying at Europe's doorstep." *Bloomberg Business.* http://www.bloomberg.com/graphics/2015-migrant-rescue-in-the-mediterranean/

Wilcox, A., Christmann, K., Rogerson, M., and Birch, P. 2009. *Tackling the demand for prostitution: A rapid evidence assessment of the published research literature.* Home Office, Research Report 27. http://socialwelfare.bl.uk/subject-areas/services-activity/criminal-justice/homeoffice/141533horr27b.pdf

World Bank. 2009, December. "Human trafficking: A brief overview." *Social Development Notes. Conflict, Crime and*

Violence No. 122. http://siteresources.worldbank.org/ EXTSOCIALDEVELOPMENT/Resources/244362-1239390842422/6012763-1239905793229/Human_ Trafficking.pdf

Yen, Iris. 2008. "Of vice and men: A new approach to eradicating sex trafficking by reducing male demand through educational programs and abolitionist legislation." *The Journal of Criminal Law and Criminology, 98*(2), 653–686.

Yie, Sallie. 2010. Trafficking in part(s): The commercial kidney market in a Manila slum, Philippines. *Global Social Policy, 10*(3), 358–376.

Zimmerman, C., Hossain, M., Yun, K., Roche, B., Morison, L., and Watts, C. 2006. *Stolen smiles: A summary report on the physical and psychological health consequences of women and adolescents trafficked in Europe.* London: London School of Hygiene & Tropical Medicine.

This chapter introduces the reader to human trafficking issues from the perspective of experts working in the field. The contributors include academic researchers, a human rights activist, a member of a religious order, a journalist, a former prosecutor, and the director of a shelter which provides programs and services to trafficked victims. They tell stories of the challenges faced in their work, their partnerships with other organizations, and introduce the findings of their studies on diverse topics to give the reader a greater appreciation of the complexity of human trafficking.

Estimating the Magnitude of Trafficking and Slavery
Ronald Weitzer

A growing number of people believe that human trafficking and slavery are a huge and growing problem today. Estimates of the number of victims worldwide range from 600,000 to 4 million trafficking victims and from 8 to 27 million persons in slavery. In 2010, the U.S. State Department asserted that 1.8 per 1,000 persons in the world (0.18%) are trafficked

Children like this young girl are prized in the carpet industry for their small, fast fingers. Defenseless, they do what they are told, toiling in cramped, dark, airless village huts from sunrise until well into the night. (Kay Chernush for the U.S. State Department)

every year. No sources have ever been provided to document any of these figures, yet they were quickly reported as facts in the media and by various government and international agencies.

Many of the agencies and interest groups involved in anti-trafficking efforts have laudable humanitarian goals and provide a much-needed service to victims. But other agencies and NGOs also have a vested interest in inflating the magnitude of trafficking and slavery. The larger the number of alleged victims, the greater the amount of attention human trafficking receives from the media, politicians, and the public—along with financial contributions to organizations involved in the trafficking arena, some of which have little or no expertise in the area. Many independent analysts have criticized the lack of documentation for the estimates (Fedina, 2015; Gozdziak and Bump, 2008), but they have been completely overshadowed by activists who insist the magnitude of the problem is both massive and increasing internationally.

Miscounting Victims: Two Defective Reports

Two recent "studies" have gotten international attention. Each presents terribly flawed conclusions.

The first is the Global Slavery Index produced by the Walk Free Foundation (2013). The creators of the index rank 162 nations on the prevalence of contemporary "slavery," which is defined very broadly as human trafficking, slavery, and forced labor. The index is based on a mix of sources: population surveys in a few countries; fuzzy estimates by governmental agencies or NGOs; stories in the media; and local "experts." For nations lacking any such source, the index creators engage in an "extrapolation" exercise—they simply apply an estimate from one nation to "similar" nations lacking such estimates. "For example, the prevalence ratio from the UK study was assumed to be relevant to other European island nations such as Ireland and Iceland, whereas the prevalence ratio for the USA was assumed to be relevant to developed Western European countries such as Germany." One obvious problem is why the United States is "relevant" to Europe. But more generally, imputing "similarity" to different nations ignores their unique characteristics; such "extrapolation" runs the risk of grossly distorting the prevalence of slavery in any particular country. For countries for which no extrapolation was possible, the creators of the index state that "it was necessary to fall back on secondary source information," which are anecdotal (NGOs, media reports, local "experts"). These sources are especially problematic when we remember that modern slavery and trafficking are clandestine, illicit practices that are very difficult to detect.

The slavery index identifies the 10 "worst" nations on the slavery scale. Some of these are in Africa (Gabon, The Gambia, Côte d'Ivoire, Benin, Mauritania), and the others are Haiti, Pakistan, India, Nepal, and Moldova. Some analysts would argue that we cannot have *any* confidence in victim estimates in such societies, because of the lack of reliable data. The index also identifies the 10 "best" nations—with the lowest slavery rates—all of which are rich nations in Western Europe and New Zealand.

The slavery index concludes that there are 29.8 million persons worldwide who are victims of forced labor, human trafficking, and slavery. This figure is intended to lend credence to the previous claim by Kevin Bales—founder of Free the Slaves—that there are 27 million persons enslaved throughout the world. When Bales first proposed 27 million, he justified it as simply a "guess." Most social scientists would be highly critical of both figures, and given the incredibly unstandardized and fragmented information and dubious assumptions on which the Global Slavery Index is based, it has no credibility whatsoever (Guth et al., 2014; Weitzer, 2014). Yet, many media sources, government agencies, NGOs, and international organizations have embraced these figures.

The second report (published in the journal *World Development* in 2012) seeks to determine whether countries where prostitution is legal have more or less trafficking than countries where prostitution is illegal. Using a report on 161 countries from the United Nations Office on Drugs and Crime (UNODC), economists Seo-Young Cho, Axel Dreher, and Eric Neumayer tried to determine if a nation's prostitution laws are related to the prevalence of human trafficking. In doing so, they ignored the UNODC's own caution *against* using its report as a measure of the number of victims in any country. UNODC noted the absence of a universal definition of trafficking across countries, problematic data collection, unstandardized reporting regarding suspected or confirmed victims, the diverse nature of the sources across all these countries, and the conflation of smuggling, trafficking, and irregular migration numbers by some countries. Cho and her colleagues say that their figures do "not reflect actual trafficking flows" and that it is "difficult, perhaps impossible, to find hard evidence" of a relationship between trafficking and anything else, but they then disregard these problems and draw sweeping conclusions about the relationship between trafficking and national prostitution laws.

Cho and colleagues rely on total national human trafficking figures (combining sex, labor, and other kinds of trafficking) to determine whether legalizing prostitution reduces trafficking. Thus, there is a *gross mismatch* between the aggregate trafficking figures and prostitution law; the authors should have used only sex trafficking figures in comparison to the type of legal regime. There are other serious problems with this study. The authors examine trafficking at a single time point, but it should have been tracked over time, before and after prostitution is legally institutionalized, in order to determine if legalization increases or decreases the amount of trafficking. And they ignore the important question of whether and how prostitution laws are actually enforced. Their analysis is confined to "law on the books," ignoring the ways in which the law is, or is not, implemented on the ground. In short, this study is fatally flawed in terms of both data quality and analytical procedures!

Larger Implications

- Both the slavery index and the Cho report received publicity in the international media, and have already been embraced by policy makers in some countries, especially those seeking greater criminalization of prostitution.

- If the claims or "findings" are unfounded, they risk diverting attention and funding from other worthy causes. Much money has been spent by governments and the international community on anti-trafficking programs over the past 15 years. Yet, compared to the claimed high magnitude of the problem, few victims have been located and assisted, and similarly few traffickers prosecuted worldwide.

- Even if the assertions about national-level victimization rates were roughly accurate, their macro-level nature means that they have no practical utility on the ground, where trafficking matters most. Micro-level studies (in a city or town) have clear advantages. They can provide (1) more reliable estimates of victimization because of the smaller, more measurable context, (2) insights regarding the operational methods of trafficking rings, and (3) the potential for detecting "hot spots" for targeted deployment of enforcement resources.

References

Cho, Seo-Young, Alex Dreher, and Eric Neumayer, E. 2012. "Does legalized prostitution increase human trafficking?" *World Development, 41,* 67–82.

Fedina, Lisa. 2015. "Use and misuse of research in books on sex trafficking." *Trauma, Violence, and Abuse, 16*(2), 188–198.

Gozdziak, E., and Bump, M. 2008. *Data and research on human trafficking.* Washington, DC: Institute for the Study of International Migration.

Guth, Andrew, Robyn Anderson, Kasey Kinnard, and Hang Tran. 2014. "Proper methodology and methods of collecting and analyzing slavery data: An examination of the Global Slavery Index." *Social Inclusion, 2*, 14–22.

Walk Free Foundation. 2013. *Global slavery index, 2013.*

Weitzer, Ronald. 2014. "New directions in research on human trafficking." *Annals of the American Academy of Political and Social Science, 653*, 6–24.

Ronald Weitzer is Professor of Sociology at George Washington University in Washington, D.C. He has conducted research on various aspects of prostitution, including clients' attitudes and experiences, prostitutes' rights organizations, debates regarding prostitution policies, and the dynamics of legal prostitution systems in Europe. He is the author of the book, Legalizing Prostitution: From Illicit Vice to Lawful Business *(New York University Press, 2012), and is editor of two editions of another book,* Sex for Sale: Prostitution, Pornography, and the Sex Industry *(Routledge Press, 2000 and 2010). He coedited a special journal issue on human trafficking: the May 2014 issue of the* Annals of the American Academy of Political and Social Science.

Labor Exploitation of Migrant Workers in the Netherlands
Joanne van der Leun

In the Netherlands, labor exploitation was brought under Criminal Law in 2005, the current section 273f, in accordance with the Palermo Protocol of 2000 and the European legal and policy framework to combat human trafficking (including the 2011/36/EU Directive on Trafficking in Human Beings and the EU Strategy toward the Eradication of Trafficking in Human Beings, 2012–2016). Since the formal criminalization and attention for exploitation outside the sex industry, labor inspectorates increased investigations against illegal employment. Fines for employers were raised significantly. This increased attention resulted in an increase in the number of detected victims of trafficking in the Netherlands (from 424 in 2005 to 1,437 in 2013, with a peak in 2012 of 1,711 "registered victims"; see the reports of the Dutch National Rapporteur at http://www .dutchrapporteur.nl/reports/).

The majority of victims are registered after identification by the police. A small minority of these known cases involve victims of trafficking outside the sex industry (178 of 1,437 victims in 2013). There are no reliable estimates of the "real number" of victims, but it is clear that the actual number of victims is likely to be much higher than these registrations suggest. Many people who are exploited will not easily approach the authorities. The latter holds in particular for unauthorized migrant workers who might fear expulsion from the country once in contact with the authorities. This makes them often overlooked and particularly vulnerable to exploitation.

Baking Shrimp Chips in The Hague

One of the first major cases in the Netherlands involving labor exploitation occurred in 2009. It is generally seen as a breakthrough in the combat against trafficking outside the sex industry. The case first came to light when people in the neighborhood heard noises in the house and noticed numerous people coming in and out of the house—indications that seemed to point to a business. Neighbors reported their suspicions to the police. An investigation was started, in which different agencies cooperated and shared information. The Dutch Inspectorate SZW (the organization tasked with ensuring safe working conditions and protecting the socioeconomic security of workers in the Netherlands) and the police detected a criminal network involved in exploiting illegal workers from

Indonesia in The Hague. When the labor inspectorate arrived together with the police, 11 workers were found in a single home, making products such as shrimp chips and chili paste for an Indonesian store, which belonged to the owner of the house. Migrant workers who resided in the country without a residence permit had to work excessive hours (10–15 hours per day) for a small salary (€25–€30 per day), and deductions were made for a mattress on the floor. Circumstances were unhygienic and unhealthy. The workers were apprehended by the Immigration Police. During the interviews, suspicion arose that they had been exploited. The owner of the house, his wife, and an assistant were arrested. When the case went to court much later, the owner of the house was found guilty of human trafficking, jointly committed with others, and sentenced to four years imprisonment. This conviction for human trafficking was seen by many as a breakthrough, as in previous years and in similar cases judges often did not see them as cases of trafficking.

Policy Challenges

Gradually, an integrated approach has been developed in the Netherlands based on the so-called barrier model. This preventive model for tackling organized crime, which has been adapted for preventing trafficking in persons, is based on establishing barriers at each step that human traffickers have to take in order to execute their criminal activities. For each step, such as entry and recruitment, accommodation, identity, employment, and finance, the model indicates organizations or agents that might be able to raise thresholds or barriers for those involved in trafficking, either as a perpetrator or as a facilitator (Aronowitz et al., 2010). Sharing information and combining a criminal law with an administrative law-based approach are pivotal in this integrated approach. The government installed not only a National Rapporteur on Trafficking in Human Beings and Sexual Violence Against Children, but also a special

Task Force on Human Trafficking to promote and coordinate the combat against human trafficking.

Despite having made important steps toward a more effective and coordinated approach, there are still serious challenges as well which result in many cases going unreported and unpunished. An important and often neglected reason is that, apart from combating human trafficking, there is also the policy realm of migration control (based on the rights of States to curb illegal or unauthorized residence and labor). On the one hand, this may lead to police officers or other law enforcement officials not recognizing potential labor exploitation because they primarily think along the lines of "unauthorized or illegal migrants should not be working here, this person must be expelled from the country." On the other hand, migration control considerations also cause governments to be reluctant to extend employment protections to irregular workers. This also hampers their access to fundamental rights to which they should have access (van der Leun and Van Schijndel, 2016).

Second, both the general public and law enforcement officers still tend to think that exploitation in the sex industry is more important than other forms of exploitation, and this, in turn, may hamper the identification of victims. Despite attempts to raise awareness among the public at large, as well as among labor inspectors, police officers, prosecutors, and judges, this still holds. Figures on sentences imposed do not distinguish between different types of trafficking, so there is no clear answer to the question whether this translates into lower sentences. However, there is wide consensus that trafficking for labor exploitation implies a lower likelihood of being detected and recognized. In the case where a victim of trafficking in persons is also a suspect of a crime, for instance because he or she has used false documents to enter the country or work, the prosecutor may decide not to investigate or prosecute this crime further, and the court may decide not to apply any punishment or measure on the basis of the so-called nonpunishment principle. Again, however, this means that victims need to be recognized as such, which is problematic for unauthorized migrants.

Where to Go from Here?

In many countries, unauthorized workers contribute to the economy in an "invisible" way. They live an "underground" existence and they work largely outside the protection of labor-related enforcement agencies or unions. They also lack working permits and do not pay taxes. Increasing controls have pushed them even further underground, and criminal networks have stepped in with shady complex cross-border "job posting" arrangements. Recognizing this, important steps to combat labor exploitation have been made over the last decade. There is more awareness and increasing cooperation in order to detect cases of exploitation. Yet, migration control sometimes hampers the fight against human trafficking and, paradoxically, strict controls even appear to encourage rather than discourage trafficking in human beings.

These fundamental barriers could only really be solved by (1) providing more opportunities for temporary labor in a legal and regulated manner and (2) by attempting to bring unauthorized workers out of the shadows, and by encouraging them to assist enforcement agencies to investigate and prosecute people who really benefit—the traffickers, "gangmasters," and mala fide employment agencies. If workers fear deportation, the latter remains unlikely to happen. Labor exploitation not only arises out of the will of migrants to look for a job elsewhere or of criminals to exploit workers, but it is also the consequence of the contradiction between increasingly restrictive admission and control policies with respect to workers in the lower segments of the labor market in combination with persisting demand for cheap and flexible labor. This message tends to be forgotten, because in the political discourse so much emphasis is placed on criminal networks and "evil" traffickers.

In practice, though, government agencies end up punishing lower-level migrant workers.

Thinking of Rights

The outcome of these processes is that in practice, victims of labor exploitation are currently not provided the same services as victims of sex trafficking in the Netherlands, as in many other countries. They have the same right to shelter and other forms of victim support, and additionally the right to a temporary residence status, but they are less likely to be able to exercise their rights. In a highly publicized case of labor exploitation on an asparagus farm in the south of the Netherlands some years ago, potential victims were seen as unauthorized workers. They were immediately put on a bus and returned to their home country instead of being recognized as potential victims that needed protection. In other cases, workers are offered shelter and support and treated as passive victims, whereas what they really want is being recognized as workers, receiving monetary compensation for unpaid work, and safe return to their home country. In sum, a broader view focusing on the interests and rights of those who are exploited in our labor markets is needed.

References

Aronowitz, Alexis A., Theuermann, Gerda, and Tyurykanova, Elena. 2010. *Analysing the business model of trafficking in human beings to better prevent the crime.* OSCE: Vienna. http://www.osce.org/files/documents/c/f/69028.pdf. Accessed on January 15, 2016.

EU Directive on Trafficking in Human Beings. http://eur-lex .europa.eu/LexUriServ/LexUriServ.do?uri=OJ:L:2011:101: 0001:0011:EN:PDF. Accessed on January 20, 2016.

EU Strategy towards the Eradication of Trafficking in Human Beings (2012–2016). http://ec.europa.eu/home-affairs/ doc_centre/crime/docs/

trafficking_in_human_beings_eradication-2012_2016_en.pdf. Accessed on January 17, 2016.

Leun, J. P. van der, Schijndel, and van, A. 2016. "Emerging from the shadows or pushed into the dark? The relation between the combat against trafficking in human beings and migration control." *International Journal of Law, Crime and Justice*, 44, 26–42.

Joanne van der Leun is professor of Criminology at Leiden Law School and Scientific Director of the Institute for Criminal Law and Criminology. Her research interests lie in the field of crime, migration, and policy. She is a member of the Advisory Committee of Immigration Affairs of the Ministry of Security and Justice, the Netherlands.

American Girls: Victims of Human Trafficking
Aaron Cohen

On a cool Fall day in September, I journeyed to New York City to investigate human trafficking. Working undercover, I posed as a "john" to look for victims of forced prostitution. For many years now, working to combat slavery as a human rights activist, my field work has been mostly abroad, in places like Haiti, Colombia, or Cambodia. But New York is a major hub city for human trafficking, so we wanted to find out firsthand how pervasive exploitation is in the world's oldest "profession" in the Big Apple.

For our New York mission, the goal was to try to help as many people as we could, to win the trust of the victims, and assist them to get out of "the life," learning as much as possible along the way. In so doing, for almost a month, we surveyed an underbelly of society that exists largely in the shadows, and what we found ran the emotional spectrum from bazaar to heartbreaking.

We assembled an all-star vice team with AbolishSlavery.org, headed by the former Las Vegas detective, Chris Baughman.

In Las Vegas, Baughman pioneered innovative techniques to combat trafficking. He knows how traffickers and pimps think—and operate. We established a command center in New York and surveyed hundreds of ads online, looking for key indicators that a woman was being trafficked and under pimp control. We scanned through ads on BackPage.com, RedBook. com, AdultFriendFinder, and free porn sites, looking for encrypted phone numbers or encrypted names written strangely like Di amon*d. The use of spaces and symbols in names and numbers make it difficult for law enforcement to track the traffickers. Names like "Diamond" also objectify the women as upscale objects to be desired. As we scanned the ads, some of the online pictures screamed—under "Pimp Control"—with the women having tattoos like crowns or dollar signs burned into their flesh, the result of their pimps actually branding them. Another giveaway is when you search a number and find several different cities listed for that ad. Sex trafficking victims are moved from city to city to keep the pimp's roster fresh and to prevent the women from ever feeling comfortable or at home anywhere for too long.

Our calls resulted in early success as we set up encounters with trafficked women. I was the undercover who called the girl's ad and set up a "date," playing the role of a john in one hotel room, while Chris Baughman and the security detail monitored the encounter via video in another room. When the girls would ask for their "donation" (fee), I would tell them that I just wanted to talk—that I didn't mind paying only for their time and that I was seeking friendship in a lonely city. Almost without fail, during our encounters, the women were being carefully monitored by their pimps, via text messaging. The majority of the women we met with were living under pimp control, although they would universally deny it. They would be sending and receiving texts during the encounter to their pimps, and Baughman and I would be texting back and forth as well. "In the culture," Chris explains, "the girls are trained to say there is no pimp, I'm doing this on my own."

We even captured on camera several women who had sworn they were independent—meeting up with their abusive pimps afterwards.

And this might surprise a lot of people but, yes, most of the women were American. And where do they come from? Well, every year in the United States, almost a half million teenagers run away from home. These victims are vulnerable, often coming from dysfunctional situations, making them susceptible to the siren song of traffickers and pimps. Many end up in hub cities for trafficking and the sex trade: Houston, Chicago, Los Angeles, Las Vegas, and New York City. A study by Melissa Farley of ProstitutionResearch.com found that 89 percent of women in the sex trade would leave "the life" if they were empowered to do so. The statistics seem to indicate that in most cases, prostitution is *not* a victimless crime.

Fortunately, New York is finally making dramatic changes in how they combat human trafficking. Manhattan District Attorney Cy Vance is instituting new get-tough policies that are established practices in countries where the human trafficking rates are lowest, places like Norway and Sweden. Today, New York City is arresting more and more traffickers and johns. This is what needs to be done—arrest the traffickers and johns and not the victims who make up the supply. By attacking human trafficking among those who are perpetuating the trade, fewer and fewer victims will be lured, coerced, and subjugated under threat of violence to satisfy the growing online demand for sex.

And what of our efforts? Over the few months of our encounters, we were able to retrieve and transition a number of trafficked victims out of harm's way. One woman, whom I will call "Veronica," was fairly new to "the game." After a couple of meetings, she let us know she was living under the control of a violent pimp, and I revealed to her that we could help.

She gratefully agreed. It was intense (and dangerous) getting her out from under the trafficker's shadow, but soon we were driving her several hundred miles back home. There, we witnessed a tearful and emotional reunion with her mom. We were lucky with Veronica, but the ones that break your heart are the victims you cannot get out. After a number of meetings with a girl we will call April, she texted me that she wanted help. She was beaten in public by her "boyfriend" who was prostituting her, and he was arrested. I raced to get to her, but by the time we got to Manhattan, he was out on bail and made it to her first; she backed out. As far as I know, April is still living under pimp control.

The question I am most frequently asked about human trafficking is why these women do not just walk away? The majority are not locked up or in real chains. But as April's case shows, traffickers and pimps know how to persuasively intimidate their victims into compliance and acceptance. It usually starts by luring victims under the guise of romance, then they up the ante, coaxing them to work at "high-end" escort services or strip clubs. What the girls eventually discover is that these establishments are commonly used as "legal" fronts for pimping, drugs, and prostitution. Then, before they know it, there are no choices left. The trafficked women are soon subjugated to a fear-based life of abuse, beat downs, drug addiction, and yes, often times, murder.

So, what can we do? We need to fund places like Breaking Free in Minnesota, an organization devoted to helping victims begin their lives anew. And we need to better enforce the federal laws against moving prostituted women across state lines. The laws are mostly there—they just need to be enforced properly.

On a state or local basis, let us make asset seizure legislation more common. When a human trafficker is arrested, his assets, from the Ferrari to his jewelry, even the Amex Black Card, need to be seized. Finally, we need to start a merciful revolution in peoples' minds about what freedom means today. The United States may be the home of the brave, but is America truly the Land of the Free? Well, certainly not for the tens of thousands of domestic women and girls who are living under pimp control.

Aaron Cohen is the author of the book Slave Hunter: Freeing Victims of Human Trafficking *(Simon & Schuster). A new documentary series based on his efforts was produced by MSNBC.*

Human Trafficking and Terrorist Groups
Elif Isitman

The link between human trafficking and terrorist groups can be examined through two case study groups: Islamic State and Boko Haram. Both groups are notorious for practices of forced marriage, sexual violence, and abuse of women and girls, although group characteristics and the means through which they conduct their practices appear to differ.

Islamic State in Iraq and Greater Syria

The Islamic State in Iraq and Greater Syria (ISIS) is a predominantly Sunni jihadist group. The self-proclaimed leader and caliph is Abu Bakr al-Baghdadi, a former prisoner of the U.S.-led Camp Bucca in Iraq. ISIS seeks to establish a caliphate: a single, transnational Islamic State based on Sharia-law (Laub and Masters, 2014). The militant group, characterized by the use of brutal violence and force to gain ground, has been held accountable by the United Nations for large-scale human rights abuses and war crimes. Amnesty International reports that the group has been engaged in ethnic cleansing on a historic scale.

Kidnapping Yazidi Women and Girls, Mount Sinjar

In August 2014, ISIS invaded the northwestern Sinjar region in Iraq, home to Yazidi communities. The Yazidi's are a minority in Syria and Iraq. They adhere to polytheistic religious views, and thus are viewed as infidels and labeled "devil worshippers" by Muslim extremists. Hundreds of Yazidi men were killed and others were forced to convert to Islam. At least 2,500 women and children were abducted by ISIS fighters. Younger women and girls were separated from their parents and older relatives, and sold, given as gifts, or forced to marry ISIS fighters and supporters (Amnesty International, 2015). The women and girls have been subjected to torture, rape, and other forms of sexual violence.

Up to 300 of those abducted have managed to escape captivity in Iraq and parts of Syria. However, the majority of them are still being held captive. They are frequently moved from place to place in order to escape detection (Amnesty International, 2014). The University of Bristol's Gender and Violence Research Center (2014) estimates that around 4,600 women are still missing.

Victim Testimonies of Escaped Yazidi Women and Girls

Yazidi women have undergone abhorrent treatment under ISIS control, ranging from systematic rape to sexual slavery and forced marriage. Many of them have attempted to commit suicide, with some of them succeeding. ISIS fighters regularly threaten to kill or harm victims' relatives if the women attempt to kill themselves (Amnesty International, 2014).

Twenty victims (11 women and 9 girls, including 2 who were 12 years old) who have escaped ISIS tell harrowing tales of rape. Almost all reported being sold or given as gifts and forced into marriage (Human Rights Watch, 2015).

ISIS held about 150 girls and women in their *maqarr* (headquarters) in the northern Iraqi city of Mosul. Various news reports have documented how terrorists conducted live slave markets, and ISIS has released videos in which their fighters brag about buying and trading sex slaves. ISIS demonstrates widespread use of social media, both in recruiting foreign fighters as in spreading propaganda in general (Barret, 2014).

Following the large-scale kidnapping of Yazidi women and children, the militant group released a pamphlet on how to conduct "sexual jihad," or how to capture, treat, keep, and sexually abuse female slaves. Researchers speaking with news reporters describe the women as being "treated like cattle" (Damon, 2015).

The ISIS pamphlet explains that it is permissible to take non-Muslims captive, and particularly points out Jews and Christians as targets. "Unbelief" in Islam is enough to make someone a slave, the pamphlet sets out. According to the ISIS rules, it is permissible to rape a female slave immediately after taking her captive if she is a virgin. If she is not, however, "her uterus must be purified first." Moreover, the pamphlet endorses and encourages child sexual abuse, saying that it is allowed to have intercourse with female slaves who have not yet reached puberty, as long as they are "fit for intercourse." It also allows fighters to buy, sell, and give female slaves as a gift because women are "merely property." There have even been reports of some fighters attempting to sell female sex slaves on social media (Warrick, 2016).

The hostage taking and sexual slavery of women is not limited to Yazidis. In 2015, the *Washington Post* reported that 26-year-old Kayla Mueller, an American humanitarian worker, was used as a sex slave by the leader of the Islamic State, Abu Bakr al-Baghdadi (Goldman and Miller, 2015).

New Form of Human Trafficking by ISIS

The U.S. Government has obtained documents produced by ISIS that sanction the removal of organs from infidels to save the life of a Muslim. The January 31, 2015, document, in the form of a *fatwa* (religious ruling), states: "The apostate's life and organs don't have to be respected and may be taken with impunity." There is no objection to removing the captive's organ, even if this results in the death of the captive. Although accusations of organ trafficking have been levied against ISIS by Iraq, there is no proof that the organization has yet been involved in this activity. The fatwa does, however, "provide religious sanction for doing so" (Strobel et al., 2015).

Boko Haram

Boko Haram, an Islamic extremist group based in northeastern Nigeria, is also active in Chad, Niger, and northern Cameroon. The group, founded in 2002, is led by Abu Bakr-Shekau and has alleged links to Al Qaeda. In March 2015, Abu Bakr Shekau announced the group's allegiance to ISIS. The aim of the group is similar to that of ISIS—to establish a "caliphate" (Islamic State) in Nigeria. The group is notorious for being opposed to Western-style modern education. Members of the group believe it lures students away from following Islamic teaching as a way of life. This embodies the group's name: "Boko Haram" means "Western education is forbidden." The group believes that the Nigerian government, by fostering schools, has interfered with traditional Islamic education (Okpaga et al., 2012).

Boko Haram has been targeting Western-style schools since 2010, and has killed and abducted hundreds of students in the process. Girls are kidnapped rather than killed, and used as cooks or sex slaves. In line with radical Islam, Boko Haram does not believe girls and women should be educated (Onuoha, 2010).

Boko Haram and the Chibok Girls, 2014

One of the most prominent mass abductions by Boko Haram took place on the night of April 14–15, 2014. Members of the militant group, posing as guards, kidnapped 276 female students from the Government Secondary School in the town of Chibok in Borno State, northeastern Nigeria. More than 50 girls managed to escape during the journey, but 219 of them have been living in captivity ever since (Amnesty International, 2015). They are believed to have been forced to convert to Islam and forced into marriage with members of Boko Haram. The bride price for the girls is 2,000 naira each, the equivalent of US$12.50. Many of the girls have been taken across the border to neighboring countries such as Chad and Cameroon.

On May 5, 2014, Boko Haram's leader claimed responsibility for the Chibok kidnapping in a recorded message, proclaiming that "Allah instructed me to sell them . . . I will carry out his instructions," and that "Slavery is allowed in my religion, and I shall capture people and make them slaves." The group believes that girls as young as nine years old are suitable for marriage, and thus sexual intercourse.

Chibok is a village dominated by Christians, and Boko Haram acknowledged that many of the girls who were kidnapped are not Muslims. "The girls that have not accepted Islam, they are now gathered in numbers, and we treat them the way the Prophet Muhammed treated the infidels he seized," Abu Bakr Shekau is quoted as saying in his video. Later, the terrorist group released a video showing about half of the kidnapped girls dressed in a *hijab* and a long Islamic chador.

Since then, there have been a number of attempts by the Nigerian government to rescue the girls. In May 2015, the Nigerian military reportedly had reclaimed most of the areas previously controlled by Boko Haram, including many of the camps in the Sambisa forest where the Chibok girls allegedly had been kept. Many women were freed, but none of the Chibok girls had been found. They may have been killed or transported elsewhere.

Victim Testimonies of Boko Haram Escapees

No victim testimonies are available for the kidnapped Chibok girls, as none of them has managed to escape. However, Amnesty International has collected victim testimonies from other escapees.

Aside from committing other forms of war crimes, such as conducting mass killings and enlisting child soldiers, Boko Haram has been conducting various forms of sexual violence against populations in Nigeria. From victim testimonies and reports, forced marriages seem to be the primary way in which Boko Haram militants conduct sexual violence against female detainees.

The militant group has abducted women and girls during raids on towns in northeastern Nigeria and has kept them under control in camps (Amnesty International 2015). Women and girls who have managed to escape Boko Haram reported that many of them were forced to marry members of the militant group.

Young women in captivity were reportedly separated from the older women. In Boko Haram camps, women who were considered infidels were told to convert to Boko Haram's interpretation of Islam, after which they received religious instruction classes and were forced into marriage with one of the fighters. Women speaking to Amnesty International testify that, in captivity, they were given food once a day and that many had suffered from a lack of safe drinking water. In many instances, women who drank the water given to them had contracted severe illnesses or died.

People who have lived for extended periods of time in Boko Haram camps or in territories controlled by the militants have told Amnesty International that sexual violence and rape of abducted women is strictly forbidden under Boko Haram's version of Sharia law. However, women have reported that militants raped them secretly at night or in the bush. Others were subjected to forced marriage and rape by their "husbands" afterward. Victims report that many militants do not use condoms or other form of protection, so they fear unwanted pregnancies and contraction of sexually transmitted diseases (STDs).

Terrorism and Human Trafficking

The systematic abduction, sexual exploitation, sale, forced marriage, forced child soldiers, trafficking in organs, and human rights abuses of women and children by terrorist organizations has created a new vehicle to traffic persons on a scale not seen since the abolition of slavery in the previous centuries. Combating this form of human trafficking will require eradication of patriarchal and extremist religious ideology, and the terrorist groups involved in this modern-day slavery.

References

Amnesty International. 2014. *Escape from hell—torture and sexual slavery in Islamic state captivity in Iraq.* London: Amnesty International.

Amnesty International. 2015. *'Our job is to shoot, slaughter and kill'—Boko Haram's reign of terror in north-east Nigeria.* London: Amnesty International.

Barret, R., and Myers, J. 2014. "Foreign fighters in Syria." *Carnegie Council for Ethics in International Affairs*, 1–17. http://soufangroup.com/wp-content/uploads/2014/06/TSG-Foreign-Fighters-in-Syria.pdf. Accessed on November 6, 2016.

Damon, A. 2015, April 14. "A Yazidi captive's tale: Sold by ISIS as a sex slave." *CNN*, http://edition.cnn.com/2015/04/14/middleeast/yazidi-sex-slaves-isis-damon/index.html

Goldman, Adam, and Miller, Greg. 2015, August 15. "Islamic State leader used U.S. hostage as sex slave." *The Washington Post,* 1.

Human Rights Watch. 2015, April 14. "Iraq: ISIS escapees describe systematic rape." https://www.hrw.org/news/2015/04/14/iraq-isis-escapees-describe-systematic-rape. Accessed on January 15, 2016.

Laub, Z., and Masters, J. 2014. "Islamic State in Iraq and Greater Syria." *Council on Foreign Relations*, 1–4. http://www.cfr.org/iraq/islamic-state/p14811

Okpaga, A., Chijioke, U. S., and Eme, O. I. 2012. "Activities of Boko Haram and insecurity question in Nigeria." *Arabian Journal of Business and Management Review 1*(9).

Onuoha, F. C. 2010. "The Islamist challenge: Nigeria's Boko Haram crisis explained." *African Security Review, 2*(19), 54–67.

Strobel, Warren, Landay, Jonathan, and Stewart, Phil. 2015, December 24. "Report: ISIS sanctions harvesting of human organs." *The World Post.* http://www.huffingtonpost.com/entry/isis-sanctions-harvesting-organs_567cc1a1e4b06fa6888016ed. Accessed on October 15, 2016.

Warrick, J. 2016, May 28. "ISIS fighters seem to be trying to sell sex slaves online." *The Washington Post.* https://www.washingtonpost.com/world/national-security/isis-fighters-appear-to-be-trying-to-sell-their-sex-slaves-on-the-internet/2016/05/28/b3d1edea-24fe-11e6-9e7f-57890b612299_story.html. Accessed on November 15, 2016.

Elif Isitman (1987) received her MSc in International Crimes and Criminology and an MA in Journalism from VU University in Amsterdam. Her MSc dissertation concerned the trafficking of women and girls in post-conflict areas, using Bosnia and Herzegovina and Kosovo as case studies.

Following her studies, she interned and worked at the Bureau of the Dutch National Rapporteur on Trafficking in Human Beings and Sexual Violence Against Children (BNRM), where she conducted research into child pornography and corresponding perpetrator profiles. She is currently working as a journalist and editor at the Dutch weekly magazine Elsevier *in Amsterdam.*

The First European Anti-trafficking NGO Is Born
Patsy Sörensen and Klaus Vanhoutte

While in the last decade national and international legislation has taken major steps in the struggle against trafficking in human beings, on an operational and judiciary level, the fact that a prostitute might be a victim of trafficking is still quite often a subject of dispute. When is a person a freelance sex worker and when is he or she a victim of human trafficking?

If that is the case today, imagine what it was like in 1987. The acknowledgment of "trafficking in human beings" as a crime, or even as a mere reality, was light years away from any kind of agenda, political or otherwise. Prostitutes, regardless of their origin, physical or mental coercion, and working conditions, were simply too insignificant to be given any serious consideration. Prostitution was regarded as a "profession," and no one seemed to be interested in the story behind the women's entry into prostitution or the personal story beyond their "profession," no matter how painful that story was. They were simply "prostitutes," and society was indifferent to them. Persons focusing on assistance or showing too much interest in these "fallen women" were themselves regarded as being of dubious moral character.

Nonetheless, in spite of the prejudice, indifference, sometimes even opposition and threats, Payoke, smack in the middle of Antwerp's red light district, realized something had to be done. The coercive factors leading to the appalling conditions in which these women and girls were forced to live and work caught the attention of Patsy Sörensen, then a teacher and artist with profound social and political engagement in her neighborhood. Initially, the assistance offered the women in prostitution took the form of a room in Patsy's private home, where prostitutes and victims could be offered a cup of coffee. Attention was given to their deplorable situation. This, in 1988, was the birth of the first formally registered NGO in Europe focusing on aid to prostitutes. What began as a cup of coffee and someone to listen to them in Patsy's home grew into an organization offering victims of forced prostitution and forced labor, physical, legal, and social protection.

Traffickers Enter the Picture

Initially, Payoke's activities were directed toward practical support and protection of victims. Patsy gave these girls refuge in her own home with no public acknowledgment and no funds but her own, while struggling to provide them with some kind of recognition as victims of coercion and inhuman treatment. Even at this time, many of these women were migrants and this made the intervention on their behalf more stressful and complex. These were not local women but foreign girls flown in from various countries across the world ending up in forced sex work. Their deplorable situation moved Patsy to become involved and start the investigation into the root causes of this misery. Patsy, through her initial work, discovered that these girls were in fact merely pawns in large international criminal structures. This knowledge took Payoke to focus on a whole new and far more complex approach. Patsy began to systematically collect information and investigate the involvement of transnational organized criminal groups. In each individual case, this holistic approach (giving competent social and legal counselling, protection, anonymity, compensation to victims as well as preparing the files for prosecution of criminals) taken by Payoke has, since the very beginning, met with a large dose of skepticism and neglect by the authorities on all levels. For several years, until the beginning of the 1990s, Payoke stood on its own with little more than the conviction that breaches of human dignity, human rights, and serious crime were taking place, and that action must prevail over fear.

An Unexpected Visitor

In 1992, a book entitled *They Are So Sweet, Sir* by Chris de Stoop described the international trafficking of women as a prima facie form of organized crime. This book created a tidal wave of such dimensions it even reached the shores of the Royal Palace. Amidst national indignation, the only organization addressing the problem turned out to be an insignificant NGO from Antwerp, Payoke. King Boudewijn of Belgium, shocked by the idea that modern-day slaves were living in his country, decided to visit Payoke, the only place he could visit to show his concern. The symbolic value of this visit was a sign that someone finally started listening. In that same year, "Saralek" was founded as an organization within Payoke, to specifically help women who were victims of traffickers. Although the core business of these criminal organizations was to exploit victims by forcing them into prostitution, other forms of forced labor abuse began to surface as well, and a different kind of victim entered the Payoke action radius. Subsequently, the "Saralek" target group was extended so both men and women who fell victim to "trafficking of human beings," regardless the type of forced labor (including forced prostitution), could be assisted. An operational standard was set.

Step by Step

A parliamentary commission was established in 1992 with the mandate to thoroughly investigate the phenomenon. In 1994, it presented its conclusions and recommendations toward a structural national policy opposing the international trafficking of women. As a result, a coherent and well-coordinated approach for police and prosecution was developed, most of it, once again, at that same Antwerp kitchen table. As improbable as this seems, the reality was in fact as unbelievable as it was simple. Payoke was the only place where actual operational expertise could be found. These legal foundations aimed at the entire judiciary, police, social support, protection, and rehabilitation structures were formulated in an official Belgian Law Decree in 1994. Apart from two added governmental guidelines in 1997 and 2003, the original design shaped a national multidisciplinary statutory platform in the fight against human trafficking and the support and protection of victims for more than 10 years. On the humanitarian side, Belgium managed to develop a specific system coordinating aid and support for victims of human trafficking 10 years before Europe was able to react accordingly. Not bad work for what began at a kitchen table in Patsy Sörensen's home.

Payoke's expertise and work resulted in a number of legal acknowledgments for the organization and the victims it represented. In July 1994, Payoke was officially mandated to prepare the files of trafficking victims, so these victims could be granted residence and work permits in Belgium. Since 1995, Payoke's mandate in legal protection has been extended, allowing the organization to represent the victims of trafficking as a civil party in court proceedings. The assistance procedure for approved victims of human trafficking and victims of smuggling with aggravating circumstances was legalized in 2006. All of the above was settled in a unique text, legally finalized in the law of April 18, 2013, and implemented through a governmental circular letter in 2015. If Payoke needed anything to bridge the last 30 years on a political level, it must have been without a shred of doubt, patience.

No Top without a Bottom

Gross violation of human dignity may, through time, force legislators to react, but new laws are of little use if those "on the ground" have not been properly instructed, educated, and trained. A law will remain irrelevant if there is no coherent and operational organization of shelters that can provide concrete aid and support. Realizing that something needs to be done is one thing; actually doing it and "getting your hands dirty" is quite another. While an obvious observation, as usual, it is not all together in line with the political reality. On the one hand, top-down directives are necessary, but they are doomed to remain little more than admirable intentions if they are not supported by solid instructive, educational, and operational structures. On the other hand, small initiatives to help and support victims are as admirable, if not more, but they can never outgrow the concept of local and limited charity without a governmental overarching multidisciplinary framework. This is something Patsy Sörensen realized at a very early stage. As such, it became inevitable that Patsy would have to enter, and then a few years later, leave politics. But in her time as a politician, she put the need for a multidisciplinary approach on the agenda, both at the local level as a member of the city council in Antwerp, and on a European level as a member of the European Parliament. Apart from her groundbreaking work "on the ground" directly with trafficked victims, recognizing and endorsing the need for an all-encompassing structure to tackle the problem is probably her most important contribution to combating human trafficking. It is precisely the knowledge obtained through years of hands-on experience "on the ground" that enabled her to develop this vision. In her case, both sides of the coin—the practical and the political—are united in a rare symbiotic unity constantly fueling one another. Unfortunately, these are exactly the kind of people both sides usually tend to lack. If so, and various partners are required to provide a comprehensive understanding of the problem, it is paramount they all regard one another as equally important collaborators with equally important contributions and responsibilities to the development of the process.

Not There Yet

Since 1987, Payoke's effort to have governments and the European Union recognizing trafficking in human beings as a form of modern slavery, serious organized crime, and a breach of human rights has been crowned with success. Thus, Payoke's almost 30 years of perilous work has received gradual recognition, formal, material, and financial support for its daily work and engagement in protecting victims' human rights, giving them physical, social, and legal protection, and strengthening their personal integrity as well as introducing measures against those exercising violence and coercion leading to forced prostitution.

The organization now faces new challenges on a domestic and international scale. Over the last few years, the "loverboy" phenomenon has become more prevalent. These young men are brutal, local traffickers. They seduce young insecure girls, some as young as 12 years, then alienate them from their social backgrounds, to finally lure them into prostitution. Because in court the most avid defenders of these offenders are in fact the young victims themselves, they are not easy targets to tackle.

Foreign victims from EU countries require assistance. Already in 1993, Payoke noticed and reported an increase of Hungarian girls trafficked into prostitution. The vast majority knew they would work as prostitutes when they left their home countries. None of them, however, signed up for the exploitation—40 customers a day, constant mental and physical abuse, and hardly any income. The prosecution of the traffickers remains difficult. Fortunately, due to the persistent efforts of Payoke and partners, from police and prosecution services, today there is a close cooperation between Hungary, the Netherlands, and Belgium to tackle these organizations simultaneously.

On a national and international level, due to the extensive migration of large numbers of both war and economic refugees, the challenges have increased exponentially. To separate actual victims from those with far less acceptable motives is a massive undertaking and a problem that shelters and police are confronted with on a daily basis. The challenge now lies in how to detect and identify a trafficking victim, taking into consideration the fact that they all, victims and imposters alike, are desperate to obtain a resident permit. It takes experienced and well-trained collaborators from government agencies and civil society at various levels to combat the problem. We must continue to remain vigilant and flexible to adapt to new situations to ensure our continued support of trafficked victims.

Patsy Sörensen is the founder, director, and driving force behind Payoke. She established the NGO Payoke in 1987, originally fighting for the rights of prostitutes. Today, the organization fights for the rights of all people who have been trafficked. She is recognized as an international expert in trafficking and is highly sought around the world to provide victim-centered approaches to counter-trafficking efforts. Patsy's current and former roles include victim advocate, politician (former MEP and alderman of the city of Antwerp), assistance provider, international trafficking expert, and former member of the Expert Group on Human Trafficking for the European Commission. She is often sought out by foreign governments, the military, start-up NGOs and shelters, and other institutions to provide input in the form of technical expertise or training, on counter-trafficking measures and victim protection schemes.

Klaus Vanhoutte started his professional career in 1998 as project manager for several humanitarian aid projects in Bosnia and Herzegovina. From 2002 to 2006, he was a lecturer at the Saint Lucas College in Brussels. From 2007 on, Klaus has had several leading functions in the private sector, developing his editorial and management skills. Over the years he has shared his skills, editorial and management, in several projects concerning human trafficking, both as a professional and volunteer.

The Dutch Religious Community and Its Work against Trafficking in Women
Ivonne van de Kar

The religious community in the Netherlands has been involved in combating human trafficking for over two and a half decades. In the Netherlands, our organization Religious Network against Trafficking in Women (*Stichting Religieuzen Tegen Vrouwenhandel* or SRTV) was one of the first organizations to focus attention to this problem. Our organization expresses something about our inspiration, our commitment, our history, and our working method. The focus has been and continues to be on trafficking in women and young girls for the purpose of sexual exploitation.

The Early Years

In 1991, it dawned on Sister Michel Keesen (a Dutch sister working within the religious order) that the religious community could not just sit idly by and watch the suffering inflicted upon trafficked women (at that time, a synonym for forced prostitution). It became clear that many foreign women—often brought illegally into the country—were being coerced into prostitution. Concern was not being raised about Dutch women, who, after all, had valid residence documents, were articulate and were aware of their rights. Shortly after our early work, we also began raising awareness of trafficking of Dutch women and girls.

Sister Michel placed an appeal in a religious magazine asking for allies in the struggle against the trafficking of women for forced prostitution. Some 15 people from the religious community responded to the call. All were religious sisters from 13 different congregations and almost all of them had just returned from missionary work abroad. The sisters realized that they could play a role in providing information and raising awareness about the subject of women trafficking. They also realized that people in the Netherlands should be aware of what was happening. Missionaries working in source countries found it important to raise awareness among anyone who would listen of the horrors of exploitation in Western European nations. The sisters had a wide social network after having been actively involved in projects for women, schools, and hospitals through their missionary work. The work originally initiated by missionary workers was later continued by local sisters of the same religious congregations.

Information and Awareness

The sisters found and still find it essential for people in the Netherlands to realize that young girls and women have come to this country seeking work because in many cultures, women and girls carry the responsibility for the well-being of children, parents, and even for the future of the entire family. It is necessity rather than greed that drives young women from Africa into prostitution in the Netherlands.

During the first years of the SRTV's existence, the sisters made sure that awareness-raising information was available in many languages for people here in the Netherlands as well as for women and young girls in their own country. Much of the local awareness raising focused on warning potential victims, in their own language, of the dangers of traveling to Europe in search of a well-paying job. Many migrants are unaware of the fact that unemployment is present in Europe, and that people need recognized qualifications for employment. But, perhaps, the most important part of the leaflet is the part that warns: "If you still want to take the chance. . . ." The leaflets contain tips and suggestions for women who are about to migrate: "Your passport is yours, don't give it to anyone. If someone offers you a job, make inquiries before you leave: find out if this job really exists. Make sure to leave a copy of your travel document with your family (if they need to find you they can more easily locate you)." These suggestions are simple, but they are often very effective.

Leaflet Campaign

Initially, these leaflets were translated by the sisters and were later translated and distributed by volunteers and sisters worldwide. The leaflets are currently available in 53 languages and distributed in over 80 countries. The sisters requested their fellow sisters in different countries to discuss the leaflet with women's groups, schools, and anywhere else where groups of women and girls came together. Over the course of the last 20 years, hundreds of thousands of leaflets have been distributed. Many women and young girls have been made aware of the dangers of human trafficking and have been informed about the reality of life in the West. The myth that "Europe is a Paradise" has been soundly refuted.

Networks and Project Safe Return

The SRTV is a small organization with two professional staff members and about 50 volunteers. Personal involvement and professionalism go together hand in hand as we continue to combat this serious problem. The SRTV is embedded in a European and global network of organizations, each with similar objectives, especially within the world of the religious community.

The SRTV has helped to build several networks. The organization was involved in the founding of the African Network Against Human Trafficking in 2007, and it co-initiated the Religious in Europe Networking against Trafficking and Exploitation (RENATE) in 2009. It is extremely important for organizations sharing the same commitment and background to be aware of each other's work and thus achieve cooperation. For example, problems which have been detected in one country have possibly gone unnoticed in another. In addition, with the help of international networks, victims can be repatriated if they so desire. As an organization from one country sometimes needs information about the situation in another country, short lines of communication are crucial, as was witnessed in our work overseas in the 1980s. In several countries, the religious community has slowly recognized the importance and has had to overcome resistance toward working with women involved in prostitution.

Fighting human trafficking is not just about raising awareness, but also about assisting trafficked victims. The SRTV was one of the partner organizations in the Netherlands, Nigeria, and Bulgaria involved in Project Safe Return. The project's goal is to assist in the safe return and reintegration of foreign victims of trafficking who were unable to obtain a residency permit to remain in the Netherlands. Trafficked victims are provided a realistic picture of their future and are assisted in developing skills to become independent rather than dependent upon assistance. The SRTV was instrumental in developing contacts with the sisters of Cosudow, the network of Nigerian sisters involved in anti-trafficking work in Lagos and Benin City. Sisters from Nigeria and workers from the organization Animus in Bulgaria contributed to the development of the program and have since been trained in its implementation.

Supported by Pope Francis

Ever since the Catholic Church has welcomed Pope Francis in 2013, all religious sisters working against human trafficking have been supported by his words and actions. Pope Francis has asked all people, but nuns and priests especially, to take care of people in the margins of society. In several recent messages (see the reference section), he spoke of poverty, lack of education, and environmental disasters being some of the root causes of human trafficking and slavery. He supports our view that women suffer the most because of the uncertainty in the lives of people in the present time.

Pope Francis, in his speech for World Day of Peace, complimented "the silent work done by so many religious congregations, especially the religious community of women who have been providing support to victims. They work in very difficult situations, dominated at times by violence, as they work to break the invisible chains binding victims to traffickers and exploiters." Pope Francis asks us: "Where is your brother or sister who is enslaved? [Gen 4:9] Human trafficking is an open wound on the body of contemporary society, a scourge upon the body of Christ. It is a crime against humanity. The work against Human Trafficking is an immense task, which calls for courage, patience and perseverance, deserves the appreciation of the whole Church and society."

References

Evangelii Gaudium (2013, November 24); https://w2.vatican .va/content/dam/francesco/pdf/apost_exhortations/ documents/papa-francesco_esortazione-ap_20131124_ evangelii-gaudium_en.pdf

Laudato Si (2015, June). http://w2.vatican.va/content/dam/ francesco/pdf/encyclicals/documents/papa-francesco_ 20150524_enciclica-laudato-si_en.pdf

Message for the celebration of the world day of peace (2015, January 1); *Pope's speech for World day of peace.*

https://w2.vatic; an.va/content/francesco/en/messages/
peace/documents/papa-francesco_20141208_messaggio-
xlviii-giornata-mondiale-pace-2015.html

Message for World Day of Migrants and Refugees 2015
(January 18, 2015).

Project Safe Return; Safe Return Methodology, http://
ivastudio.nl/uploads/safe_future_methodology/#p=4.
Accessed on January 2, 2016.

Ivonne van de Kar worked for six years as a teacher for migrants in asylum centers in the Netherlands. In 1996, she started working for the Religious Sisters against Trafficking in Women as an assistant to Sister Michel Keesen, the founder of the SRTV. Ivonne was the main organizer of the first European Conference for Religious Sisters against Trafficking in Women. In 2006, Ivonne van de Kar was appointed coordinator of the SRTV. She took the initiative to organize a gathering of religious organizations in Europe to form a network, resulting in RENATE (Religious in Europe Networking Against Trafficking and Exploitation). Ivonne is a member of the Interdepartmental Consulting Group (five government ministries, five NGOs, and the Dutch National Rapporteur).

Declining Assistance: Understanding Trafficked Persons' Decisions, Choices, and Resiliency
Rebecca Surtees

Reintegration assistance is often critical for trafficked persons as they recover and move on from trafficking. Well-designed reintegration and assistance programs can provide vital, even life-saving, services to trafficked persons and their families facing the challenging task of rebuilding their lives. Such programs also address the preexisting vulnerabilities that often contributed to individuals being trafficked and widen the life choices available to them. Nonetheless, some trafficking victims decline assistance and support after trafficking, choosing instead to try to cope on their own. Knowing why some victims do and do not decline assistance tells us a great deal about the condition of people's lives after trafficking, what challenges they face, and what opportunities are available to them. It also helps us to identify factors that could ease transition and reintegration after trafficking.

In 2006, my colleague and I undertook a research project in the Balkans to understand why and under which circumstances trafficking victims declined assistance, what happened as a result of declining support, and what paths their lives took over time (Brunovskis and Surtees, 2007). Our starting point was that declining assistance could be the right decision for trafficked persons that did not want or need help. And we found that in some cases, trafficked persons in the Balkans did decline assistance for the following reasons. One young woman we interviewed was working and studying and had recently married. Only her mother knew about her trafficking experience, and she was able to talk to her about it when she needed to. As she put it, "When I met some women at the shelter [abroad], I saw that they needed help for their studies and the job. For me, I have studies and a job. What help do I need?" Similarly, in a study of reintegration I conducted in the Mekong region in 2011 and 2012, 37 of the 252 trafficked persons declined some aspect of assistance. Some refused certain types of assistance; some declined to be assisted altogether. In addition, a number of respondents said that they would have *preferred* to decline assistance but were not able to do so given their dire situation or because of the obligatory nature of assistance in some destination countries (Surtees, 2013).

At the same time, other trafficked persons who declined assistance would have benefitted from this reintegration support but were not able to accept assistance for different reasons. Reasons for declining assistance were myriad. Nonetheless, across both studies, it is possible to talk about three broad reasons for trafficking victims to decline assistance: (1) linked to personal circumstances; (2) difficulties in the assistance system; and (3) issues of trust and victim identity.

Personal Circumstances: Financial need was a significant factor for many trafficked persons; assistance was not an option when it limited their ability to earn money (e.g., due to compulsory shelter stays). Said one victim, when offered assistance at a shelter: "What shelter? I want to work." In the Mekong region, some trafficking victims avoided being identified and assisted in the destination country because assistance would have translated into being returned home where economic options are few. One man from Myanmar trafficked for fishing in Thailand suffered severe violence on the boat. And, in spite of being pursued by his traffickers after escaping, he did not go to the police for help as he knew that this meant going back to Myanmar. Instead, he looked for another job in Thailand on his own and with the help of other migrants while trying to avoid his exploiters.

Families also significantly influence decisions about assistance. Unsurprisingly, many trafficking victims and their families simply want to be reunited after their separation as a result of the trafficking. Assistance that interfered with this choice was, therefore, not desirable. This was the view of one mother whose support was unequivocal in spite of her daughter returning home pregnant, a common source of tension and even rejection by families: "We couldn't wait to see her when she came back. We were so worried. We were so excited to have her back that we accepted the baby."

Moreover, some families were mistrustful of assistance programs. When "Julia" came home after trafficking, her mother would not let the social worker speak to her. Julia persuaded her mother to let her accept help through a shelter program, but nevertheless her mother worried that she was being mistreated somehow: "My mother would demand that I show her that they didn't hurt me—that there were no bruises." In certain environments, there was also the expectation that when a victim needed support, it should be provided within the family. As one woman said: "The child is mine, so she should be helped by me, not others."

Difficulties in the Assistance System: Some victims decline assistance because of how assistance is arranged. When programs are seen as restrictive, victims were more likely to decline. This was particularly the case with closed shelter programs, but it was also an issue when programs restricted contact between victim and family, rendering the "cost" of assistance too high. One Cambodian woman trafficked to Thailand was offered a range of services through a shelter program, including training and help in setting up a small business. All would have been useful in the long term, but she declined because she wanted to immediately reunite with her children. Similarly, one Cambodian man trafficked for fishing was offered assistance to train as a mechanic in a nearby town, but he refused as he was desperate to be with his wife and care for his children.

Some programs offered services that did not align with the individual needs and circumstances of trafficked persons. For example, training and economic opportunities were often limited and not necessarily in line with victims' specific skills, interests, capacities, or the local economy. One Vietnamese woman was offered vocational training, but declined because she did not have the capital to set up a business after finishing the training. She explained that, for her, assistance in finding a job would have been more helpful. Similarly, one Cambodian woman trafficked abroad for domestic work requested support to raise cows, because she had done so in the past and knew how to do this. However, the assistance organization said that they could only help her with pig breeding, which she did not know how to do, nor did they offer her training in how to raise and market pigs.

Some trafficked persons, when offered assistance, were not in a position at that stage to make an informed decision. Having just left trafficking situations, many were anxious to go home and did not wish to think or make plans beyond this. Many were also stressed and even traumatized and not able to sufficiently process information about assistance or the future. Not understanding the services offered was a relatively common reason for some victims to decline assistance. Even victims who accepted assistance described confusion when first offered services. Confusion was seemingly linked to a number of issues, including insufficient or confusing information and a victim's lack of capacity to understand the services offered (e.g., due to a fragile state of mind, issues of comprehension or information not being provided in a language the victim could understand).

An associated aspect of how assistance is designed is that, in some cases, trafficked persons were unable to receive support and services because they were essentially "declined" by service providers (Surtees et al., 2015). In some instances, a victim being "declined" is a function of not only being formally identified as trafficked, but it is also because of a lack of assistance for some forms of trafficking (e.g., labor trafficking, begging), and some types of victims (e.g., men and boys), and uneven geographical distribution of services (Surtees, 2008).

Trust and Victim Identity: Trust was pivotal in decision-making around assistance. Declining was, in some cases, due to suspicion of assistance. For instance, some victims were wary of whether there would be hidden costs or debt if they accepted help. Negative experiences of assistance in the past also influenced the degree to which victims trusted assistance offers. For others, the identity of "trafficking victim" (a precondition for being assisted) was at odds with their self-image and declining assistance was, in essence, declining this victim identity. Most trafficking victims we have interviewed in different countries and regions are migrants whose desire to support their family was their motivation for migration. They are used to taking care not only of themselves but also their families and relating to the role of "trafficking victim" or even "victim" generally was in conflict with this role within the family and continuing responsibilities to be a source of support for their families (Brunovskis and Surtees, 2007).

In some cases, trafficked persons faced multiple barriers to accepting assistance. For example, a Cambodian man who was trafficked for work on a fishing boat in Indonesia declined assistance not only because it did not meet his needs (he was offered vocational training but had requested capital for a small business), but also because of his family situation (he needed to work and earn money for his family as his wife was pregnant and unable to work).

These points notwithstanding, very few victims either wholeheartedly accept assistance or unequivocally decline. Decisions are generally not "either/or," with victims often selecting and declining services from various options available in the country of destination, transit, or origin, over a period of weeks, months, and even years. Victims made different decisions at different stages of their post-trafficking lives, as their situation evolved, the assistance offered, and in response to the conditions of receiving different forms of assistance. This suggests a complex and, arguably, contradictory decision-making process, making it more appropriate to speak about a continuum of decisions that most victims make.

Declining assistance means different things to different victims and at various stages of their post-trafficking lives. A part of this discussion necessarily needs to be an enhanced understanding of the experiences and decisions of those who are unassisted (voluntarily or not) and how they navigate reintegration in their families and communities. (This is the focus of a current research project NEXUS is undertaking in Indonesia, "Protecting the Unassisted and Underserved," funded by the U.S. Department of State.) One Vietnamese woman trafficked to China had, since her return, married and had a child. Her husband was working and relations within her family were healthy and positive. She was planning to train in bridal makeup application and then open a salon. She explained that she could reach her goal on her own and could also rely on her family for support. Factors that helped victims overcome their trafficking experiences without receiving any formal assistance require careful and further study, but initial findings indicate the importance of time, positive and healthy family relationships, informal support, and a positive social environment.

Research across several countries clearly demonstrates that, while each experience is different and involves a myriad of factors that uniquely impact reintegration trajectories, there are nevertheless important lessons from the research for policy makers and practitioners. Understanding the reasons, experiences, and perceptions of trafficked persons who decline (and accept) assistance can play an important role in developing and tailoring services to increasingly meet the needs of the diverse population of trafficking victims.

References

Brunovskis, A., and Surtees, R. 2007. *Leaving the past behind? When victims of trafficking decline assistance.* Norway: Fafo and Washington, DC: NEXUS Institute.

Surtees, R. 2008. "Trafficked men, unwilling victims." *St. Antony's International Review,* 4(1), 16–36.

Surtees, R. 2013. *After trafficking: Experiences and challenges in the (re)integration of trafficked persons in the greater Mekong sub-region.* Bangkok: UNIAP and NEXUS Institute.

Surtees, R., Johnson, L. S., Zulbahary, T., and Daeng Caya, S. 2015. *Going home. Challenges in the reintegration of trafficking victims in Indonesia.* Washington, DC: NEXUS Institute.

Rebecca Surtees is an anthropologist and senior researcher at NEXUS Institute. She has experience both in the implementation of anti-trafficking programs and as a researcher in Asia, Europe, the former Soviet Union, and West Africa. She has worked for the United Nations, international organizations, and NGOs, before joining NEXUS in 2005. Her particular area of interest is in terms of reintegration and assistance to trafficked persons and in exploring less considered forms of trafficking. Recent research includes reintegration of trafficked persons in Southeast Asia and the Balkans, children born into trafficking, trafficking of fishers and seafarers, why some trafficking victims decline assistance, and trafficking in men.

Female Human Traffickers
Dina Siegel

In the literature on human trafficking, women are generally portrayed as victims, whereas men are usually seen as offenders. However, the active role of women in the recruitment of other women for prostitution and other forms of exploitation is as old as prostitution itself. All around the world, women have been (and are being) deceived for profit by female perpetrators. In all periods of history, we can find instances of the witty, elegant, diplomatic, merciless "madam," from France to the United States and from Russia to Thailand. Nowadays, too, we find this type of female criminal, operating either independently or in collaboration with organized crime groups. In Japan, for example, Thai *mama-sans* maintain connections with the Yakuza, and sometimes these women are the girlfriends or spouses of Yakuza crime bosses (Brown, 2000). Phenomena such as the Dutch *besteedster* or the Ukrainian *monetkas*, women who managed to gain positions of power within human trafficking organizations, can serve as additional examples.

In contemporary research on organized crime in general and human trafficking in particular, many authors have found that the role of women in this type of crime is unjustly underexposed (Kleemans et al., 1998). They argue that women often fulfill supporting roles, for example, as the partners of principal offenders or as facilitators. However, women can also perform crucial tasks such as liaising with other criminal networks or with the families of the victims.

Based on our research of prosecution case files of human trafficking cases in the Netherlands (Siegel and de Blank, 2010), we divided the roles and tasks of female offenders in human trafficking into three categories: supporters, partners in crime, and madams. This division is based on an increasing degree of independence, on the content of the tasks, and on the degree of equality in the relationship. The supporters (50) were in a large majority—25 cases were categorized as partners in crime and 10 cases as madams. In four cases, we could not find enough information or found the information too controversial to put the women in any of the three categories.

Women were regarded as "supporters" when they were subordinate to the leading female or male traffickers and, either under threat or voluntarily, executed the orders of the leader or other members of the trafficking networks. This means that they played a supporting role, mostly limited to controlling or instructing other women.

We considered female offenders to be "partners in crime" when they were in a relationship with a man and collaborated with him, in principle, on the basis of equality, by carrying out various tasks and activities. Partners in crime include women who, together with their partners (spouse, boyfriend, or business partner), voluntarily took up human trafficking. The roles these female "partners" fulfill can vary between an equal division of work and profits ("50–50") to a managing role where the male partners occupy themselves with one task only: the use of violence. The relationships between the partners can vary from intimate to "symbolic" or "businesslike." In some cases, women were the "brains" behind the operation, in other cases they played a more passive role and were only involved in the recruitment of young women or in their supervision after arrival in the Netherlands. Some female partners were able to easily recruit girls in their native country because they were familiar with the local circumstances and could instill trust in potential victims. These female recruiters were generally better educated and in possession of good communication skills (see also Denisova, 2001). They advertised the benefits of working in the Netherlands (profits, good working conditions, enough clients) and negotiated with corrupt officials. The role of these female partners was influential and they shared in the profits on an almost equal basis. This type of partners-in-crime relationship can be described as symbiotic.

The final category consisted of so-called madams: female offenders who played a central role, were in charge of criminal organizations, and coordinated human trafficking activities. These were women who were not dependent on a man. The madams directed their subordinates, coordinated the trafficking process, managed the prostitutes, and controlled the finances. The networks led by such women can vary from small groups (one or two members) to sizable organizations operating on an international scale.

Today, Nigerian madams in particular (even though some madams are from Ghana and Cameroon) have become associated with women trafficking (Becucci, 2008; Siegel, 2007). The explanation as to why Nigerian female offenders are over-represented in this category is perhaps to be found in the historical background of the phenomenon. In the 1980s, they came to Europe as prostitutes and discovered that there was a great demand for African girls. Working as prostitutes themselves and by recruiting other girls, they managed to convince male sponsors to invest in the sex industry, which turned out to be an extremely lucrative business. The madams often work in pairs (sometimes with close relatives). One of them, a "Nigerian madam," stays behind in her native country to recruit potential migrants, while the "Italian," "Dutch," or "French" (Nigerian) madam settles in Europe to receive and control the newly arrived girls.

With the creation of new markets, African women succeeded in obtaining leading roles in criminal organizations involved in large-scale human trafficking and, in the process, left their male competitors behind. Unlike women in the Italian mafia, who took over the positions of their imprisoned husbands and sons, the Nigerian and Ghanaian offenders took the initiative themselves, by planning, establishing contacts, and performing a range of tasks in the human trafficking business.

The phenomenon of "women traffickers" can be explained by both socioeconomic developments in the position of women in their native countries and by the opportunities of making quick money in Europe. Economic necessity forces women from all parts of the world to look for a better life in Europe, and many decide on a career in the sex industry, with some of them eventually climbing to the position of madam.

The human trafficking activities of female crime bosses underline the transnational character of organized crime. Women are seizing new opportunities to explore and develop new markets around the world, by acting as active participants in legal and illegal economies. The advantages of open borders and the unprecedented new possibilities offered by increased mobility, technology, and communication are now being exploited by female crime bosses. The transnational and fluid opportunities and the attractive image of crime (which is associated with wealth, power, and freedom) seduce women into entering the criminal world.

The concrete examples of successful madams inspire other women to follow in the footsteps of these female crime bosses. The Nigerian madams operating in Europe invest significant amounts of capital in businesses and real estate in Nigeria. When a successful madam walks the run-down streets of a Nigerian city, she is the perfect advertisement for criminal activities (i.e., human trafficking). Many young girls, often encouraged by their families, knowingly apply for the opportunity to travel abroad and work for the madams as sex workers. After repaying their travel and housing expenses, these girls hope to earn enough money to improve their own and their families' economic situation, to build a house, open up a shop, or become madams themselves and recruit other young prostitutes.

Another possible explanation of the position of Nigerian women in organized crime has to do with the fact that successful female crime bosses have become "role models" for young women. The media contribute directly or indirectly to the circumstance that young women identify with famous people, including successful madams, and imagine sex work to be worthwhile and even desirable. Many young Nigerian women seize the opportunity to make a career in sex work in Europe and, if possible, rise to the position of madam. Their profits are based on the exploitation of women who, just like the madams, first came to work in Europe as prostitutes out of economic necessity.

The changing character of organized crime provides women with new criminal markets and clients. Today, organized crime is increasingly transnational and the role of women should be analyzed specifically with regard to transnational flows, new markets, products and clients, and international migrations. As long as there are differences between countries in terms of supply and demand, criminalization, economic conditions, political and ethnic conflicts, and wars, women will try to take advantage of the situation and profit from criminal activities.

References

Becucci, S. 2008. "New players in an old game: The sex market in Italy." In D. Siegel and H. Nelen (Eds.), *Organized crime: Culture, markets and policies* (pp. 57–69). New York: Springer.

Brown, L. 2000. *Sex slaves: The trafficking of women in Asia.* London: Virago Press.

Denisova, T. 2001. "Trafficking in women and children for purposes of sexual exploitation: The criminological aspect." *Trends in Organized Crime, 6*(3), 30–36.

Kleemans, E. R., van de Berg, E., and van de Bunt, H. G. 1998. *Georganiseerde criminaliteit in Nederland; rapportage op basis van de WODC-monitor* (Onderzoek en Beleid 173). Den Haag: WODC.

Siegel, D., and de Blank, S. 2010. "Women who traffic women: The role of women in human trafficking networks—Dutch cases." *Global Crime, 11*(4), 436–447.

Siegel, Dina. 2007. Nigeriaanse madams in de mensenhandel in Nederland. *Justitiële verkenningen, 33*(7), 39–49.

Dina Siegel is professor of Criminology, Utrecht University, the Netherlands. She has studied and published on post-Soviet organized crime, women trafficking, prostitution and prostitution policy, women in organized crime, and East European criminal organizations. She is one of the founders of the Center for Information and Research on Organized Crime (CIROC) and former president of the IASOC (International Association of Studies on Organized Crime) of the American Society of Criminology.

What Are the Challenges in Prosecuting Human Trafficking Offenses?
Glynn Rankin

While a key priority for the European Union (EU) is the increased prosecution of traffickers, the UNODC Global Report 2014 indicates that despite legislative progress, there are still very few convictions for human trafficking. The EU Strategy toward the Eradication of Trafficking in Human Beings 2012–2016 states that more attention is being paid to the prosecution and investigation of human trafficking cases, but the total number of cases prosecuted remains low. Throughout Europe, there were only 7,704 prosecutions over a two-year period between 2010 and 2012, although the data do show slight increases over the same period (Eurostat statistical working paper 2015). The issue of low convictions has been clearly identified; however, there is no definitive answer as to why it is occurring. Arguably, it could be because the role of the prosecutor is not fully understood and the number of convictions is an arbitrary measure. Prosecutors are committed to reducing the harm caused by trafficking; however, it does not automatically follow that all trafficking cases must result in a prosecution. There are viable alternatives to prosecution including disruption (interrupting criminal activities) that can be used where the level of risk to a victim necessitates an immediate response or where it is impossible to undertake an investigation for operational, legal, or resource reasons.

The prosecution of human trafficking cases can be difficult, and there are a number of factors that may contribute to the low conviction rate. These factors must be addressed if countries hope to increase prosecutions. The most important factor is that all prosecutions should be victim centered, with human rights of the trafficked victim being the primary consideration throughout the entire course of criminal proceedings.

Prosecutors face the challenge of what offences to charge and how to explain the definitional problems inherent in human trafficking legislation to the courts. They have to build and bring a case to court, ensuring it is effectively managed, and that victims are protected, and those victims who suffer from physical or psychological problems are able to provide testimony. Prosecutors have to balance the victim's needs with the responsibility to undertake a prosecution, when deciding whether to instigate proceedings. There are a number of challenges when prosecuting human trafficking cases that, either individually or in combination, have to be resolved.

Reliance on Victim Testimony

Article 27 of the Council of Europe Convention on Action Against Trafficking in Human Beings states that "investigations into or prosecution of offences established in accordance with this Convention shall not be dependent upon a report accusation made by a victim." While human trafficking is an offence that can be prosecuted without a complaint, without victim testimony and cooperation, prosecutions are rarely successful.

Prosecutors need to take cognizance of the victim's gender and culture. Women and men, girls and boys are trafficked into different situations and they require gender-specific assistance and support. The culture and/or religion of the victim can influence a victim's willingness to give testimony. A victim from a collectivist culture (where honor and shame reflect not only upon the individual, but upon the victim's family as well) may fear rejection from their family/community due to the shame of them being trafficked, particularly into forced prostitution.

Victims may be unable or unwilling to give testimony because of the trauma they have experienced as a result of being trafficked. The process of giving testimony, especially in an adversarial system, can potentially retraumatize victims as they have to recall the trafficking situation and can be subjected to an examination by the defense advocate.

Because of fear, cultural influences, religious belief, or other factors, victims may not be able to give truthful testimony. Examples in the United Kingdom have included trafficked victims who had an abortion and could not admit to this fact because of their religious beliefs. Victims have also lied because they believed if they told the truth they would be deported.

Victims of forced labor exploitation may be hesitant to testify, as their primary objective is not the conviction of the trafficker, but restitution/compensation for the work they have undertaken. It is also important to realize that many victims take significant risks and can be in fear of the consequences of giving testimony against their traffickers because of the threat of what might happen to them or their families.

Victim Protection

Victim protection and assistance is a primary consideration in all human trafficking cases, and experience has proven that where the victim's psychological needs are met, their level of cooperation increases. Prosecutors should familiarize themselves with the services available to trafficked victims and, at all stages of the investigation and prosecution, consider the special needs of trafficked victims. If witness protection measures are not used, it could potentially lead to the retraumatization of trafficked persons and related decisions to withdraw their complaints against the traffickers.

Obtaining Evidence

The interviewing of trafficked victims is an essential part in obtaining evidence and those conducting the interview should respect the rights, choices, and autonomy of the victim. Interviewing can be problematic because victims may deny involvement, have impaired decision-making powers, and difficulty in providing a coherent and consistent account that can lead to fabricated stories and contradicting evidence. Therefore, it is important that both the interview organization and the testimony are carefully managed.

There are ethical questions and safety concerns raised when interviewing a victim and interviewers should adopt the "Do No Harm" principle (WHO Ethical and Safety Recommendations for Interviewing Trafficked Women, 2003). This principle is particularly significant in the context of trafficking given the risks associated, and it is important that no steps are taken that make the situation more perilous for the victim.

Obtaining evidence can also be difficult because of language barriers and the necessity for interpreters because neither the victim nor the trafficker understands the language of the country where the prosecution is being undertaken. Victims may wish to return to their home country prior to giving testimony or after giving testimony, and international cooperation may be required to obtain evidence or to allow victims to give testimony (e.g., by video link).

Legislation

The first internationally recognized definition of human trafficking is in Article 3 of the UN Trafficking in Persons Protocol. The legal concepts, which may have been adopted into national legislation, are ambiguous, are difficult to prove, resulting in legislative problems for prosecutors. These problems may explain why there are a limited number of convictions and traffickers are charged with alternative offences, which have a lesser evidential burden and are easier to prove (such as migrant smuggling or pimping).

There are no common definitions of recruitment, deception, or coercion, and exploitation is not defined (it is only described), allowing states to elaborate other forms of exploitation when defining "human trafficking" in national legislation. Trafficking has also been conceptualized within the framework of transnational organized crime, and Article 5 of the United Nations Convention on Transnational Organized Crime refers to the criminalization of participation in an organized crime group. Article 2 refers to "organized criminal group" and "structured group." These definitions appear to preclude the commission of human trafficking offences by individual traffickers or criminal networks that are either randomly formed or not structured, although the prosecution of individual traffickers is addressed in domestic legislation.

International Cooperation

Prosecutors, both legally and practically, need to build and promote international cooperation to remove obstacles to the prosecution of human trafficking cases, many of which are transnational. Human trafficking cases present complications and challenges due to the fact that often victims, witnesses, and perpetrators are located in different countries. A further complication could be that the criminal offense(s), or the recruitment or transportation, may also have taken place in another country. Traffickers may have been arrested outside the jurisdiction, which may necessitate extradition proceedings (transferring the accused from the country in which he or she is arrested to the country seeking to prosecute), possibly following an international arrest warrant.

International cooperation can also be used to protect and assist victims and to support financial investigations by identifying and seizing the profits of the crime. Although international cooperation can be challenging due to legal, cultural, political, and language issues, there are legal rules and procedures to guide and facilitate cooperation.

Corruption

Human trafficking could not occur, on the scale it does, without the complicity and collusion of corrupt officials with traffickers. Corruption can obstruct prosecutions and criminal proceedings. Corrupt officials are either directly involved in the human trafficking process or through their omissions they enable the process to flourish. They may knowingly use the services of trafficked women, sell investigative information, or assist traffickers in evading prosecution.

Emerging Methods, Markets, and Types of Crime

Human trafficking relates not only to sexual exploitation and forced labor exploitation, but also there is an increasing awareness of emerging forms of exploitation that constitute trafficking. Examples of these in the United Kingdom have been trafficking for forced work in marijuana cultivation and forced participation in benefit fraud. In addition to emerging forms of exploitation, the traffickers who are responsible for the exploitation are continually changing and evolving their modus operandi. Examples include traffickers taking greater care of victims and using less violence, and in a growing number of cases, letting victims keep some of the money they have earned. This makes it more difficult to get victims to testify against their traffickers. The Internet is also playing an increasingly important role in the recruitment of victims and the advertising of their services.

Prosecutors need to recognize and understand the evolving forms of exploitation and modus operandi of the traffickers and develop the skills necessary to successfully prosecute these new forms of trafficking.

To combat human trafficking, the prosecution of traffickers should be a priority and prosecutors need to be well resourced. Specialist prosecutors, with the requisite skills to manage and the ability to recognize human trafficking offences, are essential. International and regional cooperation, using formal and informal channels of communication, is necessary. Financial investigations should be undertaken in all cases and new types of investigative techniques considered. Partnerships with the civil society and the private sector would help protect victims while increasing prosecutions.

References

Eurostat. 2015. *Report on trafficking in human beings 2015.* https://ec.europa.eu/anti-trafficking/sites/antitrafficking/files/eurostat_report_on_trafficking_in_human_beings_-_2015_edition.pdf. Accessed January 14, 2016.

(The EU Strategy towards the Eradication of Trafficking in Human Beings 2012–2016). http://ec.europa.eu/home-affairs/doc_centre/crime/docs/trafficking_in_human_beings_eradication-2012_2016_en.pdf. Accessed on November 6, 2016.

UNODC *Global Report on Trafficking in Persons.* 2014. https://www.unodc.org/documents/data-and-analysis/glotip/GLOTIP_2014_full_report.pdf. Accessed on November 6, 2016.

WHO *Ethical and Safety Recommendations for Interviewing Trafficked Women.* 2003. https://www.who.int/mip/2003/other_documents/en/Ethical_Safety-GWH.pdf. Accessed on November 6, 2016.

Conventions/Directives

Council of Europe Convention on Action Against Trafficking in Human Beings. https://www.conventions.coe.int/Treaty/EN/Treaties/Html/197.htm. Accessed on November 6, 2016.

DIRECTIVE 2011/36/EU OF THE EUROPEAN PARLIAMENT AND OF THE COUNCIL of 5 April 2011 on preventing and combating trafficking in human beings and protecting its victims. https://ec.europa.eu/anti-trafficking/sites/antitrafficking/files/directive_thb_l_101_15_april_2011_1.pdf. Accessed on November 6, 2016.

United Nations Convention Against Transnational Organized Crime. https://www.unodc.org/documents/treaties/UNTOC/Publications/TOC%20Convention/TOCebook-e.pdf. Accessed on November 6, 2016.

UN Protocol to Prevent, Suppress and Punish Trafficking in Persons, Especially Women and Children. https://www.unodc.org/documents/treaties/UNTOC/Publications/TOC%20Convention/TOCebook-e.pdf. Accessed on November 6, 2016.

Glynn Rankin is a barrister and a former Chief Crown Prosecutor in England and Wales and a founding member of the U.K. Human Trafficking Centre. He is an independent anti-trafficking specialist and has worked for the OSCE, UNODC, and ICMPD. Glynn is a Practitioner Fellow in Policing at Liverpool John Moores University, Fellow of Liverpool University, and a Senior Research Fellow at Sheffield Hallam University.

This chapter profiles people and organizations that have been or are still active in the field of antislavery and human trafficking. Their work as individuals or organizations has contributed to awareness raising, prevention, research, victim protection and assistance, and the emancipation of slaves. These individuals and organizations are only a small number of those actively working around the world to eradicate trafficking and help survivors. They should serve as examples of good practices from which other individuals, countries, and regions may learn.

Kathryn Bolkovac (1960–)

Kathryn Bolkovac was a Nebraska police officer and investigator for 10 years before being hired by DynCorp Aerospace Operations, Ltd., a private company contracted by the United States, to support the United Nations Mission in Bosnia and Herzegovina. Between 1999 and 2001, Kathryn served as a human rights investigator for the International Police Task Force for the United Nations Mission to Bosnia and Herzegovina (UNBiH). In 2000, she was promoted to the gender affairs unit based in Sarajevo at the main headquarters of the United

Afghani journalist Najibullah Quraishi poses with one of the numerous awards he has won for his documentaries portraying forms of human trafficking and child exploitation in *The Dancing Boys of Afghanistan, Opium Brides, Taliban Child Fighters,* and *ISIS in Afghanistan.* (Evan Agostini/ Invision/AP Photo)

Nations and was tasked with oversight of all investigations related to violence against women.

Bolkovac's first case of human trafficking was uncovered when the local police of Zenica delivered a young woman to her office, after finding her beaten and stumbling on the side of the road. The young woman gave information about potential criminal activity taking place at a bar near Zenica. Upon arrival at the bar, it was empty; however, subsequent investigation uncovered a large amount of cash in U.S. dollars and passports of women from Eastern Europe. Behind a locked door on the second floor of the bar, Bolkovac discovered seven women trapped inside the room. Scattered around the room were used condoms and two bare mattresses.

Bolkovac uncovered a network of human trafficking and forced prostitution of young women to the region. Her investigation of these human rights abuses led to the involvement of DynCorp colleagues and UN personnel. These men were not only using the services of trafficked victims, but one U.S. police officer was involved in purchasing a woman for use as a sex slave. Through bribery and corruption of local police officials, the operation continued unhampered. Bolkovac's repeated attempts to protect these women fell on deaf ears and met resistance from her superiors. Her investigations were stymied and shutdown at every turn.

Bolkovac was able to document the involvement of officers linked to Dyncorp and UN peacekeepers. After bringing this evidence to her superiors, she was demoted, falsely accused of tampering with timesheets, and was subsequently fired. Fearing for her safety, Bolkovac fled the country. But before this, Madeline Rees, the High Commissioner for Human Rights in Sarajevo, organized a secret meeting between Bolkovac and Angela King, a Jamaican diplomat. She was advised to go public with her accusations of trafficking and human rights violations.

Bolkovac's firing and the attempt by the UN Mission in Bosnia and Herzegovina to cover up media reports implicating its officials in human trafficking created international headlines both in Europe and the United States. Bolkovac cooperated with Human Rights Watch investigations during her time in the mission, to help expose the gross human rights violations that were occurring. This included the use of trafficked women and young girls as prostitutes and sex slaves. Thanks to the evidence she collected, she won a lawsuit against DynCorp, finally exposing them for what they had done and the complicity of the United Nations in the attempt to protect their own and their reputation.

Bolkovac's story, and that of the women she was able to assist, and the people and institutions she fought, is told in her (2011) coauthored book *The Whistleblower, Sex Trafficking, Military Contractors, and One Woman's Fight for Justice*. A movie based on her experiences, entitled *Whistleblower*, was released in 2012.

Bolkovac encourages the protection of whistleblowers and fights for changes in the way the United States and the United Nations and its Member States oversee criminal activity and sexual violence cases, perpetuated by those seconded to the missions. International employees and peacekeepers of UN missions involved in criminal sexual activities are typically removed from missions and sent home or rotated to other missions with no investigation, prosecution, or repercussion from the United Nations or their contributing country. If diplomats are involved, steps were and are taken to "protect" them (Central African Republic 2014). Victims become part of the dysfunctional system through inadequate, ineffective investigations and interviews, to repatriation by nongovernmental organizations (NGOs), rendering them unprotected and unavailable to give proper testimony and vulnerable to further abuse.

Bolkovac speaks worldwide at universities, NGOs, and government symposia about topics that include antihuman trafficking, government and corporate accountability, codes of conduct and ethics, UN peacekeeping operations, and protecting public disclosures. She has been invited to speak and tell her story at the International Criminal Tribunal for the Former Yugoslavia and the United Nations in New York. "For her continuing efforts to call international attention to the problems and abuses of the private military and security business," Bolkovac was nominated for the Nobel Peace Prize in 2015 and 2016. She is a shining example of how, in the face of adversity and danger, one person can make a difference in the life of vulnerable victims of trafficking.

CNN Freedom Project: Ending Modern-Day Slavery

In 2011, CNN International launched the CNN Freedom Project to bring attention to modern-day slavery and similar practices, including sex and labor trafficking, forced and bonded labor, and child labor. The interactive website allows visitors the opportunity to read blogs by leading activists in the anti-trafficking field, from NGOs to industry leaders, documentary makers to victims, and profiles trafficking patterns around the world.

Information on the website allows the visitor to identify charities or international agencies working in particular countries (with information on contacting these groups), hotlines around the world, a brief parents and teachers guide instructing teachers how to incorporate the theme of human trafficking into social studies themes, and suggestions on how to take a virtual stand against modern slavery. The website also provides direct links to a form to anonymously report a case of trafficking to CrimeStoppers, and a separate link to report a case of human trafficking in the United States and Mexico to the National Trafficking Resource Center.

Perhaps, most importantly, the CNN's Freedom Project provides exposure to numerous forms of trafficking and anti-trafficking heroes through news articles on its website and award-winning documentaries on television and the website.

In "Operation Hope," one of the most shocking documentaries on child trafficking, senior correspondent Sara Sidner tells the story of a seven-year-old Bangladeshi boy who stood up to traffickers who had tried to force him into begging. When the child refused, the traffickers smashed a brick on his head, cut his stomach and throat, and castrated him, leaving him to die. CNN's story, which aired internationally, attracted the attention of U.S. businessman-turned-philanthropist Aram Kovach, who, with the help of CNN and generous doctors at Johns Hopkins hospital who agreed to perform surgery, arranged for the child to be brought to the United States for reconstructive surgery. This award-winning story ultimately changed the life of this young boy and raised greater awareness of the mafia-style gangs that maim and force children into begging.

The CNN Freedom Project has produced a number of documentaries on topics as broad as child sex trafficking in Cambodia (see "Every Day in Cambodia: A CNN Freedom Project Documentary"), forced marriage and child brides, abuses in the cocoa industry ("Cocoa-nomics"), deception and exploitation in the kidney trade in Nepal ("Nepal's Organ Trail"), "Branded: Sex Slavery in America" and "The CNN Freedom Project: Children for Sale."

Coalition of Immokalee Workers

The Coalition of Immokalee Workers (CIW) was founded as the Southwest Florida Farmworker Project in 1993, with the objectives of improving the pay and working conditions of agricultural workers. Within five years, the organization helped farmworkers win raises of 13–25 percent, amounting to several million dollars annually for the community. It further aimed to end the modern-day slavery so often found in the agricultural sector. It is, according to the organization, "a worker-based human rights organization internationally recognized for its achievements in the fields of social responsibility, human trafficking, and gender-based violence at work." The organization focusses on three major programs.

The Fair Food Program was launched in 2011. This groundbreaking model is based on Worker-Driven Social Responsibility—a unique partnership between farmworkers, Florida tomato growers, and large retail buyers which participate in the program. These include Ahold USA (Giant and Stop & Shop), Aramark, Bon Appetite, Burger King, Chipotle Mexican Grill, Compass, McDonald's, Sodexo, Subway, Taco Bell, The Fresh Market, Trader Joe's, Walmart, and Whole Foods. The program was expanded to strawberries and peppers in Florida and to tomato growers in the U.S. states of Georgia, Maryland, North and South Carolina, New Jersey, and Virginia.

Under this program, CIW conducts education sessions for workers during their working hours. They are educated on the labor standard set forth in the program's Fair Food Code of Conduct. Workers receive increased wages and protection of their human rights in the workplace. Workers are trained as frontline monitors of their own rights.

A third-party monitoring system conducts regular audits and investigations into complaints, and monitors resolutions. The Fair Food Standards Council is unique in the United States. This monitoring council staffs a 24 hour a day worker complaint hotline, carries out comprehensive audits on participating farms, and mediates and resolves complaints. Since its inception in 2011 (through September 2015), CIW has interviewed 12,000 workers, has disseminated "know your rights" materials to 135,000 workers, has educated 33,000 workers face-to-face, and has addressed 1,100 complaints.

Buyers who participate in this program pay a small Fair Food premium to farm owners who pass on the premiums to workers (CIW reports that US$20 million in premiums were paid into the program between January 2011 and October 2015). Participating buyers are legally bound to cease purchase from growers who do not comply, and purchase tomatoes only from growers in good standing with the Fair Food Program code of conduct. The program has been recognized by the UN Working Group on Business and Human Rights as a model that could be replicated elsewhere in the world.

The program received recognition in the documentary film *Food Chains*, which premiered at a number of international film festivals. It has further received numerous human rights awards. The most recent of these are the Roosevelt Institute Freedom from Want Medal in 2013; the Clinton Global Citizen Award in 2014 for the groundbreaking impact of the Fair Food Program; and Secretary of State John Kerry awarded the CIW and Fair Food Program the Presidential Medal for Extraordinary Efforts to Combat Human Trafficking in 2015.

Since the 1990s, the organization has helped liberate over 1,200 exploited farm workers held against their will. CIW's Anti-Slavery Campaign has been involved in nine major investigations and assisted in the prosecution of slavery operations on farms in states across the Southeastern United States in seven of the operations. The organization pioneered the worker-centered approach to slavery prosecution and cofounded the Freedom Network Training Institute attended by local, state, and federal law enforcement officials. In 2010, CIW was recognized with the Department of State's Trafficking in Persons Hero Award, for the organization's "determination to eliminate forced labor in supply chains."

Sunita Danuwar and Shakti Samuha

At the age of 14, Sunita Danuwar was drugged by two men her family trusted and brought to Mumbai where she was forced to work as a child prostitute in an Indian brothel. She and hundreds of other young girls and women were rescued during coordinated police raids around the country in 1996. Of the 500 rescued victims, 200 were Nepalese. Danuwar had spent five months in an Indian brothel, only to be rescued and locked in a shelter in Mumbai, India, for another seven months.

The Government of Nepal was reluctant to repatriate the trafficked victims, fearing an increase in HIV/AIDS, and using the argument that many of the young girls and women did not have citizenship papers. Seven NGOs (ABC Nepal, CWIN, Shanti Punasthapan Griha, Strishakti, Maity Nepal, Nabajyoti, and WOREC Nepal) pressured the government to repatriate the victims. The government was reluctant to pay for the repatriation. It took Bollywood star Sunil Shetty, with the support of Save the Children India, to pay for the airfare and help repatriate 128 girls and young women back to Nepal.

An uncertain future awaited the young returnees. The media portrayed them in the most derogatory terms with headlines such as "Prostitutes returning home land with Package of HIV" and "HIV bombs exploding in capital city, Kathmandu." As part of their "rehabilitation," the girls and young women were forced to undergo HIV/AIDS testing. Through the dedication and care of Dr. Renu Rajbhandari (WOREC, Nepal), Danuwar and other girls were provided training. Part of this training was to help the victims understand that their trafficking experience was not their fault. This realization led Danuwar and 15 other victims of trafficking, repatriated together from India, to establish the organization Shakti Samuha, which in Nepali means "a group that empowers."

Shakti Samuha is the first NGO in Nepal to be established and run by survivors of trafficking. Danuwar is quoted as saying during an interview, "We work for 'our' rights whereas other organizations work for 'their' rights."

The idea that trafficking survivors could start an NGO met with resistance from government officials, who derided the women for being poorly educated and for being ostracized by and isolated from family. The survivors persisted and Shakti Samuha was officially registered in 2000. It is now run by 168 trafficking survivors with the group's founders.

Shakti Samuha strives to empower trafficking survivors to lead a dignified life. The organization collects data on trafficking survivors, provides income-generating practices and skills for survivors, advocates and lobbies for changes in the law, raises awareness among at-risk groups, and maintains an emergency shelter and support for survivors (including legal, counseling, and employment services). Danuwar and Shakti Samuha want to prevent human trafficking, but if this is not possible, Danuwar wants victims returning to Nepal "to feel like they are coming home to a family." The organization provides support to hundreds of girls and women and works in 11 districts in Nepal.

Danuwar has since completed her high school education and is now studying for a bachelor's degree in social work. She has been transformed from a trafficked victim to a survivor to a leading social activist. She stands as an example of the strength, self-determination, and vision trafficked survivors can exhibit. Through her work, she passes these same qualities on to others in her country.

Declaration of Istanbul Custodial Group

Exploitation of the poorest and most vulnerable in the organ trade has been documented by numerous organizations. The shortage of donor organs, the increased demand by recipients, and the transplant tourism that brings poor donors and wealthy recipients together, sometimes in situations tantamount to human trafficking, generated a response by the World Health Assembly in 2004 to address the problem. It urged Member States to take measures to protect the vulnerable donors. Two years later, representatives from the International Society of Nephrology met with representatives of the Transplantation Society and devised the idea of developing a formal declaration to express consensus among those engaged in battling unethical practices in organ transplantation. The declaration should define organ transplant tourism and commercialism, organ trafficking, establish principles of practice, and provide recommendations to address the shortage of organs.

One hundred and fifty-two participants from 78 countries around the world, representing country liaisons of the Transplantation Society and medical bodies, representatives from the Vatican, social scientists (sociologists and anthropologists), ethicists, and government officials gathered at a summit in Istanbul, Turkey, in April 2008 to draft the Declaration of Istanbul. Working groups developed different parts of the declaration and presented their work at plenary sessions for approval—the declaration was reached by consensus of those participating at the summit meeting. The Declaration of Istanbul was published in July 2008 in the renowned medical journal *The Lancet.* It has been translated into 15 languages.

The Declaration of Istanbul is based upon values espoused in the Universal Declaration of Human Rights and the World Health Assembly Resolution 57.18 on human organ and tissue transplantation. It encourages countries not only to increase deceased organ donations, but also to ensure the protection and safety of living donors. Recommendations aimed at protecting donors include psychosocial screening, ensuring informed consent is obtained, the provision of patient care (at the time of donation and for any short- or long-term postoperative medical problems), health and medical insurance for donors, and transparency in the transplantation process.

The Declaration of Istanbul is an internationally recognized, nonbinding instrument; it is not a legal document. It has no power to compel compliance; rather, it offers principles and proposals that should serve as guidelines in the transplantation of organs. Creators of this document have sought its endorsement. The declaration has been endorsed by 114 different organizations comprising national bodies (societies of nephrology and transplantation in countries across the world), regional bodies (e.g., the Council of Europe, European Committee on Organ Transplantation, the Asian Pacific Society of Nephrology or La Sociedad Latinoamericana de Nefrología e Hipertensión), and international organizations (e.g., Global Alliance of Eye Bank Associations or the International Pediatric

Nephrology Association). Endorsement promotes ethical practices amongst health authorities who support the Declaration of Istanbul, and encourages policy makers to adopt legislation to facilitate these goals.

The Declaration of Istanbul Custodial Group (DICG) continues to work toward a comprehensive strategy aimed at governments, pharmaceutical companies, professional societies, and other bodies involved in transplantation practices to achieve the goals set forth in the declaration. The website of the organization provides more information on the role of the DICG members, resources, and news related to the shortage of organs, organ trafficking, organ trafficking in conflict zones, and the Declaration of Istanbul in the news.

If the DICG and its supporters are able to achieve these ambitious goals, they may save the lives of countless people waiting for an organ, and eradicate organ trafficking and the abusive practice that endangers poor and vulnerable donors.

ECPAT

In 1990, ECPAT began as a campaign to End Child Prostitution in Asian Tourism. The organization, headquartered in Bangkok, Thailand, has grown to a network of 90 civil society organizations operating in 82 countries around the world. ECPAT coordinates advocacy, research, and action, and is recognized as the only international nongovernmental organization/network with the sole goal of eradicating the sexual exploitation of children. ECPAT's three main issues address the sexual exploitation of children online, ending sexual exploitation of children in the tourist and travel industries (by both locals and travelers), and ending child trafficking (including commercial sexual exploitation of children or CSEC and child marriages).

The organization conducts cutting-edge research and develops reliable data in order to inform evidence-based advocacy to strengthen national justice and protection systems.

It encourages countries to bring their legislation in line with international (United Nations) and regional (e.g., ASEAN—the Association of Southeast Asian Nations—or the African Union) standards and agreements. Furthermore, ECPAT sustains partnerships with governments, local (NGO), national, and international law enforcement agencies (INTERPOL), and industry experts (e.g., in the case of online sexual exploitation of children, ECPAT liaises with the Child Online Protection initiative established by the International Telecommunication Union and the Virtual Global Taskforce—an alliance of international law enforcement agencies and the private sector).

The organization is a hub for the most recent resources on the issue. Documents date back to 1996. They include journals, research reports, guidelines for campaigns and advocacy, and to teach children how to stay safe online, frameworks for interventions, and training and toolkits (many of these documents are in multiple languages), and all can be downloaded from the resources page. For an example of ECPAT's extensive network and academic and policy-oriented research, see the 2016 study "Offenders on the Move: Global Study on Sexual Exploitation of Children in Travel and Tourism."

Advocacy involves keeping the issue of child sexual exploitation high on the political agenda, both nationally and internationally. ECPAT holds international stakeholders accountable for their commitments and advocates at the national level for multisector collaboration, stronger legal frameworks, more effective prevention and protection systems, and better implementation thereof.

ECPAT initiated the Global Study on Sexual Exploitation of Children in Travel and Tourism (SECTT), which involved 67 partners (from the United Nations, NGOs, and the private transportation and tourism sector). Together they produced over 2,500 pages of experience and expertise in the first comprehensive global study on this topic, resulting in 7 main findings and 46 recommendations.

ECPAT believes in involving children in all aspects of its work—awareness raising, research, monitoring, and evaluation. Particularly important are the contributions of child survivors. To this end, the organization has launched the "Access to Justice and Remedies Project," which addresses the experiences of child survivors with the judicial system and recovery and reintegration programs. The program aims to produce a document for children, educating them to their right to be free from violence and how to access support. The Global Youth Participation Project (YPP) works with survivors of child sexual abuse and prepares them to be Peer Supporters, Youth Motivators, and Advocates. Their experiences are told in child-friendly guides, journals, and studies available as ECPAT resources. Evaluations of the YPP projects showed that they empowered survivors and those they supported (at-risk youth) "to realize their fundamental right to influence matters affecting their lives."

International Justice Mission

Prior to founding the International Justice Mission (IJM), Gary Haugen directed the UN investigation into the Rwandan Genocide in 1994. Three years later, IJM became a reality and one of the most powerful antislavery organizations of its time. This international, faith-based NGO, with headquarters in the United States, maintains 18 field offices in countries in Africa (Ghana, Kenya, Rwanda, and Uganda), Latin America (Bolivia, Dominican Republic, Ecuador, Guatemala, and Peru), South Asia (various cities within India), and Southeast Asia (Cambodia, Philippines, and Thailand). IJM has partner offices in Australia, Canada, Germany, the Netherlands, and the United Kingdom. Over 600 people are employed by the organization, 95 percent of whom are nationals of the countries in which they work.

Its mission is to partner with local authorities to address issues of violence, rescue victims, restore survivors, bring offenders to justice, and strengthen criminal justice system responses. This is accomplished through the Justice System Transformation approach, focusing on the four Rs (rescue, restore, restrain, and represent). These four focal areas are not mutually exclusive. IJM works with law enforcement to rescue victims and restrain offenders. Through training programs for, and working together with district administrative officials, law enforcement, prosecutors, and judges, IJM ensures that officials truly understand their national law, and that offenders are caught and sufficient evidence is collected to result in successful prosecutions—which was not always a given prior to IJM's measures. IJM helps survivors gain the strength to testify at trial against their exploiters, and equips police to gather evidence and prosecutors with the resources to get a conviction. IJM works to ensure criminals are brought to trial without delay. Through work in Cebu, the Philippines, IJM was able to ensure that child sex traffickers were brought to trial, which lasted seven to eight months rather than the usual five years. Long trials increase the likelihood of dismissal, sending out the message that the criminal justice system provides no justice for victims and that traffickers can operate with impunity.

The organization addresses topics of sexual violence and sex trafficking, forced labor, child sexual assault, property grabbing (vulnerable people, often widows and orphans, are chased from their homes and property by members of their own family or community), citizenship rights abuse (members of minority ethnic groups entitled to citizenship are denied this, and thus unprotected under the law), and police brutality and abusive detention. Within each country, IJM investigators, social workers, lawyers, and trained volunteers work together with local authorities to prevent violence and help protect the poor, identify weaknesses in the justice system, and introduce measures to rectify these.

Once problems are identified, IJM works to "fix the system" by providing *resources* (a motorcycle was given to police in Mukono County, Uganda, to reach victims of property-grabbing schemes in rural areas), *training* (hundreds of officers in Cambodia were trained on victim-centered interviewing and evidence gathering), *accountability* (IJM worked with the government in Cebu, the Philippines, to establish a special anti-trafficking police unit when it was found that corruption among street-level police was hindering enforcement of the country's anti-trafficking law), and *hope* (convictions of notorious traffickers and slave holders give people trust in their governments and hope for a future without violence and oppression).

Tackling problems in developing nations requires good measurement and reliable data. IJM conducts studies and provides reports of these analyses and research to scholars, human rights advocates, practitioners, and policy makers (see IJM's analytical report on "Commercial Sexual Exploitation of Children in Cambodia").

The organization's countless programs are documented on its website and in its annual (or semiannual reports). Together with local authorities and its partner, the National Adivasi Solidarity Council, IJM rescued an entire village of 96 people (including a 10-year-old child) in India from bonded labor as fishermen. In another dramatic case, five years after IJM rescued 511 slave laborers from a brick kiln in Chennai, India, in 2011, the same kiln was again operating with bonded slave laborers. The owner had been detained briefly in 2011 but had been released, and he later returned to his operation. IJM once again staged a rescue, this time freeing 564 men, women, and children. IJM provided urgent medical care and assisted the families to return to their home villages. IJM continues to support these survivors through its two-year aftercare program (which also includes helping survivors find jobs). This time, IJM ensured the arrest of the brick kiln owner. It is the belief of the organization that "if criminals remain free, these violent crimes will continue. But if laws are enforced and traffickers go to jail, slavery will end."

In its most recent midyear report, IJM shows sweeping improvements over its accomplishments in 2015. The organization has, within the first six months of the year, been involved in the rescue of 2,551 victims of oppression, the restraint of 101 perpetrators of violent crimes, and the provision of aftercare services to more than 3,300 victims and their families. Additionally, IJM has provided training to more than 18,500 community members and justice system officials. Having received recognition for its important work in the field of antislavery, this organization aspires to break these records and increase services in the coming years.

International Labour Organization

In 1919, at the end of World War I, the International Labour Organization (ILO) was created, based on the belief that social justice could produce universal and lasting peace. The executive bodies of this tripartite organization brought together representatives of governments, employers, and workers. The aim of the organization was to protect workers' rights and ensure regulation of adequate wages, working conditions, and freedom of association. The ILO drafted numerous Conventions, and within less than two years, 16 International Labour Conventions and 18 Recommendations were adopted by Member States. The ILO became a specialized agency of the newly formed United Nations in 1946, and currently has 187 Member States.

The ILO sets international labor standards for decent employment, promotes the creation of jobs, and the strengthening of workers' rights and social protection, while fostering dialogue between governments, employers, and employees on work-related issues.

A unique supervisory system exists at the international level to ensure that countries implement the ILO conventions they ratify. Under the Standard Supervisory System, the ILO regularly examines the application of standards in Member States and indicates where these could be improved. Where the application of standards is weak, the ILO encourages social dialogue and provides technical assistance to Member States. Within the framework of the regular system of supervision, the ILO examines reports submitted by Member States, as well as on observations sent by workers' and employers' organizations. Special procedures are invoked when the ILO receives a complaint.

The ILO is credited with playing a major role in supporting the legitimacy of the independent self-governing trade union Solidarność ("Solidarity") leading to the emancipation of Poland from dictatorship. After the imposition of military law and the suspension of the trade union in 1981, ILO delegates at the 1982 International Labour Conference filed a complaint against Poland for violations of conventions the country had ratified: the Freedom of Association and Protection of the Right to Organise Convention, 1948 (No. 87) and the Right to Organise and Collective Bargaining Convention, 1949 (No. 98). Under pressure from the ILO, and numerous countries and organizations, the government of Poland gave Solidarność legal status in 1989. Lech Walesa, leader of Solidarność and later President of Poland, noted: "The Commission of Inquiry created by the ILO after the imposition of martial law in my country made significant contributions to the changes which brought democracy to Poland."

The ILO's International Programme on the Elimination of Child Labour (IPEC), in operation since 1992, has worked globally toward the eradication of the worst forms of child labor. ILO-IPEC does this through raising awareness, promoting policy reform, and introducing concrete measures to eliminate exploitative child labor. The actions of ILO-IPEC have resulted in the prevention from entering the workforce, or the withdrawal of hundreds of thousands of children from exploitative and dangerous work, and their rehabilitation. Child labor monitoring continues to occur.

The fight against forced labor and human trafficking is one of the ILO's main priorities. Since 2002, the Special Action Programme to combat Forced Labour (SAP-FL) has spearheaded the organization's work in this field. In addition to its awareness-raising role, the ILO develops training materials and key indicators to identify situations of forced labor and human trafficking and implements pioneering programs that build capacity of law enforcement and labor market institutions, and provide direct support for prevention and rehabilitation programs. The global fight against forced labor, human trafficking, and slavery-like practices was given new impetus in June 2014, when governments, workers, and employers voted to adopt a legally binding protocol and a recommendation that supplement the Forced Labour Convention, 1930 (No. 29), by providing express guidance on effective measures to eliminate all forms of forced labor. The protocol advances protection, prevention, and compensation measures.

In 2005, the ILO developed a well-respected methodology to estimate the prevalence of human trafficking and forced labor worldwide; the methodology was updated in 2012. The organization conducts in-depth qualitative and quantitative research worldwide on topics related to child (exploitative) labor, forced labor, and human trafficking in different industries, and is initiating a research program to document the state of affairs with regards to national and international initiatives to measure forced labor, human trafficking, and slavery. As part of the ILO's statistical work, the organization maintains the ILOSTAT database containing over 100 indicators for more than 230 countries. Research also focusses on legal and policy analysis, as well as child labor monitoring and program evaluation. The ILO has become a center of thematic studies, statistical data, good practices, guidelines, and training materials on fair and exploitative labor practices.

International Organization for Migration

In 1951, following the displacement of people in Western Europe after the end of World War II, the Provisional Intergovernmental Committee for the Movement of Migrants from Europe (PICMME) was born. The organization underwent a change in name and mandate from an operational logistics agency to support the move of 11 million Europeans uprooted by the war, to a migration agency whose mandate extends worldwide. The organization took the name International Organization for Migration (IOM) in 1989, and adheres to the belief that "humane and orderly migration benefits migrants and society." IOM has 165 Member States (and 8 more holding observer status), more than 9,000 staff in over 150 countries, and was involved in more than 2,400 active projects worldwide in 2014. It is the leading international agency working with governments, intergovernmental, and nongovernmental partners to promote understanding of migration issues and uphold the human dignity and well-being of migrants, refugees, and (internally) displaced persons. The organization has no legal protection mandate; however, its activities contribute to protecting the human rights of those involved in migration.

IOM works to promote the safe and humane management of migration, to search for practical solutions to migration problems, and assist migrants in need. In order to accomplish these goals, the organization works in four broad areas of migration management. These are migration and development, regulating migration, facilitating migration, and forced migration. The organization addresses these goals by promoting international migration law, guiding policy, and protecting migrants' rights and health.

With the increased number of migrants on the move, and horrific stories of their exploitation and unexpected deaths (on November 4, 2016, 5,610 deaths of migrants had been recorded worldwide; the majority of these deaths were in the Mediterranean), the work of IOM is becoming increasingly more important. A study by the organization of almost 1,400 migrants and refugees interviewed in Italy between June 24 and August 3, 2016, found that 76 percent experienced incidences of exploitation bordering on human trafficking—from not being paid for work performed to being held against their will, kidnapping, and torture.

Since 1994, IOM has been working in the area of counter-trafficking, particularly as it occurs within the context of migration. In addition to providing for the mental, physical, and social well-being of trafficked persons, the organization focusses on institutional capacity building of governments and civil society to achieve sustainability. IOM focusses on prevention by conducting information campaigns aimed at the general public and vulnerable persons to arm them with information necessary to protect themselves.

IOM conducts quantitative and qualitative research at both the national and regional level to better support cooperation between countries to combat cross-border trafficking. To support these efforts, considerable research in the areas of legislation and policy are conducted. The organization also developed and maintains the Global Human Trafficking Database, containing information on trafficked persons assisted by the organization. It is the largest global database with primary data on victims of trafficking. It serves as a standardized counter-trafficking data management tool, facilitating the management of all IOM direct assistance to trafficked persons. Mapping victims' trafficking experiences provides the organization valuable information on understanding the vulnerabilities of trafficked persons and the modus operandi of traffickers.

Technical cooperation activities and publications aid government and civil society institutions to better address human trafficking. These activities include training NGOs and government officials, such as police, providing technical support in developing counter-trafficking legislation, policies, and procedures. This is accomplished, in part, through publications such as "Caring for Trafficked Persons: Guidance for Health Providers," "Handbook on Direct Assistance for Victims of Trafficking," and a "Handbook on Performance Indicators for Counter-Trafficking Projects." IOM's "Handbook on Direct Assistance for Victims of Trafficking" provides advice and guidance on effectively delivering the full range of assistance to victims of trafficking.

One of the most important contributions IOM makes is the comprehensive, direct assistance it offers to trafficked persons, including accommodation in safe shelters, medical and psychosocial care, skills development and vocational training, and safe repatriation and reintegration assistance. Specialized protection is offered to minors. In 2015, IOM provided assistance to 7,000 persons, the majority of whom were adult male victims (55%) of transnational trafficking (85%) for forced labor (74%). Since its involvement in counter-trafficking, IOM has assisted approximately 70,000 trafficked persons with safe return to their home countries, safe reception centers, care, and sustainable reintegration programs.

La Strada International

As a result of a trilateral anti-trafficking project between the Czech Republic, the Netherlands, and Poland in 1994, La Strada was launched a year later. Six years after that, the organization had expanded to include an additional five European members (Belarus, Bulgaria, Macedonia, Moldova, and Ukraine). The organization takes its name from a famous Federico Fellini film *La Strada*, in which a young girl is sold to work in a circus. The word "la strada" in Italian means the street, and represents, as described on the organization's website, "the streets on which many women have to work, the long way out of their exploitative situation and the long road the founders of La Strada saw in front of them toward effective strategies to deal with the issues." The organization operated under the auspices of the Dutch Foundation against Trafficking in Women and then the Coordination Center Human Trafficking (CoMensha) until it became an independent international association in October 2004. La Strada International is a leading European NGO anti-trafficking network comprising eight independent organizations which work at the grass roots level. Therefore, each of the eight country offices manages programs and projects aimed at the needs of its population.

La Strada takes a human rights approach to trafficking—putting the human rights of those at risk and those trafficked at the center of prevention and protection programs. Trafficked persons should not be viewed as instruments to assist in prosecution but should be empowered to understand and exercise their rights. This is accomplished through a number of strategic objectives which include, but are not limited to, strengthening the role and financial sustainability of NGOs that work with trafficked persons and those at risk and to strengthen La Strada's network and partnership with external stakeholders.

La Strada represents its network of NGOs at the international level and lobbies for independent special rapporteurs (as in the Netherlands) as well as civil society influence on policy making and monitoring. It advocates changes in policy focusing on the human rights approach to combating trafficking. La Strada maintains close contact with the EU Group of Experts on Trafficking in Human Beings, the OSCE's Office of the Special Representative on Trafficking in Human Beings, and the nongovernmental Human Rights and Democracy Network (HRDN).

The organization's documentation center provides access to over 1,700 documents that can be downloaded in pdf format via the searchable database. The documents, meant for practitioners, policy makers, academics, and trafficked persons, include background documents on human trafficking as well as legislation. The organization's quarterly newsletter provides readers with international developments in the field of migration and human trafficking. Stakeholders are, thus, provided background information and analysis on publications, policy changes, and new trends in the field of anti-trafficking from a human rights and service-oriented perspective.

The international branch of La Strada not only supports the work of and partners with its eight affiliate organizations, but also engages in independent projects with non–La Strada partners. Perhaps, one of the most important projects implemented by La Strada International, in coordination with

Anti-Slavery International, was the COMP.ACT project. Together with partners in 14 countries (Austria, Belarus, Bosnia and Herzegovina, Bulgaria, Czech Republic, Germany, Ireland, Italy, Macedonia, Moldova, Poland, Spain, Ukraine, and the United Kingdom), the project aimed to increase awareness of the existing possibility to compensate victims for their exploitation and unpaid wages and remove obstacles to trafficked persons being compensated. Partner organizations conducted research, formed national coalitions on compensation, and developed guidelines and recommendations. They were involved in international advocacy and campaigning. In participating countries, partners introduced projects to assist trafficked persons obtain compensation while supporting them through the process. COMP.ACT partners supported over 50 trafficked persons in obtaining compensation (the highest amount granted was €54,000). The COMP.ACT project contributed to the inclusion of compensation to victims of trafficking in the EU Directive on Preventing and Combating Trafficking in Human Beings and Protecting the Victims EU/2011/36 and the EU Strategy towards the Eradication of Trafficking in Human Beings 2012–2016.

Because of its important role as a regional anti-trafficking network partner in Europe, La Strada International is partnering with Polaris (United States) and Liberty Asia on the Global Human Trafficking Hotline Network.

Liberty Asia

Founded in 2011, Liberty Asia is an anti-trafficking NGO registered in Hong Kong, providing services to stakeholders in East and Southeast Asia. The focus of the organization is strategic collaborations with NGOs, corporations, and financial institutions, providing legal advocacy and technological interventions to prevent human trafficking.

Liberty Asia gathers intelligence on slavery in the region and passes this on to the private sector. Through online platforms, the organization facilitates the exchange and sharing of data, expertise, and best practices with network partners. Liberty Asia provides training and education to raise awareness of slavery and facilitate change in all sectors of society. The organization takes a human rights–based approach, emphasizing the need to restore victims' human rights. An important element of the organization's work is to build a stable communications network of Asia hotlines to assist NGOs to build up their capacity to support (repatriated) victims.

The legal program provides resources and tools through its Legal Resource Center. This center provides briefing papers on the U.K.'s Modern Slavery Act (and its implication for Asia), a section on case law (contains cases from international as well as Hong Kong courts) on cases involving sexual exploitation, debt bondage, forced labor, forced marriage, and domestic servitude. In addition to Liberty Asia's publications (e.g., a *Victim Identification Toolkit* 2016), the organization provides information on best practices, guidelines, learning tools, and recent news. Legal gap analysis is also conducted to determine what gaps exist and need to be filled to successfully prosecute cases. The consultation section will send relevant legislation, case law, research, or policy, in response to queries from practitioners concerning human trafficking cases.

The emphasis of the Information Strategies is to provide information concerning traffickers—those who generate a profit from their exploitation of victims—to the financial service sector, to aid them in business dealings (under the auspices of the Anti-Bribery and Corruption and Anti-Money Laundering regulatory requirements). Information obtained from media or local cases is made available to "due diligence specialists" such as Thomson Reuters WorldCheck (used by many financial institutions in the "Know Your Customer" and "Client Due Diligence" procedures). Within the year, August 2015—July 2016 (the website is updated monthly), Liberty Asia covered 11 countries, working together with 16 NGOs which contributed to the program. The names of 3,020 traffickers were submitted for profiling. There were 5,200 financial institutions screening for matching the names to profiled traffickers.

With respect to data and technology, Liberty Asia partnered with Verizon and Alfresco to offer, free of charge, a cloud-based evidence and document management system to those working in anti-trafficking investigations; the organization provides training on the system, data protection, and data security. A victim-based case management system offers NGO partners the ability to store and share their client data to improve services to victims. The communication division has connected frontline NGOs with advance call handling options. This has facilitated cross-border collaboration, which is important in providing services to repatriated victims. In line with the IT focus of Liberty Asia, the Freedom Collaborative provides a platform for users to network, read, and share information and obtain legal support.

Liberty Asia differs from many other NGOs, in that it does not collect data, nor does it provide direct victim assistance. This organization serves as a pivotal point in bringing other anti-trafficking stakeholders together and providing the tools necessary to enhance their work. Because trafficking in the region is often cross-border, it is essential to link NGOs working in source and destination countries together to increase the likelihood that repatriated victims receive the care they need.

Liberty Asia, together with two other anti-trafficking organizations (Polaris Project and La Strada International), will share a US$3 million Google-funded Global Impact Award. It will be used to build an international database and response system that will facilitate the sharing of data and best practices to improve services to victims and strengthen initiatives to combat human trafficking.

Loretta Lynch (1959–)

As a child, Loretta Lynch showed an interest in court and spent hours with her father watching trials in Durham, North

Carolina. Years later, she would graduate with a juris doctorate degree from Harvard University.

While her legal career spans three decades, she is perhaps best known for her work as the U.S. Attorney for the Eastern District of New York, where she was responsible for overseeing all federal and civil investigations and cases in Brooklyn, Queens, and Staten Island, as well as Nassau and Suffolk counties on Long Island. It was in this capacity that Lynch proved her ability to systematically prosecute and convict traffickers involved in the forced prostitution of children and young women. She was known to colleagues as "one of the country's premier guardians of victims of sex trafficking." The deputy mayor of New York City, who worked closely with Lynch's office during her tenure as the U.S. Attorney for the Eastern District, attests to the fact that Lynch made the prevention of young girls falling prey to trafficking an important focus of her work. Lynch made it a personal priority to prosecute human trafficking cases and emphasized a victim-centered approach.

The Eastern District, under Lynch, led the country in federal trafficking prosecutions (often against violent Mexican gang members that trafficked young Mexican girls into the United States for forced sexual slavery), rescuing more than 110 victims, and delivering more than 55 indictments in human trafficking cases. Lynch's office was successful in obtaining lengthy convictions for sex traffickers.

Lynch has been a protector of children subjected to horrific sexual abuse and child pornography cases as well. Her office obtained convictions of a number of men and women charged with sexually abusing or photographing children for the purpose of child pornography.

Project Safe Childhood was launched as a nationwide initiative by the Department of Justice in 2006 to respond to the epidemic of child sexual abuse and exploitation cases. The project was led by the Criminal Division's Child Exploitation and Obscenity Section and the U.S. Attorneys' Offices. Under Project Safe Childhood and Lynch's guidance, the Attorney

General's Office of the Eastern District brought 173 prosecutions for child pornography and child exploitation.

In 2015, Loretta Lynch became the first African American woman to become the U.S. Attorney General, the highest ranking official in the Department of Justice. Following in the footsteps of her predecessor, Attorney General Eric Holder, Lynch plans to continue and expand the Anti-Trafficking Coordination Team Initiative (ACTeams) from its initial six cities to include six more cities in Phase II. The number of cases filed and convictions obtained for trafficking and sexual abuse of children more than doubled in the two years after initiation of ACTeams in the Phase I cities. These multidisciplinary teams comprised of federal law enforcement agents and prosecutors are responsible for "high-impact" federal investigations and prosecutions, dismantling trafficking networks, and protecting the rights of victims. Under Lynch's guidance as U.S. Attorney General, it is becoming easier to protect victims and bring human traffickers to justice.

Steve Maman (1975–)

A Canadian Jewish businessman with Moroccan roots is the unlikely savior of Christian and Yazidi women held as sex slaves by ISIS fighters in Iraq. Yet, Steve Maman, who has become known as the "Jewish Schindler" (after Oskar Schindler, known for having saved more than 1,200 Jews from Auschwitz during World War II), is credited with rescuing 140 Christian Yazidi girls and women.

Maman's call to action occurred after the ISIS attack on Sinjar province in 2014, when thousands of Yazidis were murdered and young Christian and Yazidi women were taken as ISIS brides or sold into slavery. The turning point for Maman was an incident in which children were caged while an ISIS combatant stood before them with a torch, threatening to burn them—a simple reminder of what had happened to a captured Jordanian pilot. Maman decided something had to be done to liberate the children, and founded the organization Liberation of Christian and Yazidi Children of Iraq (CYCI) in 2015.

Steve Maman runs a crystal wholesale business and classic car dealership in Montreal, Canada. In search of cars, his business brought him to countries worldwide, among them Iraq. Maman befriended a Christian Assyrian who had contacts with the governments of Kurdistan and Iraq. Funding for the rescues was provided initially through Maman's business friends from the Jewish community in Canada, and later through GoFundMe and PayPal accounts. To date, Maman and the CYCI have raised 766,000 Canadian dollars in donations to finance the rescues.

Maman's organization works closely with B. Jajju Dawood, the adoptive son of the priest Andrew White, known as the Vicar of Baghdad. B. Jajju Dawood is a Christian Iraqi soldier who has worked with the U.S., Canadian, and British military. He and other CYCI team members on the ground in Kurdistan (a U.S.-trained hostage negotiator and other U.S.-trained terrorism prevention personnel) negotiate with brokers and intermediaries for the release of women and girls. CICY does not deal directly with ISIS. Since September 2014, 140 children and women have been safely extracted from Mosul and have been provided medical care and short-term shelter in a secure location in Northern Iraq.

The organization has met with some criticism. Detractors are concerned that purchasing the freedom of women and children will encourage ISIS to increase kidnappings and take more hostages. Maman disagrees, stating that ISIS is unable to expand. He exclaims that the US$1,000–3,000 that he pays per child is paltry compared to the US$4 billion that ISIS is worth.

In addition to the rescues, Maman's organization continues to provide medical care to those in need. Due to worsening conditions in Iraq that have put the lives of CICY team members at risk, negotiations in the country have been discontinued. The organization provides services for Yazidis in camps who were able to reach Greece. In collaboration with the Greek government, Petras Camp, a camp solely for Yazidi refugees, was opened. CICY assists asylum seekers in the camp and has provided financial assistance, safe passage to Germany, and food for over 2,310 refugees.

Maman claims that his Jewish heritage dictated that he become involved. What happened to the Jews during the Holocaust should not happen to the Yazidis in Iraq under the rule of ISIS. He reminds his critics that the 1,200 Jews rescued by Oskar Schindler were liberated "unlawfully"—Schindler gave money to the Nazis to secure their safety. What has become a mantra for Steve Maman is a quote from the Talmud, the book of Jewish law: "One who saves a life, saves a world."

National Agency for the Prohibition of Trafficking in Persons, Nigeria

The Nigerian Trafficking in Persons (Prohibition) Law Enforcement and Administration Act of 2003 required the creation of a National Agency for the Prohibition of Trafficking in Persons (NAPTIP). NAPTIP was founded in August the same year. This multidisciplinary agency's mandate is to combat human trafficking through a four-pronged approach of partnership, prevention, prosecution, and (victim) protection. NAPTIP coordinates law enforcement and prosecution, prevention, and victim protection initiatives by government and nongovernmental agencies working on issues of human trafficking. The organization is mandated to provide services to victims—temporary shelters, access to justice, counseling, and rehabilitation and reintegration—in the 36 states and the Federal Capital Territory, Abuja. The mandate of the agency was expanded with the enactment of the new Trafficking in Persons (Prohibition), Enforcement and Administration Act, 2015, to include, among others, the responsibility to freeze and confiscate assets derived from human trafficking or related offenses, and to conduct research on the factors contributing to trafficking.

In order to ensure a multidisciplinary approach to understanding and dealing with the problem, the governing board of the agency is comprised of representatives from the Ministries of Justice, Women Affairs, Labour and Productivity, the Nigeria Police Force, the National Intelligence Agency and the National Planning Commission, Nigeria Immigration Service, and two representatives from civil society organizations. NAPTIP has six specialized departments with operational responsibilities: Investigation and Monitoring, Legal and Prosecution, Counseling and Rehabilitation, Public Enlightenment, Research and Program Development, and Training and Manpower Development.

In its ongoing attempts to protect victims of human trafficking, NAPTIP has launched a National Referral Mechanism for the Protection and Assistance to Trafficked Persons in Nigeria (NRM). The NRM will ensure that service providers understand and effectively operate within the principles of the National Policy on Protection and Assistance to Trafficked Persons in Nigeria. The development of guidelines for the NRM organizes service providers into service clusters and geographical areas to provide increased assistance and protection services to trafficked persons using a human rights–based approach.

By 2015, NAPTIP had investigated 2,987 cases of human trafficking and related crimes, had obtained the conviction of 280 persons, and had rescued 9,453 victims, the majority of whom are women and girls.

A single agency with the authority to investigate and prosecute crimes *and* the mandate to provide services to victims of trafficking is a rarity. NAPTIP represents the most integrated and comprehensive model to fight human trafficking that currently exists. The agency draws upon the motivation and dedication of its Director General Beatrice Jefy-Agba, who was selected by the U.S. Department of State as one of the 2014 trafficking-in-persons heroes. Under her guidance, NAPTIP has transformed the antihuman trafficking landscape in Nigeria by incorporating anti-trafficking issues into national development dialogue, planning, and policy.

National Association to Protect Children

The National Association to Protect Children (PROTECT) was founded on June 24, 2002. It is a national nonprofit organization with a "pro-child, anticrime" agenda. The organization's pro-child agenda is accomplished through advocacy for legal reporting and adequate funding for services for children. Its anticrime agenda focuses on surveillance of released sex offenders, and advocacy to increase funding for law enforcement and stronger criminal sentencing. The organization is nonpartisan and is represented by members in all 50 U.S. states. In the past, the organization has been involved in a number of projects and campaigns including advocating for long-term and lifetime probation and parole for convicted sex offenders (under the Real Safety campaign) and reform of laws allowing preferential treatment to offenders who sexually abuse their own children (Circle of Trust campaign). Laws were changed in Arkansas, California, Illinois, New York, North Carolina, and Virginia.

The organization is currently actively involved in three projects and can claim success in each. The Sunlight and Accountability Project aims to hold public servants accountable for their decisions involving the safety of children in the system and punishment of offenders. A particularly powerful project involved investigation into and subsequent release of Judicial Accountability reports in 2012, 2013, and 2014, documenting the lenient sentences that judges—particularly those up for reelection—were handing down in cases of child pornography and (sexual) abuse in the state of Virginia. In this "naming and shaming" document, PROTECT examines the sentences handed down by individual judges. The relatively mild sentences obtained through plea bargains were blamed by judges on the prosecution service, but in fact judges must approve the plea bargain deal. The project will be expanded in Virginia to examine performance data on the practices of the prosecution department and child protective services. The plan is to expand the project to other states.

The National Association to Protect Children has been working with federal agencies and Congress since 2006, to recruit private industry and scientific experts to develop new technology to aid law enforcement to detect child pornography and stop child abuse. The center has funded research and development and provided software and equipment for law enforcement agencies, including "law enforcement information-sharing and deconfliction systems, secure law enforcement image repositories, computer forensic processing, investigative protocols and tool development." The Weiss Center also provides training for participants in the HERO Child Rescue Corps. Future developments in technology will improve communication between agencies dealing with children and will allow for children to be tracked through the child protection system.

Perhaps, one of the greatest contributions made by this organization in the battle to protect children is the establishment of the HERO Child Rescue Corps (http://www.herocorps.net/), a joint project of the National Association to Protect Children, U.S. Immigration and Customs Enforcement (ICE), and the U.S. Special Operations Command, in partnership with the national Internet Crimes Against Children (ICAC) task force program. The program recruits wounded U.S. veterans from elite military units, provides intensive training, and embeds them in law enforcement agencies as "human exploitation rescue operatives" or HEROs. ICE hired the first class of graduates. The program is being expanded and law enforcement agencies plan to hire 200 HERO graduates by 2018.

Since its inception, the National Association to Protect Children has fought and won campaigns in 28 states, has influenced the passage of 51 federal and state laws, has contributed to the development of software, secured over US$230 million in government spending assistance to law enforcement agencies, and helped train and employ 70 wounded veterans in the battle against child pornography.

National Rapporteur on Trafficking in Human Beings and Sexual Violence Against Children, the Netherlands

Following a ministerial conference on trafficking in women organized by the European Union and with the adoption of The Hague Declaration in 1997, the European Union recommended the appointment of national rapporteurs to report on the scale and nature of trafficking in human beings in European countries. National rapporteurs were encouraged to exchange ideas and promote mutual cooperation. Emphasis was placed on the need for reliable and comparable data on human trafficking in the European Union.

Following this Declaration, the Netherlands appointed A. G. Korvinus as the first National Rapporteur in 2000. It was the first country in the European Union to appoint an independent rapporteur on human trafficking. Six years later, in 2006, Corinne Dettmeijer-Vermeulen succeeded Korvinus in the role of National Rapporteur.

By a decision of the Ministry of Justice in 2009, the mandate of the Rapporteur was expanded to include investigating and reporting on child pornography and sexual crimes against children. In a subsequently published report, the National Rapporteur suggested to enlarge the mandate of its office to include monitoring and reporting on sexual violence as a whole. In 2012, the government implemented this recommendation and widened the mandate, changing the official name of the office to "National Rapporteur on Trafficking in Human Beings and Sexual Violence Against Children." In 2013, the position of the National Rapporteur was established by law preserving the independence of the office (The Second Chamber, Parliamentary year 2012–2013, 33 309, nr. 7).

The Act establishing the position of the National Rapporteur requires the Rapporteur:

"a) to conduct research into developments in the scale and nature of trafficking in human beings and sexual violence against children, as well as the effects of policy measures taken to tackle trafficking in human beings and sexual violence against children;

b) to provide advice to the government on policies to prevent and suppress trafficking in human beings and sexual violence against children;

c) to report periodically to the government by sending reports relating to trafficking in human beings and to sexual violence against children to the Minister of Security and Justice."

The Bureau of the Dutch Rapporteur maintains contact with and gathers information from governmental agencies and NGOs involved in the prevention, detection, prosecution, and the protection of victims of human trafficking and sexual violence against children. The Bureau of the National Rapporteur has access to all files held by the police, prosecution services, and judicial authorities. Because there is an international element to cases of human trafficking and sexual violence against children, the Bureau also has many contacts abroad and cooperates with international organizations. Due to her expertise in sexual violence against children, the Dutch National Rapporteur was recently asked to provide an amicus curiae brief to the lawyer of a victim appearing before the U.S. Supreme Court involving a case of child pornography (see *Paroline v. United States*).

The Bureau of the National Rapporteur releases periodic reports. The reports contain information on relevant regulations and legislation, as well as information on prevention, criminal investigations (regarding human trafficking, child pornography, and sexual violence against children), prosecution of perpetrators, and victim support. Reports contain information on the demographics of victims and offenders as well as government and NGO responses. They also contain policy recommendations aimed at improving the fight against human trafficking. In order to provide a solid report, the bureau collects data from stakeholders such as the police, prosecution service, courts, NGOs providing victim support, and has access to criminal files held by police and judicial authorities. The reports, the most detailed produced by any country in the world, can be downloaded from the website.

The Bureau of the National Rapporteur has placed the problem of human trafficking high on the political agenda in the Netherlands. It has increased awareness among police, prosecutors, and judges and has driven home the need for a victim-centered approach in investigations and trials and the need to tailor victim care to the specific needs of the victim. The National Rapporteur has made more than 200 recommendations to the Dutch government since its establishment in 2000. Many of these recommendations have been adopted by the government.

The Dutch model has proved so successful that it is frequently cited as a model of best practice. In its "Explanatory Report on the Convention on Action Against Trafficking in Human Beings" (para. 298), the Council of Europe explicitly refers other state parties to the Dutch model.

In 2009, an informal EU Network of National Rapporteurs or equivalent mechanisms was established in line with the EU Directive 36/2011 on human trafficking. They are tasked with the collection of national data and the monitoring of the implementation of anti-trafficking policy in their respective countries. Under the coordination of the European Commission, the network meets twice a year.

Office to Monitor and Combat Trafficking in Persons (U.S. Department of State)

The Office to Monitor and Combat Trafficking in Persons (TIP Office), of the U.S. Department of State, was established under the mandate of the U.S. Trafficking Victims Protection Act (TVPA) of 2000. Together with input from international organizations, foreign governments, civil society, and the private sector, the TIP Office works toward developing and implementing effective measures to combat human trafficking and slavery. Consistent with the emphasis of the UN Protocol to Prevent, Suppress and Punish Trafficking in Persons, especially Women and Children, supplementing the United Nations Convention Against Transnational Organized Crime, the TIP Office "pursues policies, partnerships and practices" to guarantee the implementation of the three Ps: prevention, (victim) protection, and prosecution (of offenders). There are a number of sections within the TIP Office tasked with different responsibilities.

The Public Engagement section liaises with the media, civil society, the private sector, academics and research institutes, international organizations, government agencies and Congress to build partnerships, raise awareness of the problem of human trafficking, and help strengthen efforts to combat it.

The International Programs section is responsible for the disbursement of funds (over US$250 million since 2002) in foreign assistance to more than 800 anti-trafficking projects in countries around the world. This section monitors projects and provides assistance to those organizations receiving grants. The four focal areas within this section are Research and Innovation (supporting projects that examine new approaches to combating trafficking), Training and Technical Assistance (to both civil society and governments), Bilateral and Regional (support to multiyear projects promoting the three Ps), and Emergency Victim Assistance.

The Reports and Political Affairs section is responsible for engaging foreign governments to improve their approach to the "three P" paradigm. Representatives from the TIP Office and U.S. missions meet with foreign government officials to identify trafficking trends and assess progress in anti-trafficking measures. This section is responsible for contributions to the annual U.S. Trafficking in Persons, or TIP report.

The TIP report appraises government efforts to implement measures to comply with the standards set forth in Section 108 of the U.S. Trafficking Victims Protection Act. The report, published since 2001, now includes 188 countries and territories, which are ranked into tiers based upon their efforts to comply with the minimum standards set forth in the TVPA. Country reports delineate measures and programs in all countries and territories and each country report contains recommendations for improvement. Additionally, the annual reports contain information on current or new patterns of trafficking. The 2016 TIP report highlights ways in which governments can identify at-risk populations and reduce their vulnerability to trafficking, as well as such timely topics as human trafficking in conflict zones. Each year the report highlights organizations and individuals who have made a special contribution to combating trafficking, whether through victim protection, law enforcement, and prosecution, or prevention measures. The TIP report is the most comprehensive international report on measures being implemented worldwide to address human trafficking.

Polaris Project

Moved by what they had learned about in a class, two Brown University students, Katherine Chon and Derek Ellerman, created a nonprofit organization focused on eliminating human trafficking and modern-day slavery in 2002. They named the organization Polaris Project, after the North Star that guided escaped slaves using the Underground Railroad to freedom in the North. The Polaris Project was one of the first NGOs in the United States to focus attention on sex and labor trafficking affecting men, women, and children. It has since expanded its activities to deal with victims of trafficking for forced criminal activities and domestic service, and trafficking affecting the LGBT (lesbian, gay, bisexual, and transgender) community.

The organization is based on a three-part model to systematically disrupt trafficking by immediately and effectively responding to victims, by equipping important stakeholders and communities to prevent and address human trafficking, and by implementing targeted campaigns to disrupt the business of human trafficking. The goals of the organization are achieved through a number of programs.

Polaris has been running the National Human Trafficking Resource Center (NHTRC) Hotline since 2007. This is a 24 hour/7 days a week/365 days a year toll-free hotline manned by trained anti-trafficking advocates in English and Spanish. Communication in more than 200 languages is available using a teleprompting service. Between December 2007 and April 2013, the hotline took 72,000 calls, reported 3,000 cases of human trafficking to law enforcement, and connected 8,300 survivors to support and services. In 2013, the organization launched the BeFree Textline. In addition to the national hotline, which services victims and survivors as well as others who wish to anonymously report a suspected case of human trafficking, the NHTRC provides technical assistance, innovative training, and capacity-building support. The NHTRC online Referral Directory provides a list of organizations by geographical area and services provided to trafficked victims and survivors.

In Washington, D.C., Polaris provides immediate services to trafficked victims, including crisis intervention, counseling, and case management.

Polaris has been pivotal in advocating for improved legislation and government policy to strengthen anti-trafficking laws and improve services to victims. Its expertise is extended to the public and private sectors where Polaris provides solutions tailored to the needs of its stakeholders. In close collaboration with the International Labor Recruitment Working Group and the Alliance to End Slavery, Polaris is working to support state and federal legislation that protects workers on temporary visas from exploitative labor and trafficking.

Data analysis is another important aspect of Polaris's work. The organization publishes statistics on the number of calls and text messages received by the NHTRC and the number of cases investigated and provides a breakdown of the cases by type of exploitation and by state. The data are used to understand the markets into which people are trafficked as well as the scope and size of the problem in the United States.

The organization has expanded beyond the borders of the United States and has begun collaboration with governments, law enforcement, service providers, and hotlines to share data and strategies to impact regional cross-border trafficking. Noting that trafficked victims in the United States are often from outside of the region, Polaris has begun conducting hotline training in Mexico and countries in the Middle East, Eastern Europe, and Southeast Asia, hosting the first bilateral meeting between workers on hotlines in Thailand and Vietnam. Polaris is becoming a global player in identifying an international network of support for victims and for facilitating the creation of hotlines in countries around the world. Together with La Strada International and Liberty Asia, and with the support of Google's US$3 million Global Impact Award in 2013, Polaris launched the Global Human Trafficking Hotline Network.

Of significance is the Global Modern Slavery Directory, which contains to date information on 2,055 organizations. Searches can be conducted by country (or by state in the United States or by city in other countries). Information on each organization indicates the population served, the type of exploitation (sex trafficking, labor trafficking, forced marriage, etc.), the services provided by the organization and the languages spoken by personnel working at the establishment. The directory enables stakeholders—law enforcement, advocates, service providers, and policy makers—to identify organizations providing service to victims in countries around the world. The mapping exercise also allows Polaris to identify areas where services for victims are absent.

Najibullah Quraishi

Najibullah Quraishi grew up and attended high school from 1986 to 1990 in Mazar-e-Sharif, Afghanistan. From 1991 to 1995, he studied production and directing (BA degree) at Balkh University in the same city. Between 1995 and 1997, Quraishi worked as a reporter for the Afghan Ministry of the Interior, followed by work as a producer of a social affairs program for Afghan national television, and as a cameraman and reporter for a weekly program on youth issues. In 2001, Quraishi left Afghanistan after being almost beaten to death while investigating the massacre of prisoners during the war.

Quraishi moved to the United Kingdom in 2002, and has since worked as chief investigator, cameraman, reporter, and director for the documentary film company Clover Films, covering topics in the Middle East and Asia. Since then, Quraishi has produced a number of award-winning documentary films: *Afghan Massacre—The Convoy of Death; Behind Taliban Lines; The Dancing Boys of Afghanistan; Fight for Al-Qaeda; Opium Brides; Taliban Child Fighters; The Other Side of War; Growing Up Behind Bars; The Lions Last Roar?; The Girls of the Taliban; Living Beneath the Drones; ISIL and the Taliban/ISIS in Afghanistan.*

In 2009, he founded Quraishi Films, a London-based documentary production company focusing on stories from conflict and post-conflict zones. His company works closely with Clover Films, the producer of *The Dancing Boys of Afghanistan.*

Through award-winning investigative journalism, Quraishi exposes practices of human trafficking involving child soldiers through the (forced) recruitment of children as suicide bombers (*Taliban Child Fighters* 2013), the exchange of young children as payment for debt in Afghanistan (*Opium Brides* 2012), and the enslavement and sexual abuse of young boys (*Dancing Boys of Afghanistan* 2010). All three of these films have won numerous prestigious awards.

In *Opium Brides*, Quraishi shows the terrible consequences of the eradication and crop substitution programs of the UN Office on Drugs and Crime and the Afghan government's good intentions to destroy poppy crops. Under the protection of NATO and International Security Assistance Forces (ISAF), Afghan government officials themselves, or by forcing farmers, destroy fields of poppies. The terrible consequence of the eradication of their crops is that farmers, some of whom have taken out loans from smugglers to purchase more land, end up with debts that cannot be paid off. As repayment for the debt or failed crops, drug smugglers have been known to kidnap or bargain with the parents to obtain a child, often a girl as young as six or seven, who is sold into marriage to a drug smuggler or drug lord. The documentary won an Emmy for outstanding investigative journalism.

Quraishi's film, *Taliban Child Fighters* introduces Niaz, a young boy kidnapped at the age of eight and primed by the Taliban for a suicide mission at a military checkpoint. The child escaped the Taliban at night and turned himself in to Afghan police. He is now in an orphanage. Other children, as young as 12, have been arrested for planting mines or preparing ambushes on ISAF troops. These adolescents are locked in a juvenile prison in Gazni City. In an unconfirmed video in this documentary, an adolescent boy is coaxed by Taliban fighters into becoming a suicide bomber, despite his fear and resistance.

In *The Dancing Boys of Afghanistan*, the practice of *bacha bazi* (meaning "boy play") is exposed. Boys, sometimes as young as 11, are trained to sing and dance, wear women's clothing, and perform in front of all-male audiences. The boys are often "sold" to the highest bidder, and then sexually abused. Exposing himself to danger, Quraishi's film documents a practice that everyone in Afghanistan knows exists but no one wants to admit it is occurring. The viewer witnesses crushing poverty, government corruption, and powerful mujahedeen warlords responsible for the abuse of these young boys. The documentary exposes the experiences of a number of *bacha bazi* boys, while following the training and life of a young boy identified in the film as Shafiq. Fearing for his own safety, Quraishi, at one point, is forced to leave Afghanistan. Upon returning to the United Kingdom, he and producer Jamie Doran sought the help of a powerful warlord to remove Shafiq from his owner, only to be told that Shafiq had died. With persistent efforts in finding out what had happened to Shafiq and after further investigation, it appeared Shafiq was alive. Shafiq was removed with the help of one of the most powerful warlords in Afghanistan, and, to protect him, he and his family were resettled to another district at an unknown location. Quraishi visited Shafiq on another trip to Afghanistan and brought funds and personal contributions from the producers and Frontline staff to help support the family and provide for Shafiq's education. Quraishi and Doran have made efforts to monitor the family's welfare and Quraishi makes occasional visits.

Quraishi, Doran, and the making of *The Dancing Boys of Afghanistan* have not only protected an innocent young boy from serious harm and abuse, but also this documentary has done more than anything ever written or produced about *bacha bazi* to expose the practice and the corruption that keeps it alive. When the film was broadcast in Afghanistan, it was a great source of embarrassment to the Afghan government. But that was not enough to put an end to the practice. In accepting the 2011 Hillman Prize for Broadcast Journalism for *The Dancing Boys of Afghanistan*, Quraishi explains that the number of children abused is beginning to fall. But, he argues, those perpetrating these crimes against children are former military who fought alongside British and American troops. It is essential that allied governments pressure Kabul to put an end to this practice.

STOP THE TRAFFIK

STOP THE TRAFFIK, founded in 2006, is an international movement with over 55,000 activists working in more than

60 countries worldwide. Individuals, frontline professionals, organizations, faith-based groups, schools, charities, and businesses are all part of STOP THE TRAFFIK. The global office is located in London, with eight affiliates across the world in Australia, Brazil, Canada, Germany, the Netherlands, New Zealand, the United Kingdom, and the United States. STOP THE TRAFFIK, through campaigning and using data, seeks to disrupt trafficking operations and prevent trafficking by raising awareness and making individuals and communities more resilient. The organization and its partners work together on preventing and disrupting human trafficking based on the organization's Theory of Change. "Act locally and campaign globally" calls upon individuals to educate their community to make it harder for traffickers to exploit people within the local community. Change occurs through community transformation, global campaigning, and gathering and sharing knowledge.

This advocacy organization seeks to create a "traffik free" world through numerous measures. First and foremost, the organization aims at awareness raising and educating people on what simple measures can be taken to eradicate forced labor and exploitation in their home communities in specific industries.

One of the most prominent campaigns this organization has been involved in, beginning in 2007, was the Traffik Free Chocolate campaign. STOP THE TRAFFIK has ranked the major producers of chocolate based upon the criteria of certification of the product, report on money spent, ensuring a living income for cocoa farmers, and impact assessment. STOP THE TRAFFIK raises consumer awareness and advises us how we as consumers can influence companies to eradicate trafficking in their supply chains and ensure worker safety. Leading producers of chocolate such as Cadbury, Mars, and Nestlé have taken steps toward greater transparency in their supply chains.

Similar campaigns have also been launched to raise awareness and stop exploitation in the manufacturing industry—cotton, textile, and garment supply chains—where the exploitation of young women and girls have been documented, and in the production of tea. STOP THE TRAFFIK has designed the "Make Fashion Traffik Free" Protocol—a commitment to ensure that businesses (and any manufactures, suppliers, or subcontractors across the supply chain) commit to transparency, ensuring that there is no trafficked labor and that workers' rights are protected. Regular, independent, unannounced, third party, independent auditing, and off-site worker interviews must occur to ensure protections are in place and are being abided by. Results in measures taken and audits should be made public. STOP THE TRAFFIK is encouraging retailers and brands to commit to the Protocol. Similar to this, the organization ran a third campaign—"Not My Cup of Tea"—to raise awareness of exploitation in Assam's (India's) tea gardens.

STOP THE TRAFFIK was a leader and spent two years during the consultation period in working toward inclusion of the supply chain transparency requirement in the United Kingdom's 2015 Modern Slavery Act. The organization helped influence the U.K. legislation, which requires leaders of businesses with a turnover of £36 million, to state what they are doing to eradicate modern slavery from their supply chains if they do business in Britain (section 54 of the Modern Slavery Act 2015). This makes the United Kingdom a leader in fighting modern-day slavery in business supply chains. STOP THE TRAFFIK has encouraged other countries to adopt similar legislation. STOP THE TRAFFIK has worked with law firms around the world which have donated time and resources to prepare draft laws for consideration in 28 countries.

The organization is working toward an Intelligence-Led Prevention Program, by partnering with IBM Cloud Data Service and a leading global communications marketing firm to create a center for data on human trafficking. The strategic team includes members from the law enforcement (the U.K.'s National Crime Agency) and legal community. Additionally,

STOP THE TRAFFIK provides individuals and businesses with awareness-raising tools to start campaigns and raise awareness in their communities.

The strength of this organization is its ability and willingness to reach out to the general public and provide individuals with all the tools they need to start campaigns to raise awareness in their communities. STOP THE TRAFFIK has prepared fliers with information on trafficking and the number of the national hotline for individuals to download and disseminate. It has prepared signs for hotels and taxis and for individuals working in those branches who want to take a stand against human trafficking. For those who want to do more and raise funds for STOP THE TRAFFIK, the organization provides suggestions on fund-raising events and all the tools necessary to launch the event. The organization's logo and other materials may be used in fund-raising events. STOP THE TRAFFIK has opened petitions and prepared letters for individuals to sign and email back to STOP THE TRAFFIK—the organization promises to deliver the letters to CEOs of the particular companies at which the campaign is aimed.

Truckers Against Trafficking

Truckers Against Trafficking (TAT) began in 2009, becoming an independent nonprofit educational and advocacy organization in 2011. The organization aims to educate, empower, and mobilize the trucking industry to recognize and respond to human trafficking within the context of the industry's regular jobs.

Since 2009, TAT has partnered with hundreds of public and private trucking schools and trucking companies, almost all state trucking associations, hundreds of companies, and major truck stops. The organization has also partnered with law enforcement, disseminating materials to train drivers to recognize the signs of human trafficking, how to approach potential victims, and where to report suspicious activities.

Materials include a training DVD (with interviews from trafficking survivors) and wallet cards with contact numbers and questions to ask children or women who appear to be in danger.

If solicited for prostitution, truckers are trained to ask persons if they need help. They are trained to pay particular attention to language and to avoid such words as "prostitute," "lot lizard" (a derogatory term used for women and girls soliciting for prostitution at truck stops, parking lots, and rest areas), or "john" (the customer of a prostitute), but encouraged to use the terms "prostituted person," "victim," "survivor," and "customer." They are trained to recognize that persons are not "*what has been done to them*. They aren't prostitutes. They have been prostituted" and that "there is NO such thing as a 'child prostitute' or a 'teen prostitute'." Anyone under the age of 18 being sold for commercial sex is a *victim* of sex trafficking (according to the U.S. Trafficking Victim's Protection Act). Truckers are trained to ask questions to a suspected victim, such as "Are you being watched?" or "Are you being paid?"

Truckers are not just trained to respond if solicited for prostitution; they are also trained to observe other potentially dangerous or suspicious situations—like young (runaway) girls asking for rides, a crude tattoo on a young person's neck, or a frightened, lost look on the face of a young girl who is in the company of men. This training and awareness paid off when, at a rest stop, long-haul truck driver Kevin Kimmel viewed the face of a gaunt young woman behind the black drape covering the window of a parked recreational vehicle. The woman was jerked away from the window a second later. Finding this suspicious, Kimmel called the police. His call resulted in the rescue of a 20-year-old woman who had been kidnapped, tortured, starved, and forced into prostitution.

There are more truckers out on the roads, streets, and highways than law enforcement officers. Many travel interstate and stop at places that have traditionally been used as prostitution meeting points. They are a tremendous asset to police and anti-trafficking service groups. TAT has paired up with other organizations to help raise awareness and provide information to victims. Knowing that victims are often left only to use the bathroom, organizations have started wrapping bars of soap with the hotline number and truckers are helping place them in the restrooms of gas stations and hotels across the country. Truckers also leave a stack of fliers featuring TAT's steering wheel logo and national hotline number near the road map rack at gas stations.

Outreach materials are spreading across the industry to busses and taxis, service areas, and rest stops. The window decals produced by Truckers Against Trafficking (asking "Do you need help" and containing the number of the national hotline) adorn the trucks of companies such as Walmart. Vigilante Trucking has painted entire trailers with anti-trafficking messages and parks them at truck stops.

Another awareness-raising project is the Freedom Drivers Project (FDP), a 48-foot trailer mobile exhibit used to educate members of the trucking industry and general public about domestic sex trafficking and how the trucking industry is combating it. The truck includes a theater, actual artifacts from women and children who have been victims of trafficking, and portraits of real Truckers Against Trafficking and how they are working to end human trafficking. For many, this is their first exposure to human trafficking in the United States. Visitors are educated about what steps they can take to deal with a potential situation of trafficking.

In addition to building coalitions with other organizations with which the trucking industry works closely together, other important milestones have been met. The organization has produced and distributed over 25,000 training DVDs. Over one million wallet cards have been distributed. Truckers have made over 1,464 calls to the NHTRC to report possible cases of trafficking. Four hundred and fifty-two "likely" human trafficking cases were reported, involving 992 trafficking victims, of which 270 were minors.

On April 22, 2015, TAT was lauded for its work in raising the public's awareness at the annual Congressional Victims' Rights Caucus Awards. TAT is also the winner of the Norma Hotaling Award for Demand Reduction. The State Department, via their International Visitors Leadership Program, has asked TAT to consult with a number of countries regarding its model. The United Nations honored the work of TAT by including the organization in the United Nations' 100 Best Practices list to combat human trafficking.

Harriet Tubman (circa 1820–1913)

Harriet Tubman was born into slavery in Dorchester County, Maryland. She was one of nine children. Although the exact date of her birth is unknown, she is believed to have been born somewhere between 1820 and 1825. Three of her sisters were sold by the owner's son. When another buyer came to take possession of the youngest son in the family, Harriet's mother threatened to kill him. As a result of this action, Harriet's mother not only saved her young son from being removed from her care, but may have provided Harriet a very important lesson in resistance.

As a young child, Harriet (who was born Araminta "Miny" Ross and later took the name Harriet in honor of her mother) was a house servant; as an adolescent, she was sent out to work in the fields. Her owner hired her out on a number of occasions. At one household, she was subjected to regular beatings. Harriet suffered a particularly serious injury as an adolescent, and one which would affect her for the remainder of her life. While at a store, she was told by the overseer of a slave who had left the fields without permission to restrain the slave. Harriet refused, and was accidently hit in the head by a two-pound weight that was meant to hit the runaway slave. As a result of this injury, Harriet began having hallucinations, vivid dreams, and narcoleptic seizures that continued throughout her life.

Araminta Ross married John Tubman, a free black man, and took his last name. Four years later, in 1849, Harriet, fearing she and other slaves would be sold, decided to escape the plantation. With the assistance of a white abolitionist, Tubman followed the North Star (Polaris), finally reaching Philadelphia (Pennsylvania was a free state). She worked there cleaning houses and was able to save some money before returning to Maryland the following year to rescue her niece and her niece's two children. She returned again to rescue her brother and two other men. Upon returning a third time to rescue her husband, she found out he had remarried. It was during this trip that she found other slaves and escorted them to the North. She is responsible for rescuing her 70-year-old parents, a difficult trip for Tubman as they were frail and unable to walk long distances.

Harriet Tubman became the most well-known of all the "conductors" of the Underground Railroad, earning her the nickname of Moses, for leading her people out of slavery to the promised land of freedom. Between trips, Tubman worked and saved her money in order to travel South and free more slaves. She acquired such a reputation among supporters of the Underground Railroad that they began giving her shelter and funds to support her trips. Between 1850 and 1860, Tubman made numerous trips to Southern states and escorted countless slaves, many of them family members, to freedom (a 19th-century biography of Tubman claims 19 trips and 300 slaves; Tubman herself credits her actions with saving 50 people. Historians believe she may have saved as many as 70 people via the Underground Railroad in 13 different trips). She did this at great peril to her own safety. A bounty offering a large reward had been placed on her head. Additionally, the 1850 Fugitive Slave Act threatened severe punishment to anyone assisting a slave to escape.

Tubman remained illiterate all her life. Yet her deep faith and common sense allowed her to continue dangerous journeys to free slaves. She often worked in the winter months or at night, when bounty hunters or people who may have detected the movement of escaped slaves were indoors. Saturdays were a favorite day for rescues; Tubman knew the newspaper advertisements would not appear until Monday morning, buying her two extra days before notices of escaped slaves appeared. She is said to have once "hidden in plain sight" by pretending to read—the wanted notice described Tubman as illiterate. She is said to have carried a gun on her freedom runs.

During the Civil War, Harriet Tubman served as a cook, nurse, scout, and spy. She was the first woman to lead an armed expedition and is credited with guiding the raid at Combahee Ferry, South Carolina, liberating more than 700 slaves. After the War and the Emancipation Proclamation, Tubman returned to Auburn, New York. She became involved in the suffragette movement (working together with Susan B. Anthony) and raised money to open schools for African American children. On March 18, 1869, Tubman married her second husband, Nelson Davis, 22 years her junior. In 1874 they adopted their daughter, Gertie.

Tubman continued her activism and humanitarian contributions, which brought her national recognition honoring her contributions to the nation, but left her in poverty. She was able to support herself and her family through maintaining a vegetable garden and through donations.

Harriet Tubman had always been religious. Religious visions, she claimed, had given her the strength to make the numerous rescue missions. Harriet became actively involved in the African Methodist Episcopal Zion Church in Auburn and donated a piece of land to the church with the wish that it be used as the grounds for a home for "aged and indigent coloured people." The home was opened in June 1908, and it is here that Harriet Tubman died in 1913. She was buried with semi-military honors in Auburn's Fort Hill Cemetery.

Tubman, the abolitionist, humanitarian activist, and suffragette, honored in her lifetime and in death, will appear on the US$20 bill, expected to be unveiled in 2020.

United Nations Office on Drugs and Crime

The Office for Drug Control and Crime Prevention was established in 1997 when the UN International Drug Control Programme was merged with the Centre for International Crime Prevention. In 2002, the organization was renamed the UN Office on Drugs and Crime (UNODC). The organization is headquartered in Vienna, Austria, and through a network of field and regional offices around the world, is focused on combating transnational crime and drug problems. The organization raises global awareness and assists Member States in the key areas of criminal justice and prison reform, corruption, crime and drug prevention (to include treatment and care, HIV and AIDS), human trafficking and migrant smuggling, terrorism prevention, organized crime, and money laundering.

There are three main approaches to tackling these criminal justice and crime issues. UNODC supports technical cooperation projects in the field to enhance the capacity of Member States to effectively prevent, investigate, and prosecute crimes. It supports research and analysis to provide knowledge to guide evidence-based policy and operational decisions. It further assists Member States in ratifying and implementing international treaties that deal with crime, drugs, and terrorism.

The UN Convention Against Transnational Organized Crime and the protocols thereto, in particular the Protocol to Prevent, Suppress, and Punish Trafficking in Persons, Especially Women and Children, supplementing the UN Convention Against Transnational Organized Crime, have become synonymous with UNODC. The convention and two of the protocols were adopted by the General Assembly in resolution 55/25, November 15, 2000. What has come to be known as the "Palermo Protocol" or "Trafficking Protocol" provided the world with an agreed-upon (albeit contentiously debated) definition of human trafficking, and one which focused additionally on the rights and protection of trafficked persons (Articles 6 through 8) as well as on prevention. The Trafficking Protocol entered into force on December 25, 2003. Since that time, UNODC has fought tirelessly for the ratification of the protocol by Member States and has developed a Model Law against Trafficking in Persons to assist states in developing domestic legislation in line with the Trafficking Protocol. To further strengthen a country's response to trafficking, UNODC has developed numerous manuals, such as the *Toolkit to Combat Trafficking in Persons, Combating Trafficking in Persons: A Handbook for Parliamentarians, First Aid Kit for Use by Law Enforcement Responders in Addressing Human Trafficking,* and *Assessment Toolkit: Trafficking in Persons for the Purpose of Organ Removal.* These toolkits, training materials, and strategy documents facilitate the implementation of measures to combat human trafficking.

UNODC's Blue Heart Campaign (so named because of the "cold-heartedness of those who buy and sell fellow human beings") is an initiative to raise global awareness and inspire action to combat human trafficking. The campaign aims to mobilize political support and action to fight criminals and support victims. UNODC administers the UN Trust for Victims of Trafficking in Persons, Especially Women and Children. The trust supports NGOs that provide medical and legal aid, psychological assistance, job training, and safe houses. Between its launch in 2010 and 2014, the Trust Fund supported 11 projects in Albania, Cambodia, Costa Rica, the Czech Republic, France, Kenya, Israel, Moldova, Nepal, Nigeria, and the United States, benefiting over 2,000 victims of human trafficking.

The organization's Human Trafficking Knowledge Portal comprises a case law database and a database of legislation. The human trafficking case law database includes more than a 1,000 cases of human trafficking from countries around the world, detailing trafficking routes, demographic information on traffickers and their victims, verdicts and court arguments, and sentences. The database is relevant to researchers and others trying to understand how persons are trafficked and how perpetrators are convicted. The database on legislation contains laws relevant to the Convention on Transnational Organized Crime and the protocols thereto. As of August 2016, the database contained 309 pieces of legislation relevant to human trafficking.

A recent project launched by UNODC in collaboration with the European Union, and being implemented in partnership with UNICEF and the IOM, is the four-year Global Action against Trafficking in Persons and the Smuggling of Migrants (2015–2019) or GloACT. This project will be implemented in countries across Africa (Egypt, Mali, Morocco, Niger, South Africa), Asia (Kyrgyzstan, Lao PDR, Nepal, Pakistan), Eastern Europe (Belarus, Ukraine), and Latin America (Brazil, Colombia), with the aim of assisting governments, civil society organizations, smuggled migrants, and trafficked persons. The counter-smuggling and counter-trafficking initiatives will be implemented through strategy and policy development, assistance in strengthening legislation, capacity building between government and civil society, as well as the strengthening of regional and transregional cooperation and increased protection and assistance to smuggled migrants and victims of human trafficking, in particular children.

This chapter introduces global data on human trafficking focusing on victims, markets of exploitation, human traffickers, government responses, and heroes whose anti-trafficking measures have made a difference in the world. The chapter also includes various documents from NGOs, international organizations, and government sources to help the reader develop a deeper understanding of how victims become survivors, what trafficking indicators to look for, the U.S. law dealing with human trafficking, recent U.S. legislation, the relationship between human trafficking and corruption, and how trafficking can be fought in the global supply chain.

Data

It is difficult to obtain reliable data on trafficking in persons. Due to its clandestine nature, victims and traffickers represent hidden populations. The United Nations seeks to obtain data on human trafficking for its Global Trafficking in Persons report, but warns that "the amounts of data that form the basis

---

Street kids, runaways, or children living in poverty can fall under the control of traffickers who force them into begging rings. Children are sometimes intentionally disfigured to attract more money from passersby. Victims of organized begging rings are often beaten or injured if they do not bring in enough money. They are also vulnerable to sexual abuse. (Kay Chernush for the U.S. State Department)

for the different analyses vary" (UNODC, 2014, 18), so that data may be available on the age but not the gender of victims or perpetrators (e.g., the total number of reported victims is 40,177, but data on gender according to form of exploitation are available for only 22,405 victims). The data provided in Tables 5.1 through 5.9 are generated from the 2014 UN Global Trafficking in Persons report, the most recent data available at the time this book went to publication. More recent UNODC data will be available in the Global Trafficking in Persons Report, due for release in December 2016.

Victims and Forms of Exploitation

While the data are not complete due to our inability to locate all victims, they do, however, provide insight into patterns and trafficking trends in different parts of the world where victims and traffickers have been identified. For the purpose of comparing trends over the last ten years, the reader is encouraged to access previous Trafficking in Persons reports published by UNODC.

Worldwide aggregate data (Table 5.1) show that the majority of victims are adult women (almost half of all victims) followed by girls (21%), boys (12%), and adult men (18%). Taken together, children comprise a larger percentage of identified victims (33%) than identified adult male victims. The large number of girls and women identified as victims in this sample is attributed in part to the fact that sexual exploitation was

Table 5.1   Detected Victims of Trafficking by Age and Gender, 2011

Age/Gender	Percentage
Adult Women	49
Adult Men	18
Girls	21
Boys	12

Source: UNODC, Global Report on Trafficking in Persons, 2014, p. 9.

identified as the major form of exploitation among detected victims of trafficking (53%; Table 5.2).

There has been an increase, over the years, of the number of detected victims of human trafficking for forced labor (and a subsequent decrease in the number of victims of trafficking for sexual exploitation). Between 2007 and 2011, the percentage of victims of forced labor has risen slowly from 32 percent in 2007 to 40 percent of all detected victims of trafficking in 2011. The data in Table 5.3 indicate that there are differences between regions of the distribution of detected victims of forced labor by age and gender. While adult men and boys make up the majority of detected victims in the Americas and Europe and Central Asia (68% and 69%, respectively), women and girls make up the majority in Africa and the Middle East (55%) and East Asia, South Asia, and the Pacific (77%).

Table 5.2 Forms of Exploitation among Detected Victims of Trafficking, 2011

Type of Exploitation	Percentage
Sexual exploitation	53
Forced labor	40
Organ removal	0.3
Other forms of exploitation	7

Source: UNODC, Global Report on Trafficking in Persons, 2014, p. 9.

Table 5.3 Gender Breakdown of Detected Victims of Trafficking for Forced Labor by Region, 2010–2012 (or More Recent)

Region	Adult Men and Boys (%)	Adult Women and Girls (%)
Africa and the Middle East	45	55
Americas	68	32
East Asia, South Asia, and the Pacific	23	77
Europe and Central Asia	69	31

Source: UNODC, Global Report on Trafficking in Persons, 2014, p. 10.

Table 5.4 Forms of Exploitation among Detected Trafficking Victims by Region of Detection, 2010–2012 (or More Recent)

Region	Sexual Exploitation (%)	Forced Labor, Servitude, and Slavery-like Practices (%)	Other Forms of Exploitation (%)
Africa and the Middle East	53	37	10
Americas	48	47	4
East Asia, South Asia, and the Pacific	26	64	10
Europe and Central Asia	66	26	8

Source: UNODC, Global Report on Trafficking in Persons, 2014, p. 5.

According to aggregate statistics, the largest percentage of detected victims globally was found in forced sexual exploitation. The forms of exploitation among detected victims of trafficking differ by region of detection (Table 5.4). Whereas the majority detected victims of sexual exploitation were found in Africa and the Middle East (53%) and Europe and Central Asia (66%), the opposite pattern is found in East Asia, South Asia, and the Pacific, where most detected victims of exploitation were found in forced labor. In three regions (Africa and the Middle East; East Asia, South Asia, and the Pacific; and Europe and Central Asia), between 8 and 10 percent of detected victims were identified in other forms of exploitation.

Trafficking Flows

Tables 5.5 and 5.6 show trafficking flows by geographical reach and the percentage of identified victims by subregional and transregional trafficking. Trafficking occurs most frequently within a country or between neighboring countries (or those nearby) within a subregion. These flows account for 71 percent

Table 5.5   Trafficking Flows by Geographical Reach, 2010–2012 (or More Recent)

Flow	Percentage
Transnational (transregional)	26
Cross-border within the same subregion	37
From nearby subregion	3
Domestic (within national borders)	34

Source: UNODC, Global Report on Trafficking in Persons, 2014, p. 8.

of all trafficking flows. Slightly more than a quarter (26%) of detected trafficking flows are transnational or transregional or from nearby subregions (3%) (Table 5.5).

Trafficking patterns vary according to region and subregion. While trafficking in South Asia, East Asia, and the Pacific, Sub-Saharan Africa, Eastern Europe, and Central Asia, and South America is almost exclusively domestic and subregional trafficking (between 94% and 99% of all detected victims), the subregion Middle East and North Africa shows the exact opposite pattern (Table 5.6). More than two-thirds of victims of trafficking come from outside the region. The majority are East Asians (33%), South Asians (18%), Sub-Saharan Africans (10%), and South and Central Asians (6%). This large influx of foreign workers to the Middle East (predominantly the Gulf States) can be attributed to the small local population and the high demand for unskilled migrant laborers in these states (Aronowitz, 2015a). Western and Central Europe are unique and it is the only region in which victims from every subregion have been identified. The pattern in North and Central America and the Caribbean is predominantly from within the country or the subregion (58%). With respect to transnational trafficking into this region, a quarter of all victims identified are East Asians, with smaller numbers of victims coming from Central Europe (5%), South Asia (7%), and South America (3%; UNODC, 2014).

Table 5.6   Shares of Detected Victims by Subregional and Transregional Trafficking

Region	Within the Subregion or Country	From Outside the Subregion — Transnational
North America, Central America, and the Caribbean	58%	42%
South America	94%	6%
Western and Central Europe	61%	39%
Eastern Europe and Central Asia	99%	1%
North Africa and the Middle East	32%	68%
Sub-Saharan Africa	97%	3%
South Asia	96%	4%
East Asia and the Pacific	97%	3%

Source: UNODC, Global Report on Trafficking in Persons, 2014, Map 5, p. 39.

Criminal Justice Responses to Trafficking

The number of countries around the world which have criminalized trafficking in persons has increased since 2003. Since that time, the share of countries criminalizing trafficking in persons, partially or in full compliance with the UN Trafficking in Persons Protocol has increased from 42 percent in November 2003 to 95 percent in August 2014 (UNODC, 2014). Countries in certain geographical regions of the world provide no legislative coverage (Africa and the Middle East), or partial legislative coverage (Asia and South America). Despite an increase in the share of countries providing some legislative coverage, UNODC (2014, 52) reports that "about one third of the world's population—some 2 billion people—live in a situation where trafficking is not criminalized as required by the UN Trafficking in Persons Protocol."

Conviction of human traffickers remains problematic. While some countries are extremely successful at prosecuting offenders, others, despite adequate legislation, have not been able to successfully prosecute traffickers for their crimes. UNODC reports that "While more countries in the world now have solid legislation in place, the number of convictions is stable at a very low level more or less everywhere" (UNODC, 2014, 54). If one examines the number of convictions recorded per year, 41 percent of the countries had no or fewer than 10 convictions, while only 16 percent of the countries had more than 50 convictions (Table 5.7).

Even if a person involved in human trafficking is detected, the likelihood of a conviction is low. UNODC estimates the risk of facing a conviction for human trafficking when a person has been identified by the police. At the global level, approximately one in four persons identified as being involved in trafficking will face prosecution in the first instance. Of 100 persons investigated by the police, 45 of those will be prosecuted and only 24 of those prosecuted will be convicted in the first instance (UNODC, 2014).

Worldwide, between 2010 and 2012, 33,860 suspects were identified, 34,256 persons were prosecuted, and 13,310 persons were convicted. With respect to traffickers, the majority of detected suspects of trafficking are male (62%) and 38 percent are female. With respect to prosecutions (Table 5.8), the majority of those prosecuted are males (68%) and an even greater percentage of those convicted are male (72% compared to 28% female; UNODC, 2014).

Table 5.7 Number of Convictions Recorded per Year, Share of Countries, 2010–2012

No convictions	15%
Less than 10 convictions	26%
Between 10 and 50 convictions	26%
More than 50 convictions	16%
Information not available	17%

Source: UNODC, 2014, Figure 28, p. 54.

Table 5.8   Persons as Suspects, Persons Prosecuted, and Persons
Convicted by Gender, 2010–2012

Suspects by Gender		Prosecutions by Gender		Convictions by Gender	
Male	Female	Male	Female	Male	Female
62%	38%	68%	32%	72%	28%

Source: UNODC, 2014.

A greater percentage of women are tried and convicted of human trafficking than other crimes. According to UNODC (2014, 27), "For most other crimes, the share of females among the total number of convicted persons is in the range of 10–15 percent" (citing UN Surveys on Crime Trends and the Operations of Criminal Justice Systems). In Eastern Europe and Central Asia, 46 percent of persons prosecuted were women, and women account for an astounding 56 percent of those prosecuted in the region. The figures for prosecutions and convictions are only slightly lower for South America (45% and 40%, respectively), and North America, Central America, and the Caribbean (43% and 33%, respectively; UNODC, 2014; see Table 5.9). This high number of women involved in the crime of trafficking may have to do with the more visible roles that women play in the trafficking process, recruiting, escorting, or collecting money from victims.

Globally, 64 percent of convicted traffickers are nationals of the countries in which the trafficking occurred. An additional 22 percent were from the countries in the same region. Only 14 percent of those convicted of trafficking were foreigners from other regions (UNODC, 2014). These figures differ depending upon whether one is looking at countries of origin or destination. In countries of origin, 95 percent of offenders are nationals of the country. This may be due to the fact that much of the trafficking is domestic or that offenders are arrested for recruitment. In countries of destination, 42 percent of offenders are nationals of the country, while 58 percent are non-nationals (UNODC, 2014).

Table 5.9 Suspects, Prosecutions, and Convictions by Gender and Region

Region	Suspects by Gender		Prosecutions by Gender		Convictions by Gender	
	Male	Female	Male	Female	Male	Female
Global data	62%	38%	68%	32%	72%	28%
Western and Central Europe	Not available	Not available	77%	23%	78%	22%
Eastern Europe and Central Asia	Not available	Not available	54%	46%	44%	56%
South America	Not available	Not available	55%	45%	60%	40%
North America, Central America, and the Caribbean	Not available	Not available	57%	43%	67%	33%
East Asia and the Pacific	Not available	Not available	54%	46%	Not available	Not available

Source: UNODC, 2014.

Government Responses to Trafficking

The U.S. Department of State produces an annual report on the state of affairs regarding trafficking and government responses thereto in 188 countries worldwide. The report ranks countries using the following assessment criteria:

- "enactment of laws prohibiting severe forms of trafficking in persons, as defined by the Trafficking Victims Protection Act (TVPA), and provision of criminal punishments for trafficking offenses;
- criminal penalties prescribed for human trafficking offenses with a maximum of at least four years' deprivation of liberty, or a more severe penalty;
- implementation of human trafficking laws through vigorous prosecution of the prevalent forms of trafficking in the country and sentencing of offenders;

- proactive victim identification measures with systematic procedures to guide law enforcement and other government-supported front-line responders in the process of victim identification;

- government funding and partnerships with NGOs to provide victims with access to primary health care, counseling, and shelter, allowing them to recount their trafficking experiences to trained social counselors and law enforcement in an environment of minimal pressure;

- victim protection efforts that include access to services and shelter without detention and with legal alternatives to removal to countries in which victims would face retribution or hardship;

- the extent to which a government ensures victims are provided with legal and other assistance and that, consistent with domestic law, proceedings are not prejudicial to victims' rights, dignity, or psychological well-being;

- the extent to which a government ensures the safe, humane, and—to the extent possible—voluntary repatriation and reintegration of victims; and

- governmental measures to prevent human trafficking, including efforts to curb practices identified as contributing factors to human trafficking, such as employers' confiscation of foreign workers' passports and allowing labor recruiters to charge prospective migrants excessive fees and government efforts to reduce the demand for commercial sex acts and international sex tourism." (U.S. Department of State, 2016, 36–37)

Based upon the above criteria, the Department of State (2016) has ranked countries into four different tiers. Tier 1 countries (36) "fully comply with the TVPA's minimum standards for the elimination of trafficking." The governments of countries placed on Tier 2 (comprising the largest number of countries, 78) "do not fully comply with the TVPA's minimum standards but are making significant efforts to bring themselves into compliance with those standards." More problematic are countries placed on the Tier 2 Watch List (44). While the governments of these countries have not implemented measures which fully comply with the TVPA minimum standards, they are making efforts to comply. However, "a) the *absolute number* of victims of severe forms of trafficking is very significant or is significantly increasing; b) there is a failure to provide evidence of *increasing efforts* to combat severe forms of trafficking in persons from the previous year, including increased investigations, prosecution, and convictions of trafficking crimes, increased assistance to victims, and decreasing evidence of complicity in severe forms of trafficking by government officials; or c) the determination that a country is making significant efforts to bring itself into compliance with minimum standards was based on commitments by the country to take *additional steps over the next year.*"

Last, the governments of countries placed in Tier 3 (27) neither comply with the TVPA minimum standards, nor are they making significant efforts to do so. Three countries are listed as special cases. Table 5.10 shows a list of the countries and the tiers in which they are placed as of 2016.

Table 5.10 U.S. Department of State Tier Ranking

Tier Ranking	Countries
Tier 1	Armenia; Australia; Austria; The Bahamas; Belgium; Canada; Chile; Colombia; Cyprus; Czech Republic; Denmark; Finland; France; Georgia; Germany; Iceland; Ireland; Israel; Italy; Korea, South; Lithuania; The Netherlands; New Zealand; Norway; Philippines; Poland; Portugal; Slovakia; Slovenia; Spain; St. Maarten; Sweden; Switzerland; Taiwan; United Kingdom; United States
Tier 2	Albania; Angola; Argentina; Aruba; Azerbaijan; Bahrain; Bangladesh; Barbados; Bhutan; Bosnia and Herzegovina; Botswana; Brazil; Brunei; Burkina Faso; Cambodia; Chad; Croatia; Curaçao; Dominican Republic; Ecuador; Egypt; El Salvador; Estonia; Ethiopia; Fiji; Greece; Guatemala; Guyana; Honduras; Hungary; India; Indonesia; Iraq; Jamaica; Japan; Jordan;

(continued)

Table 5.10 (*continued*)

Tier Ranking	Countries
	Kazakhstan; Kenya; Kosovo; Kyrgyzstan; Latvia; Lebanon; Lesotho; Liberia; Luxembourg; Macau; Macedonia; Madagascar; Malawi; Malta; Mauritius; Mexico; Micronesia; Moldova; Mongolia; Montenegro; Morocco; Namibia; Nepal; Nicaragua; Nigeria; Palau; Panama; Paraguay; Peru; Romania; Sierra Leone; Singapore; South Africa; Tajikistan; Timor-Leste; Togo; Turkey; Uganda; United Arab Emirates; Uruguay; Vietnam; Zambia
Tier 2 watch list	Afghanistan; Antigua and Barbuda; Benin; Bolivia; Bulgaria; Cabo Verde; Cameroon; China (PRC); Congo, Democratic Republic of; Congo, Republic of; Costa Rica; Côte d'Ivoire; Cuba; Gabon; Ghana; Guinea; Hong Kong; Kiribati; Kuwait; Laos; Malaysia; Maldives; Mali; Mozambique; Niger; Oman; Pakistan; Qatar; Rwanda; Saudi Arabia; Senegal; Serbia; Seychelles; Solomon Islands; Sri Lanka; St. Lucia; St. Vincent and The Grenadines; Swaziland; Tanzania; Thailand; Tonga; Trinidad and Tobago; Tunisia; Ukraine
Tier 3	Algeria; Belarus; Belize; Burma; Burundi; Central African Republic; Comoros; Djibouti; Equatorial Guinea; Eritrea; The Gambia; Guinea-Bissau; Haiti; Iran; Korea, North; Marshall Islands; Mauritania; Papua New Guinea; Russia; South Sudan; Sudan; Suriname; Syria; Turkmenistan; Uzbekistan; Venezuela; Zimbabwe
Special case	Libya; Somalia; Yemen

Source: U.S. Department of State. Trafficking in Persons Report, June 2016. Washington, DC. http://www.state.gov/documents/organization/258876.pdf

Country Ratings on Government Responses

Another examination of government response to trafficking—although here the organization refers to "modern slavery"—is the assessment produced by the Australian-based, global Walk Free Foundation. The organization rated 167 countries based on five criteria to determine "the strength of government responses to modern slavery." Researchers collected data to assess the following five outcomes for each country (italics added):

1. "*Survivors are identified, supported* to exit and remain out of modern slavery;

2. *Criminal justice* mechanisms address modern slavery;

3. *Coordination and accountability* mechanisms for the central government are in place;

4. *Addressing Risk* factors that enable modern slavery;

5. *Businesses and governments* through their public procurement stop sourcing goods and services that use modern slavery."

The outcomes include such measures as long-term victim assistance for women and children as well as for men, national action plans, training for law enforcement and other first responders, and regulation of supply chain transparency to guarantee that slave or forced labor is not used in the production of goods. The five objectives were measured through 98 indicators to determine the strength of a government's response (see Global Slavery Index 2016; Appendix 2; Part C: Government Responses; Walk Free Foundation).

Total scores are generated for each country. Based on the outcome, each country is given a letter rating based between AAA (the highest rating) and D (the lowest) to designate the strength of the government responses to modern slavery. In the 2016 report, no country was awarded with an "AAA" or an "AA" ranking, and only the Netherlands was given an "A."

Other countries ranked high are characterized "by strong political will, sufficient resources, and a strong civil society that holds governments to account" (Walk Free Foundation, 2016). In the "BBB" class, there are 10 countries: Australia, Austria, Belgium, Croatia, Norway, Portugal, Spain, Sweden, the United Kingdom, and the United States. Twenty-eight countries are ranked "BB". A considerable number of countries appear in class "B" (35), but the vast majority of the countries have been ranked "CCC" (44). The "CC" class contains 30 countries, closely followed by the "C" class with 9 countries. The last category, "D," comprises four countries: Equatorial Guinea, Eritrea, Iran, and North Korea. No data are available on Afghanistan, Iraq, Libya, Somalia, Syria, and Yemen.

Almost all countries score low on the factor "business and government" involvement. Exceptions to this are the United States (scoring the highest), followed by Australia and Brazil.

Table 5.11   Country Ratings on Government Responses

Response Rating	Rank	Countries
AAA		None
AA		None
A	78.43	The Netherlands
BBB	83–60	Australia; Austria; Belgium; Croatia; Norway; Portugal; Spain; Sweden; United Kingdom; United States
BB	59.79–50.55	Albania; Argentina; Brazil; Canada; Costa Rica; Cyprus; Czech Republic; Denmark; Dominican Republic; Finland; France; Georgia; Germany; Hungary; Ireland; Jamaica; Latvia; Lithuania; Macedonia; Mexico; Moldova; Montenegro; New Zealand; Philippines; Poland; Serbia; Slovenia; Switzerland
B	49.71–40.20	Armenia; Bangladesh; Benin; Bosnia and Herzegovina; Bulgaria; Chile; Colombia; Ecuador; Guatemala; Iceland; India; Indonesia; Israel; Italy; Jordan; Kosovo; Mozambique; Nepal; Nicaragua; Nigeria; Paraguay; Peru; Romania; Senegal; Sierra Leone; Slovakia; South Africa; Sri Lanka; Thailand; Turkey; Uganda; Ukraine; United Arab Emirates; Uruguay; Vietnam
CCC	39.69–30.46	Azerbaijan; Bahrain; Barbados; Belarus; Bolivia; Burkina Faso; Cambodia; Cameroon; China; Côte d'Ivoire; Djibouti; Egypt; El Salvador; Estonia; Ethiopia; The Gambia; Greece; Guyana; Haiti; Honduras; Japan; Kazakhstan; Kyrgyzstan; Laos; Lebanon; Lesotho; Liberia; Luxembourg; Malaysia; Mauritius; Mongolia; Myanmar; Namibia; Oman; Pakistan; Panama; Qatar; Rwanda; Swaziland; Taiwan; Tajikistan; Trinidad and Tobago; Tunisia; Zambia
CC	29.72–20.56	Algeria; Angola; Botswana; Burundi; Chad; Congo, Republic of; Cuba; Gabon; Ghana; Guinea-Bissau; Kenya; Kuwait; Madagascar; Malawi; Mali; Mauritania; Morocco; Niger; Russia; Saudi Arabia; Singapore; South Korea; Sudan; Surinam; Tanzania; Timor-Leste; Turkmenistan; Uzbekistan; Venezuela; Zimbabwe

Response Rating	Rank	Countries
C	19.56–10.75	Brunei; Cape Verde; Central African Republic; Congo, Democratic Republic of; Guinea; Papua New Guinea; Hong Kong, SAR China; South Sudan; Togo
D	<0–10	Equatorial Guinea; Eritrea; Iran; Korea, North
No Data		Afghanistan; Iraq; Libya; Somalia; Syria; Yemen

Source: The Global Slavery Index, 2016; Government Response; http://www.globalslaveryindex.org/findings/

Heroes Acting to End Modern Slavery

Despite limited success in identifying victims, and arresting and prosecuting offenders, the fight continues to address the trafficking problem. Since 2004, the U.S. Department of State has identified and honored "individuals around the world who have devoted their lives to the fight against human trafficking by awarding them the TIP Report Hero Acting to End Modern Slavery Award. . . . They are recognized for their tireless efforts—despite resistance, opposition, and threats—to protect victims, punish offenders, and raise awareness of ongoing criminal practices in their countries and abroad" (http://www.tipheroes.org/about/). Every year, as few as 6 and as many as 14 persons or organizations have been identified. More than 110 individuals have been recognized for their contribution to ending human trafficking. In Table 5.12 are the TIP heroes from 2015 and 2016.

Between 2004 and 2016, there were a total of 112 TIP Heroes awards; some were granted to couples or teams. They hail from 64 different countries, including Albania, Antigua and Barbuda, Argentina (2), Aruba, The Bahamas, Bahrain, Bosnia and Herzegovina, Botswana, Brazil, Burundi, Cambodia (4), Canada, Colombia (2), Costa Rica, Cyprus, Democratic Republic of Congo, Ecuador, Finland, France, Ghana (3), Greece (4), Guatemala, Guyana, Honduras, Hungary, India (7), Indonesia (5), Iraq (2), Israel (2), Italy (3), Japan (2), Jordan (2), Latvia, Lebanon, Lithuania, Madagascar, Malaysia (2), Mauritania (2),

Mexico (2), Mongolia (2), Morocco (2), Mozambique, Namibia, Nepal (4), Nicaragua, Nigeria, Pakistan (2), Peru (2), Philippines (2), Republic of Congo, Romania (2), Russia, Senegal (2), South Sudan, Sweden, Taiwan, Tajikistan, Thailand, Trinidad and Tobago, Uganda (2), the United Kingdom (2), the United States (4), Uzbekistan (2), and Vietnam.

The largest number of heroes come from or are working in Asia (33) followed by Europe (22). Twenty-three heroes are from the Americas. This region can be subdivided into North America (8), Central America and the Caribbean (8), and South America (7). The Department of State has recognized 19 African heroes and 12 from the Middle East.

The majority of the heroes (60) were recognized while working for NGOs. The second largest group recognized as heroes were working in government jobs, such as the police force, prosecution, politics, and as ambassadors. A smaller percentage of the heroes worked independently or with international organizations. Others, as victims, gained hero status after courageously fighting for justice in court, or helping others.

Table 5.12   TIP Report Hero Acting to End Modern Slavery Award, 2015–2016

Name (Year)	Sex	Organization	Country	Area of work
(2016)				
Karen G. I. Rigby	F	Ministry of National Security and Trafficking in Persons Inter-Ministerial Committee	The Bahamas	Government
Priscila Kedibone Israel	F	Public Prosecutions	Botswana	Government
Rita Theodorou Superman	F	Police Anti-Trafficking Unit	Cyprus	Government
Kiran Bajracharya	M	Superintendent of Police	Nepal	Government
Biram Dah Abeid and Brahim Bilal Rahdhane	M/M	Initiative for the Resurgence of the Abolitionist Movement (IRA)	Mauritania	NGO

Name (Year)	Sex	Organization	Country	Area of work
(2016)				
Syeda Ghulam Fatima	F	Bonded Labour Liberation Front	Pakistan	NGO
Oluremi Banwo Kehinde	M	Help Services for Nigerians in Russia	Russia	NGO
(2015)				
Moses Binoga	M	Ugandan National Counter Human Trafficking Taskforce	Uganda	Government
Betty Pedraza Lozano	F	Corporacion Espacios de Mujer	Colombia	NGO
Ameena Saeed Hasan	F	Iraqi Council of Representatives	Iraq	Government
Norotiana Ramboarivelo Jeannoda	F	National Union of Social Workers	Madagascar	NGO
Catherine Groenendijk-Nabukwasi	F	Confident Children out of Conflict (CCC)	South Sudan	NGO
Gita Miruškina	F	Safe House	Latvia	NGO
Parosha Chandran	F	Policy maker and attorney	United Kingdom	Government

Source: U.S. Department of State. "Meet the Heroes." http://www.tipheroes.org/the-heroes/

Documents

The Many Faces of Human Trafficking

The following is a collection of victim stories showing exploitation in different markets around the world. These stories show how victims become survivors and how traffickers pay a price for their involvement in exploitation.

VIETNAM | CHINA

When Ping was 12 years old, an acquaintance offered her and a friend jobs in a different city in Vietnam. Ping and her friend accepted the offer. The recruiter took them to a local bus station and placed them on a bus with their "caretaker." When they disembarked, the caretaker revealed they were in China and had been sold into prostitution with 20 other girls. When one of the girls refused to do as she was told, the owners beat her severely. Ping suffered in the brothel for almost a year before authorities raided the establishment, rescued the girls, and returned them to Vietnam. Although Ping still suffers from headaches and poor vision—including moments of blindness—as a result of her exploitation, she is training for a career in hairdressing.

HUNGARY | UNITED STATES

Michael was looking for jobs on the internet when he met Lorant, who offered him the chance to earn a lot of money working as a male escort in the United States. Michael and several other men accepted the offer, left Hungary, and traveled to Florida, where Lorant instead forced them into prostitution for 18–20 hours each day without pay. Lorant forced eight men to stay in a one-bedroom apartment, confiscated their identity documents, and threatened to kill them if they asked to leave. Police discovered the trafficking scheme after neighbors reported unusual behavior outside the men's living quarters. Lorant was convicted of human trafficking and racketeering and sentenced to 11 years in prison.

FRANCE

When Adelaide and Paul hit hard times, Paul suggested his wife consider prostitution for a year or two to supplement their income. Adelaide agreed, but when she wanted to quit, Paul forced her to continue. He took away her keys and cell phone, and would not let her leave the house or care for their son. He listed her on four escort websites, controlled what she wore and ate, and collected all the money she earned. Paul used psychological coercion and threatened Adelaide to keep her in prostitution; when she threatened to leave, he vowed he would find her. Paul was finally arrested and awaits trial, where he faces up to 10 years' imprisonment if convicted.

NIGERIA | UNITED KINGDOM

When a British-Nigerian couple offered to take Paul, 14 years old, from Nigeria to the UK, enroll him in school, and pay him to perform housework, he accepted. Once in Britain, however, the family changed his name and added him to their family passport as an adopted son. They forced him to clean their house for as many as 17 hours each day for no pay and did not allow him to go to school. They took his passport, set up cameras to monitor his movements, and limited his contact with the outside world. Paul tried several times to escape; once he contacted the police, who told him they did not handle family matters. Eight years after that, Paul heard a radio report about modern slavery and bravely reached out to an NGO. The NGO helped, and the couple was arrested a few months later after having exploited Paul for 24 years. They each received 10-year sentences, six years for servitude and four for other crimes.

GUATEMALA | BELIZE

When Janine was 13 years old, she met a woman in Guatemala who promised her a well-paying babysitting job in Belize, where the woman lived. Janine accepted and was willingly smuggled from Guatemala to Belize. Instead of a babysitting job, the woman coerced Janine to work at a bar in a small village, and also subjected her to sex trafficking. Janine was never paid and was threatened with detention for having entered the country illegally. Janine was also afraid of a complicit law enforcement official who sexually exploited her. Janine escaped a year later and received assistance from local villagers and other law enforcement officials.

Source: U.S. Department of State, *Trafficking in Persons Report* 2016. http://www.state.gov/documents/organization/258877 .pdf

Recognizing the Signs

This fact sheet for schools introduces the reader to the signs or indicators of human trafficking. Knowing these signs may help you identify a potential victim. Knowing where to report this may help save a life.

How Does Human Trafficking Affect Our Schools?

Trafficking can involve school-age youth, particularly those made vulnerable by challenging family situations, and can take a variety of forms including forced labor, domestic servitude, and commercial sexual exploitation.

The children at risk are not just high school students—pimps or traffickers are known to prey on victims as young as 9. Traffickers may target minor victims through social media websites, telephone chat-lines, after-school programs, at shopping malls and bus depots, in clubs, or through friends or acquaintances who recruit students on school campuses.

How Do I Identify a Victim of Human Trafficking?

Indicators that school staff and administrators should be aware of concerning a potential victim:

- Demonstrates an inability to attend school on a regular basis and/or has unexplained absences
- Frequently runs away from home
- Makes references to frequent travel to other cities
- Exhibits bruises or other signs of physical trauma, withdrawn behavior, depression, anxiety, or fear
- Lacks control over his or her schedule and/or identification or travel documents
- Is hungry, malnourished, deprived of sleep, or inappropriately dressed (based on weather conditions or surroundings)
- Shows signs of drug addiction
- Has coached/rehearsed responses to questions

Additional signs that may indicate sex trafficking include:
- Demonstrates a sudden change in attire, personal hygiene, relationships, or material possessions
- Acts uncharacteristically promiscuous and/or makes references to sexual situations or terminology that are beyond age-specific norms
- Has a "boyfriend" or "girlfriend" who is noticeably older
- Attempts to conceal recent scars

Additional signs that may indicate labor trafficking include:
- Expresses need to pay off a debt
- Expresses concern for family members' safety if he or she shares too much information
- Works long hours and receives little or no payment
- Cares for children not from his or her own family

How Do I Report a Suspected Incidence of Human Trafficking?
- In the case of an immediate emergency, call your local police department or emergency access number.
- To report suspected human trafficking crimes or to get help from law enforcement, call toll-free (24/7) 1-866-347-2423 or submit a tip online at www.ice.gov/tips.
- To report suspected trafficking crimes, get help, or learn more about human trafficking from a nongovernmental organization, call the toll-free (24/7) National Human Trafficking Resource Center at 1-888-373-7888.
- To report sexually exploited or abused minors, call the National Center for Missing and Exploited Children's (NCMEC) hotline at 1-800-THE-LOST, or report incidents at http://www.cybertipline.org.

Resources and Publications

One of the best ways to help combat human trafficking is to raise awareness and learn more about how to identify victims.

Information on human trafficking can also be found on the following Web sites:

- Department of Homeland Security Blue Campaign
- National Center for Missing and Exploited Children
- National Human Trafficking Resource Center
- Readiness and Emergency Management for Schools Technical Assistance Center
- United Nations Office on Drugs and Crime
- U.S. Citizenship and Immigration Services, Victims of Human Trafficking & Other Crimes

NOTE: This fact sheet contains resources, including Web sites, created by a variety of outside organizations. The resources are provided for the user's convenience and inclusion does not constitute an endorsement, by the U.S. Department of Education of any views, products, or services offered or expressed therein. All websites were accessed on January 7, 2013.

Source: U.S. Department of Education (2013). http://www2 .ed.gov/about/offices/list/oese/oshs/factsheet.html

The Human and Social Costs of Trafficking

The negative effect of human trafficking extends far beyond the immediate harm to victims. Human trafficking contributes to societal problems, erosion of government authority, and the rise of organized criminal groups.

Victims of human trafficking pay a horrible price. Psychological and physical harm, including disease and stunted growth, often have permanent effects. In many cases the exploitation of trafficking victims is progressive: a child trafficked into one form of labor may be further abused in another. It is a brutal reality of the modern-day slave trade that its victims are frequently bought and sold many times over—often sold initially by family members. Victims forced into sex slavery are often subdued with drugs and subjected to extreme violence. Victims trafficked for sexual exploitation face physical and emotional damage from violent sexual activity, forced substance abuse, exposure to sexually transmitted diseases including HIV/AIDS, food deprivation, and psychological torture. Some victims suffer permanent damage to their reproductive organs. Many victims die as a result of being trafficked. When the victim is trafficked to a location where he or she cannot speak or understand the language, this compounds the psychological damage caused by isolation and domination by traffickers.

The Human Rights Dimension. Fundamentally, trafficking in persons violates universal human rights to life, liberty, and freedom. Trafficking of children violates the inherent right of a child to grow up in a protective environment and the right to be free from all forms of abuse and exploitation.

Promoting Social Breakdown. The loss of family and community support networks makes trafficking victims vulnerable to traffickers' demands and threats, and contributes in several ways to the breakdown of social structures. Trafficking tears children from their parents and extended family. The profits from trafficking often allow the practice to take root in a particular community, which is then repeatedly exploited as a ready source of victims. The danger of becoming a trafficking victim can lead vulnerable groups such as children and young women to go into hiding, with adverse effects on their schooling or family structure. The loss of education reduces victims' future economic opportunities and increases their vulnerability to being re-trafficked in the future. Victims who are able to return to their communities often find themselves stigmatized or ostracized. Recovery from the trauma, if it ever occurs, can take a lifetime.

Fueling Organized Crime. The profits from human trafficking fuel other criminal activities. According to the U.S. Federal Bureau of Investigation, human trafficking generates an estimated $9.5 billion in annual revenue. It is closely connected with money laundering, drug trafficking, document forgery, and human smuggling. Where organized crime flourishes, governments and the rule of law are undermined and weakened.

Depriving Countries of Human Capital and Inhibiting Development. Trafficking has a disastrous impact on labor markets, contributing to an irretrievable loss of human potential. Some effects of trafficking include depressed wages, diminished workforce productivity, loss of remittances, and an undereducated generation. These effects lead to the loss of future productivity and earning power. Forcing children to work, and denying them access to education, reinforces the cycle of poverty and illiteracy that represses national development. When forced or bonded labor involves a significant part of a country's population, this form of trafficking retards the country's advancement, because generation after generation of victims remain mired in poverty.

Public Health Costs. Victims of trafficking often endure brutal conditions that result in physical, sexual, and psychological trauma. Sexually transmitted viruses and infections, pelvic inflammatory disease, and HIV/AIDS are often the result of being used in prostitution. Anxiety, insomnia, depression, and post-traumatic stress disorder are common psychological manifestations among trafficked victims. Unsanitary and crowded living conditions, coupled with poor nutrition, foster a host of adverse health conditions such as scabies, tuberculosis, and other communicable diseases. The most egregious abuses are often borne by children, who are more easily controlled and forced into domestic service, armed conflict, and other hazardous forms of work.

Erosion of Government Authority. Many governments struggle to exercise full law enforcement authority over their national territory, particularly where corruption is prevalent. Armed conflicts, natural disasters, and political or ethnic struggles can create large populations of internally displaced persons, who are vulnerable to trafficking. Human trafficking operations further undermine government efforts to exert authority, threatening the security of vulnerable populations. Many governments are unable to protect women and children kidnapped from their homes and schools or from refugee camps. Moreover, bribes paid to law enforcement, immigration officials, and members of the judiciary impede a government's ability to battle corruption.

Source: U.S. Department of State. *Trafficking in Persons Report 2006.* http://www.state.gov/j/tip/rls/tiprpt/2006/65983.htm

Summary of the Trafficking Victims Protection Act (TVPA) and Reauthorizations

The U.S. Victims of Trafficking and Violence Protection Act of 2000 (P.L. 106–386) and its subsequent reauthorizations in 2003 (H.R. 2620), 2005 (H.R. 972), 2008 (H.R. 7311), and 2013 (P.L.113–4) provide the tools to combat trafficking in persons in the United States and worldwide.

Trafficking Victims Protection Act of 2000 (TVPA 2000)

In the beginning of the 21st century, at least 700,000 people were reported as victims of international trafficking each year, 14,500–17,500 of which are women and children who are trafficked specifically into the United States. The International Labour Organization (ILO) estimates there are 20.9 million victims of forced labor, with other estimates using nongovernmental sources of information estimating that even larger numbers face modern slavery in all its forms (International Labour Office, 2012).

In order to combat the growing issue of trafficking in persons, members of the international community came together and concluded a new protocol to the Transnational Crime Commission that banned trafficking, resulting in the Palermo Protocol, which the U.S. Government helped develop and support. During this process and ultimately to provide for both implementation of the Protocol and to fill gaps in U.S. law, Congress passed the bipartisan Trafficking Victims Protection Act, and it was signed by President Clinton on October 28, 2000 (Public Law 106–386). The issue of trafficking in persons included those trafficked into the commercial sex industry, slavery, and forced labor. The TVPA 2000 was created to "ensure just and effective punishment of traffickers, and to protect their victims" (Victims of Trafficking and Violence Protection Act of 2000, Public Law No. 106–386 (2000)). In particular, there were three main components of the TVPA, commonly called the three P's:

Protection: The TVPA increased the U.S. Government's efforts to protect trafficked foreign national victims including, but not limited to:

- Victims of trafficking, many of whom were previously ineligible for government assistance, were provided assistance; and

- A non-immigrant status for victims of trafficking if they cooperated in the investigation and prosecution of traffickers (T-Visas, as well as providing other mechanisms to ensure the continued presence of victims to assist in such investigations and prosecutions).

Prosecution: The TVPA authorized the U.S. Government to strengthen efforts to prosecute traffickers including, but not limited to:

- Creating a series of new crimes on trafficking, forced labor, and document servitude that supplemented existing limited crimes related to slavery and involuntary servitude; and

- Recognizing that modern slavery takes place in the context of force, fraud, or coercion and is based on new clear definitions for both trafficking into commercial sexual exploitation and labor exploitation: Sex trafficking was defined as, "a commercial sex act that is induced by force, fraud, or coercion, or in which the person induced to perform such an act has not attained 18 years of age" (22 U.S.C. par. 7102(9)(A)). Labor trafficking was defined as, "the recruitment, harboring, transportation, provision, or obtaining of a person for labor or services, through the use of force, fraud, or coercion for the purpose of subjection to involuntary servitude, peonage, debt bondage, or slavery" (22 U.S.C. par. 7102(9)(B)).

Prevention: The TVPA allowed for increased prevention measures including, but not limited to:

- Authorizing the U.S. Government to assist foreign countries with their efforts to combat trafficking, as well as address trafficking within the United States, including through research and awareness-raising; and
- Providing foreign countries with assistance in drafting laws to prosecute trafficking, creating programs for trafficking victims, and assistance with implementing effective means of investigation.

Secretary of State Hillary Rodham Clinton later identified a fourth P, "partnership," in 2009 to serve as a, "pathway to progress in the effort against modern-day slavery."

Trafficking Victims Protection Reauthorization Act of 2003 (TVPRA 2003)

Congress re-authorized the TVPA in 2003 (herein, TVPRA 2003) (P.L.108–193). Despite significant progress to combat and prosecute trafficking in persons, additional assistance and research was still needed. Moreover, corruption was still evident among some foreign law enforcement authorities that undermined any international effort to combat this issue (*Trafficking Victims Protection Reauthorization Act of 2003*, Public Law No. 108–193 (2003)). Thus, TVPRA 2003 added provisions to expand its reach, which included, but were not limited to, the following responsibilities:

- Allowed for materials to be disseminated, which alert travelers that sex tourism is illegal;
- Created a new civil action that allowed trafficked victims to sue their traffickers in federal district court; and
- Required the Attorney General to report annually on trafficking efforts.

Trafficking Victims Protection Reauthorization Act (TVPRA 2005)

As awareness about the issue of human trafficking grew, the United States began to recognize that human trafficking impacted not just foreign national victims of human trafficking, but also United States Citizens and Legal Permanent Residents. Congress reauthorized the TVPRA in 2005 (herein, "TVPRA 2005") (P.L.109–164) (*Trafficking Victims Protection Reauthorization Act of 2005*, Public Law. No. 109–164 (2006)). The TVPRA 2005 added additional measures in particular to protect U.S. citizen survivors. These included, but were not limited to:

- Grant programs to assist state and local law enforcement efforts in combating trafficking in persons and to expand victim assistance programs to U.S. citizens or resident aliens subjected to trafficking; Programs to create comprehensive service facilities for trafficking victims;
- Programs to create rehabilitative facilities for trafficking victims; and
- Extraterritorial jurisdiction over trafficking offenses committed overseas by persons employed by or accompanying the federal government

Trafficking Victims Protection Reauthorization Act of 2008 (TVPRA 2008)

In December 2008, Congress reauthorized the TVPA through Fiscal Year (FY) 2012 with the William Wilberforce Trafficking Victims Protection Reauthorization Act of 2008 (herein, TVPRA 2008) (P.L.110–457). This bipartisan reauthorization extended and modified certain programs that form the core of the Justice Department's efforts to prevent and prosecute human trafficking and protect the victims of trafficking and slavery, as well as the Department of Labor's efforts to better document and deter the trafficking problem. It also allowed the continuation of the Department of Health and Human Services' efforts to provide services to victims of trafficking, most especially children.

TVPRA 2008 added the following provisions:

- New crimes were created that imposed penalties on those who obstruct or attempt to obstruct prosecutors' investigations of trafficking.

- The standard of proof for the crime of sex trafficking was changed to require that the government only prove that the defendant acted in "reckless disregard of the fact that such means [force, fraud, or coercion] would be used."

- The prior requirement that the defendant knew that the person engaged in commercial sex was a minor was eliminated in sex trafficking charges where the defendant had a reasonable opportunity to observe the minor.

- The crime of forced labor was expanded, providing that "force" is a means of violating the law.

- Criminal liability was imposed on those who, knowingly and with intent to defraud, recruit workers from outside the U.S. for employment within the U.S. by making materially false or fraudulent representations.

- The penalty was increased for conspiring to commit trafficking.

- A penalty was created for those who knowingly benefit financially from the participation in ventures that engage in trafficking.
- New prevention and protection measures were added to provide information to persons entering the U.S. lawfully and to establish protections for unaccompanied alien minors.

Trafficking Victims Protection Reauthorization Act of 2013 (TVPRA 2013)

In February 2013, Congress reauthorized the TVPA (herein, "TVPRA 2013") (P.L.113–4), which was passed as an amendment to the Violence Against Women Act. This authorization establishes and strengthens programs to ensure that U.S. citizens do not purchase products made by victims of human trafficking, and to prevent child marriage. It also puts into place emergency response provisions within the State Department to respond quickly to disaster areas and crises where people are particularly susceptible to being trafficked. The reauthorization also strengthens collaboration with state and local law enforcement to ease charging and prosecuting traffickers.

TVPRA 2013 added the following key provisions to:

- Provide invaluable resources to supporting holistic services for survivors and enabling law enforcement to investigate cases, to hold perpetrators accountable, and to prevent slavery from happening in the first place.
- Prevent U.S. foreign aid from going to countries that use child soldiers.
- Penalize the confiscation of identity documents, a prevalent form of coercion that traffickers use to exploit victims.
- Create a grant-making program to respond to humanitarian emergencies that result in an increased risk of trafficking, such as the situation in Haiti after the 2010 earthquake when children's vulnerability to re-trafficking escalated sharply.

- Authorize the J/TIP office to form local partnerships in focus countries to combat child trafficking through Child Protection Compacts.

- Enhance law enforcement capacity to combat sex tourism by extending jurisdiction under the 2003 PROTECT Act to prosecute U.S. citizens living abroad who commercially sexually exploit children.

Conclusion

Despite these efforts, the problem of human trafficking and slavery is still growing. These victims often experience severe trauma that requires intensive therapy, recovery, rehabilitation, and restorative services as a result of their abuse. In addition, human trafficking and slavery criminal cases are often complicated and lengthy legal proceedings that require additional resources for prosecutors as well as victims. Many of these victims require comprehensive case management provided by victim service organizations to see them through their recovery, help them navigate the legal system, and provide assistance to law enforcement necessary to prosecute criminal enterprises involved in trafficking and modern slavery.

Source: Alliance to End Slavery and Trafficking (ATEST). http://dev.endslaveryandtrafficking.org/fy2015/Relevant-Au thorization-Statutes.php

Breaking the Chain: Corruption and Human Trafficking

Corruption facilitates the commission of numerous crimes, including human trafficking. Transparency International argues for the need to include anticorruption measures in all anti-trafficking programs.

Contraband networks dealing in drugs, guns and other illicit goods have begun trading a new "commodity": people. This modern day form of slavery, known as human trafficking, is estimated to affect between 2.4 to 12 million victims around the world. Corruption is the grease that illicitly enables their movement within and across countries. Corruption is a constant companion to human trafficking and the suffering that it brings.

The Web of Trafficking

Trafficking victims are exploited in many ways: prostitution, debt bondage, forced or bonded labour and contractual servitude. Deception is used to target victims who often know the person recruiting them. Many times family members of victims serve as the recruiters, abusing trust in order to personally profit from the trafficking. Research shows that 46 per cent of trafficking victims know their recruiter. Victims that are tricked by recruiters may be searching for a way to flee poverty, unemployment or war. However, none expect the exploitation that is to come, at the hands of the recruiters and those further along the trafficking chain.

No nation is safe from trafficking and being caught up in its tangled networks. For example, a recent news report alleges that trafficked workers are being hired by third party vendors operating concessions (such as fast food restaurants) on US military installations. In the European Union, corruption allegations surround a recent case where reportedly trafficked forestry workers were being used by companies operating under a Czech government contract.

. . .

Corruption: The Currency for Trafficking

Corruption is present at every stage of the trafficking process, beginning with a victim's recruitment and transport through to their exploitation. Corruption can facilitate the transportation of victims within countries and across borders without detection or requests for paperwork. Once the victims reach their destination and the exploitation begins, traffickers rely on corruption to maintain their silence and avoid arrest. US government findings suggest that globally less than one in 10 traffickers are ever prosecuted.

Weak institutions offer weak protection. Pay-offs to police, courts and other public sector officials result in state institutions being willing to turn a blind eye to trafficking gangs or even to participate in them. Studies show that victims tend to come from countries where the public sector is perceived to be highly corrupt, as measured by our Corruption Perceptions Index.

The relatively low risk of getting caught is matched by the lure of large profits from selling the victims into prostitution, forced labour and other forms of abuse. The International Labour Organization estimates that about US$32 billion in profits are made each year from the sexual or physical exploitation of trafficked victims, affecting men and boys as often as it does women and girls.

The mix of profit and impunity through easily "bought" protection from law enforcers and politicians has created a "high reward/low risk" scenario for human traffickers and their accomplices. Trafficking networks often overlap with organised crime networks. According to the UN Office on Drugs and Crime, human trafficking brings organised crime groups their third largest source of profits, after drugs and arms.

Many criminal groups dealing in drugs and guns have added trafficked persons to their portfolio of illegal deals, according to the Financial Action Task Force. In Europe, human trafficking is tied to Albanian and Russian gangs as well as the Italian mafia. Drug gangs have been documented using victims of trafficking, many of them children, as forced labor in illegal cannabis factories across the UK and Ireland. In Asia, Chinese criminal networks and the Japanese mafia are considered the main perpetrators.

Breaking the Chain

Recognising how corruption facilitates trafficking is a critical and simple step. Government anti-trafficking programmes must include anti-corruption components as well as raise awareness about the broader development and poverty concerns that make victims vulnerable to recruiters.

International frameworks exist that can help to better link these different issues together. For example, the UN Convention Against Transnational Organised Crime (UNCTOC) and the UN Convention against Corruption (UNCAC) have provisions to deal with corruption, trafficking and criminal networks. The UNCTOC and its three protocols aim to prevent, suppress and punish trafficking, while the UNCAC includes articles that criminalise and prosecute active and passive bribery, the obstruction of justice and money laundering.

To begin bringing together work on anti-corruption and anti-trafficking, Transparency International recommends taking concrete steps, which include:

- establishing an effective review mechanism for the UNCTOC and its protocols—or at least for the Protocol on Trafficking
- forming an international working group composed of representatives from the main source and destination countries of trafficked people, including both anti-trafficking and anti-corruption experts to develop proposals to enhance cooperation
- creating national-level joint task forces combining anti-trafficking and anti-corruption experts.

In the end, solutions will only be effective when governments show political will and leadership to end trafficking. They must develop measures that break the corruption that holds together the networks involved, from recruiters and middlemen, to police and high-level officials.

September 1, 2011

Source: Transparency International. Breaking the Chain: Corruption and Human Trafficking. © 2011 Transparency International. Licensed under CC-BY-ND 4.0. http://archive .transparency.org/news_room/in_focus/2011/breaking_the_ chain_corruption_and_human_trafficking. Accessed on September 5, 2016.

Preventing Human Trafficking in Global Supply Chains

A large percentage of forced labor and exploitation occurs in the supply chain of companies producing goods that we consume and services that we use. A criminal justice, law enforcement approach will only solve part of the problem. By ensuring that no child or slave labor is used in the supply chain of companies, businesses can play an important part in eradicating human trafficking.

As the International Labour Organization (ILO) estimated in 2014, forced labor in the private economy reaps some $150 billion in illicit profits each year; most instances of what the *Trafficking in Persons Report* refers to as human trafficking are covered by ILO's definition of forced labor. These billions flood the formal marketplace, corrupt the global economy, and taint purchases made by unwitting consumers. Long and complex supply chains that cross multiple borders and rely on an array of subcontractors impede traceability and make it challenging to verify that the goods and services bought and sold every day are untouched by modern-day slaves.

Governments, the private sector, and individuals can all make a difference when it comes to addressing human trafficking in supply chains. Each has the unique ability to leverage economic power to influence existing markets, and create new ones, where workers can enjoy decent work and human dignity, and are free from coercion and the exploitation associated with human trafficking.

The Risk of Human Trafficking in Supply Chains

The fluid nature of the crime means traffickers can target vulnerable workers anywhere to fill labor shortages everywhere along a supply chain. In the electronics sector, for example, human trafficking may exist in the extractive stages (mining for raw material), in the component manufacturing stage (where separate pieces are produced or combined), and in the production stage (where a good is assembled and packaged in a factory).

Although human trafficking is found in many trades, the risk is more pronounced in industries that rely upon low-skilled or unskilled labor. This includes jobs that are dirty, dangerous, and difficult—those that are typically low-paying and undervalued by society and are often filled by socially marginalized groups including migrants, people with disabilities, or minorities.

Risks may also be higher in industries of a seasonal nature or where the turn-around time for production is extremely short. In these industries, the demand for labor increases drastically at the time of harvest or when a new product—be it a smartphone or a roadway—must be manufactured within a strict timeframe.

Finally, in industries where fierce competition leads to constant downward pressure on prices, some employers respond by taking cost-cutting measures to survive commercially, from reducing wages or ignoring safety protocols, to holding workers in compelled service through debt bondage or the retention of identity documents.

Labor Recruitment in Global Markets

Practices that lead to human trafficking often occur in the recruitment process before employment begins, whether through misrepresentation of contract terms, the imposition of recruitment fees, the confiscation of identity documents, or a combination of these. The involvement of intermediaries (for example, labor brokers, middlemen, employment agencies, or recruiters) creates additional layers in the supply chain and positions these individuals to either assist or exploit.

Labor brokers function as a bridge between worker and employer and can provide helpful guidance and assistance in matching workers with jobs and arranging visas and documentation, medical checkups, pre-departure orientation, training, and travel. In many cases, labor brokers are both legitimate and important to connect readily available laborers to employers in need of a workforce. A worker's dependence on intermediaries, however, can also increase their risk of being subjected to trafficking.

It is possible to identify areas of increased vulnerability in supply chains, including fraudulent practices in the recruitment process. Indicators of such recruitment typically include deception about job terms, living conditions, location, legal status, and wages, or more forceful methods such as document confiscation, debt bondage, isolation, or violence. Fraudulent recruitment practices can lead to exploitation at the place of employment, as an unsuspecting worker may endure excessive hours, poor living conditions, and wage theft. When workers are put or held in such situations through the use of force, fraud, or coercion, it constitutes human trafficking.

The Role of Government

Government action is crucial in prosecuting trafficking cases, protecting victims, and preventing trafficking. By strengthening efforts in these areas, and by continuing to build partnerships with civil society and the private sector, governments are making serious strides in fighting modern slavery.

Governments can also play an important leadership role in combating human trafficking in supply chains. At home, governments can model and encourage multi-stakeholder dialogue and partnerships to bring together businesses and anti-trafficking experts to generate ideas and solutions and promote voluntary responsible business conduct initiatives. Governments should set clear expectations for businesses on human rights issues and adopt policies that promote greater transparency and better reporting on anti-trafficking efforts in supply chains. For example, in March, the United Kingdom enacted the Modern Slavery Act of 2015, which requires—among other things—commercial organizations with annual sales above a certain threshold to prepare annual statements outlining the steps they have taken to prevent human trafficking from occurring in their supply chain or in any part of their business.

Of course, governments have the responsibility to enforce labor laws, treat all workers fairly, including lawfully present and irregular migrants, and root out corruption—all factors that can help prevent trafficking. International cooperation to strengthen labor migration policies and manage the increasing flows of migrant labor is critical to reducing the number of people who fall prey to human traffickers. Better regulation of private labor recruiters can also help protect workers.

Further, governments can provide a model for the private sector by better monitoring their own supply chains, which look much like those of the private sector. Tiers of subcontractors, lack of transparency, and the sheer magnitude of expenditure all make it extremely difficult for governments to ensure that taxpayer money is not supporting the illicit business of human trafficking. Nevertheless, the massive spending by governments to procure goods and services each year gives them enormous influence and leverage in the marketplace to minimize the risks of human trafficking.

Governments can, and often do, prohibit government employees and contractors from engaging directly in trafficking in persons. In addition, some governments have policies in place that require contractors and subcontractors to ensure that employees have not participated in those activities that can lead to trafficking: charging recruitment fees, engaging in contract switching, and confiscating or retaining identification documents. These prohibitions must be backed up with effective enforcement.

The Private Sector: An Opportunity to Lead

Beyond the efforts of governments, companies can also take action to reduce the likelihood of trafficking in their supply chains and respect the rights of those who work to make their businesses successful.

There are many measures businesses can take to mitigate the risks of human trafficking throughout their operations.

For starters, business leaders can create anti-trafficking policies that address the common risks in their operations and supply chains, ensure workers have the right to fair compensation and redress, train staff to understand the indicators of human trafficking, and put remediation plans in place before any allegations arise to allow for appropriate corrective action. Businesses should also work with government officials, NGOs, and recruiters in the countries where they source to gain a better understanding of workers' vulnerabilities and commit to making improvements.

A company can demonstrate its commitment to responsibly source goods and services by creating a clear and comprehensive anti-trafficking policy, which includes an enforcement mechanism that is applied throughout the company's supply chain. High-level executives should approve and promote such a policy and build it into company operations so supplier consideration goes beyond price and reliability, to include an assessment of labor practices. Among other things, an effective policy:

- prohibits human trafficking and those activities that facilitate it—including charging workers recruitment fees, contract fraud, and document retention;
- responds to industry- or region-specific risks;
- requires freedom of movement for workers;
- pays all employees at least the minimum wage in all countries of operation, preferably a living wage;
- includes a grievance mechanism and whistleblower protections; and
- applies to direct employees, as well as subcontractors, labor recruiters, and other business partners.

Such a policy sends a clear message to employees, business partners, investors, and consumers that human trafficking will not be tolerated. Coupled with effective risk assessments, monitoring, and serious remediation efforts, it can promote good labor practices throughout the supply chain.

Understanding how supply chains operate, where key suppliers are located, and what working conditions exist in those locations and sectors is vital to help a company gain control. By fully mapping its supply chain, down to the level of raw materials, a company can gain a better understanding of gaps in transparency. Companies can then create a plan to target those areas where high levels of spending overlap with industries or locations with high risks for human trafficking.

Once a risk assessment is completed, companies must begin to address problem areas, implement corrective measures, and monitor and enforce anti-trafficking policies. Monitoring often takes the form of social auditing, which—when done properly—can help to detect violations of company policies, including worker abuse. Yet, human trafficking is frequently difficult for auditors to detect. Companies that are serious about addressing forced labor in their supply chains should make sure that auditors are properly trained and equipped to look for known indicators of human trafficking, including the fraudulent recruitment practices discussed in this Report. Audits should be thorough, comprehensive, and periodic.

Finally, constant pressure on cutting costs can have a destabilizing effect on the proactive measures a company may take to prevent human trafficking. By incorporating anti-trafficking measures throughout an operation, including in company budget, training, policies, and protocols, business can make efforts to ensure that the dignity of workers throughout the supply chain is not sacrificed for higher profits.

Source: U.S. Department of State. Preventing Human Trafficking in Global Supply Chains. http://www.state.gov/j/tip/rls/tiprpt/2015/243360.htm

Publications on human trafficking produced by academicians, government agencies, intergovernmental and nongovernment organizations, investigative journalists, and former trafficked victims are numerous. This chapter introduces the reader to some of the most important publications. The sources below have been categorized into books, reports, articles, and Internet sources. The list is not exhaustive, and the reader is encouraged to visit the website of the organizations for future publications.

Books and Book Chapters

Arhin, Antonela, and Quayson, Ato, eds. *Labour Migration, Human Trafficking and Multinational Corporations: The Commodification of Illicit Flows*. New York: Routledge, 2012.

> This edited text comprises 10 chapters by leading authors in the field of labor exploitation. It focusses on migrants and how they are exploited in the labor sector, often producing goods for multinational corporations. Driven by the need to produce goods at affordable and competitive prices, corporations seek cheap labor and intentionally or unintentionally exploit workers in the process. The contributors find that subcontractors, often not monitored

Escaping desperate conditions of forced labor and political repression at home, these Burmese laborers look to commercial fishing in Thailand as a way to a better life. Like illegal or marginalized immigrants everywhere, they are prey to unscrupulous traffickers who, for a fee, sell them to greedy ship captains and exploiters. (Kay Chernush for the U.S. State Department)

by main contractors, contribute to the problem. Measures taken by governments and international agencies to address the problem are discussed in the individual chapters.

Aronowitz, Alexis A. "To Punish or Not to Punish: What Works in the Regulation of the Prostitution Market?" In Persak N. and G. Vermeulen (eds.), *Reframing Prostitution: From Discourse to Description, from Moralisation to Normalisation?* Antwerp, Belgium: Maklu Publishers, 2014, 223–251. https://biblio.ugent.be/publication/5639953/file/5639963. Accessed on May 1, 2016.

This chapter examines various prostitution markets, and contrasts and critiques the Dutch model of legalization and control with the Swedish model of limited legality. In Sweden, the purchase of sexual services is prohibited; however, the "sale" is legal. The chapter attempts to answer the question whether legalized prostitution leads to more human trafficking.

Aronowitz, Alexis A. *Human Trafficking, Human Misery: The Global Trade in Human Beings.* Westport, CT: Praeger, 2009.

After defining human trafficking and smuggling, this provides a critical view of the statistics and perspectives to explain human trafficking. The book examines regional patterns of human trafficking and different markets of exploitation. The profiles of victims, how criminals and criminal organizations traffic and exploit their victims, as well as less frequently discussed forms of trafficking—in organs, child soldiers, mail-order brides, and adoption, and the use of Internet in trafficking are discussed.

Bales, Kevin, and Soodalter, Ron. *The Slave Next Door: Human Trafficking and Slavery in America Today.* Berkeley: University of California Press, 2009.

The authors explain how and why slaves in the United States are "hidden in plain sight." Numerous cases are provided. The authors present positive measures taken by the United States to combat human trafficking, and at the same time point out areas of continuing concern.

Bolkovac, Kathryn, and Lynn, Cari. *The Whistleblower: Sex Trafficking, Military Contractors, and One Woman's Fight for Justice.* Basingstoke: Palgrave Macmillan Trade, 2011.
This is the true story of Kathryn Bolkovac, who left her work as a Nebraska (United States) police officer to join a private military contractor, DynCorp International, to work as a UN peacekeeper in Bosnia. In her capacity as a human rights investigator, Kathryn uncovered the trafficking for sexual exploitation of women into the region and the shocking fact that this was supported, condoned, and facilitated by UN Peacekeeping officers. This book tells the story of her fight to bring justice to the victims, and protect herself, when her accusations resulted in the termination of her contract and threats to her security.

Brennan, Denise. *Life Interrupted: Trafficking into Forced Labor in the United States.* Durham: Duke University Press, 2014.
The author follows the lives of survivors of human trafficking for forced labor in the United States. Global economic inequalities drive people from their homes in neighboring countries with the promise of a better life in the United States. Instead, migrant workers are exploited at the hands of employers in unprotected and un- or under- regulated sectors. This book is an account of exploitation and life after trafficking, calling for regulated migration and reform of labor sectors.

Brysk, Alison, and Choi-Fitzpatrick, Austin. *From Human Trafficking to Human Rights: Reframing Contemporary Slavery.* Philadelphia: University of Pennsylvania Press, 2012.
Numerous experts discuss how human trafficking is rooted in structural issues framed by human security, foreign

policy, gender, and labor relations. The authors' message is clear: human trafficking must be recognized as a social justice and human rights issue rather than one emphasizing sex work.

Burke, Mary. *Human Trafficking: Interdisciplinary Perspectives.* New York: Routledge, 2013.

The 16 authors contributing to this book provide insight into trafficking from the perspective of human security and development issues, rights, law enforcement, victim protection, and health and mental health. The book defines human trafficking, placing it within the historical perspective of slavery.

Cohen, Aaron, and Buckley, Christine. *Slave Hunter.* New York: Simon Spotlight Entertainment, 2009.

Aaron Cohen chose to give up a life in rock music and commit himself to rescuing persons, in particular minors, trafficked for sexual exploitation. His missions have brought him to places as far reaching as Cambodia, Sudan, and countries in Latin America. He has consulted with government officials, antislavery organizations, think tanks, and the media. Aaron's work has been recognized by the Dalai Lama, the Immoral Chaplains Foundation, and the U.S. Congress.

Gallagher, Anne. *The International Law of Human Trafficking.* Cambridge: Cambridge University Press, 2012.

This book examines human trafficking from the aspect of international legal obligation, the theories of compliance, and the doctrine of responsibility.

Hepburn, Stephanie, and Simon, Rita. *Human Trafficking around the World: Hidden in Plain Sight.* New York: Columbia University Press, 2013.

The authors highlight trafficking for sexual and labor exploitation, sex tourism, and organ trafficking across

24 nations. They describe the experiences of the victims and perpetrators involved in the trade. Through interviews, intimate accounts, and statistical data, the reader is provided with an in-depth understanding of the trafficking practices and anti-trafficking measures in the countries profiled in the book.

Hoang, Kimberly Kay, and Parreñas, Rhacel Salazar. *Human Trafficking Reconsidered: Rethinking the Problem, Envisioning New Solutions*. New York and London: International Debate Education Association, 2014.

This book comprises a collection of original essays from around the world, addressing sex and labor trafficking. Various approaches allow the reader to examine the field of human trafficking through ethnographic studies, legal approaches, and historical perspectives. The book examines the definition of trafficking, analyzes the effectiveness of current anti-trafficking measures, and discusses the challenges faced by anti-trafficking advocates on the ground.

Kara, Siddhartha. *Sex Trafficking. Inside the Business of Modern Slavery*. New York: Columbia University Press, 2009.

The author has traveled to countries on four continents to describe sex trafficking in India and Nepal, Italy and Western Europe, Moldova and the former Soviet Union, Albania and the Balkans, Thailand, the Mekong Sub-region, and the United States. Drawing on his expertise in economics and finance, the author introduces a business analysis of the sex industry and the local push factors and macroeconomic trends that contribute to the global sex industry.

Kara, Siddhartha. *Bonded Labor: Tackling the System of Slavery in South Asia*. New York: Columbia University Press, 2012.

Kara provides a legal, historical, and economic analysis of the problem of bonded labor in Bangladesh, India, Nepal, and Pakistan. He sheds light on forced labor and exploitation in the carpet, tea, rice, construction, and brick making industries. From Asia, Kara traces the supply chains back to Western consumers.

Kempadoo, Kamala, Sanghera, Jyoti, and Pattanaik, Bandana. *Trafficking and Prostitution Reconsidered, Second Edition: New Perspectives on Migration, Sex Work, and Human Rights.* Boulder, CO: Paradigm Publishers, 2011.
This second edition updates the 2005 publication introducing recent developments in research, policy, law, and international agreements. Criminologists and legal experts, feminists and abolitionists debate prostitution and sex trafficking and look at new developments in action research with migrant women around the world.

Keo, Chenda. *Human Trafficking in Cambodia.* Routledge Contemporary Southeast Asia Series, London and New York: Routledge, Taylor & Francis Group, 2014.

Lee, Maggie. *Human Trafficking.* Cullompton, Devon: Willan Publishing, 2007.
This edited volume introduces the topic of human trafficking from a number of perspectives addressing the key topics necessary to understanding the phenomenon—its place within a historical context, and the link to global crime, migration, and globalization.

Mahdavi, Pardis. *Gridlock: Labor, Migration, and Human Trafficking in Dubai.* Redwood City, CA: Stanford University Press, 2011.
The Middle East has been portrayed as a hotbed of labor exploitation, and Dubai is one of the major destinations for trafficking in the region. In a nuanced study of the problem, the author shows that not all migrants are trapped in situations of human trafficking, and that the situation for workers in Dubai is not representative of the typical cases of human trafficking which have guided

the discourse on the problem. Migrants' personal stories are set against U.S. policy showing the gap between the reality of human trafficking in the Gulf State and the policies regulating the problem.

Mahdavi, Pardis. *From Trafficking to Terror: Constructing a Global Social Problem.* New York: Routledge, 2013.
This book provides case studies from around the world and examines the confluence of the wars on human trafficking and on terror to produce moral panics. Together, they facilitate Islamophobia. This book is a plea to rethink the discourse on both trafficking and terrorism.

Malarek, Victor. *The Natashas: The Horrific Inside Story of Slavery, Rape, and Murder in the Global Sex Trade.* New York: Arcade Publishing, 2011.
This is a journalistic account of the sale and exploitation of young women into the international sex trade. Called "Natashas" in Israel, the term refers to women from Eastern Europe brought into Western countries by organized crime groups and forced into prostitution. The author purports that corrupt police officers, immigration officials, and international peacekeepers facilitate the trade.

Melrose, Margaret, and Pearce Houndmills, Jenny J., eds. *Critical Perspectives on Child Sexual Exploitation and Related Trafficking.* Basingstoke, Hampshire: Palgrave Macmillan, 2013.
From a variety of perspectives, this edited volume explores issues relevant to young people affected by trafficking and sexual exploitation. Topics include the construction of child exploitation, migrant and refugee communities, gangs, perpetrators, and international policy.

Mishra, Veerendra. *Human Trafficking: The Stakeholders' Perspective.* Los Angeles: SAGE Publications Pvt. Ltd., 2013.
This is an edited volume comprising six sections dealing with sexual exploitation, child trafficking issues,

perspectives on trafficking outside India, civil society organizations and their experiences and perspectives on human trafficking, legal provisions, state responses, and case studies and examples of good models.

Segrave, Marie. *Human Trafficking.* Burlington, VT: Ashgate Publishers, 2013.
This volume highlights four key areas: data and research; transnational organized crime; the implementation of anti-trafficking responses; and the explanation of alternative responses to human trafficking. Material is presented as a collection of essays drawing attention to recent empirical research and contemporary arguments.

Shelley, Louise. *Human Trafficking: A Global Perspective.* Cambridge: Cambridge University Press, 2010.
The author introduces the reader to the structural factors that contribute to human trafficking and discusses the consequences. Her focus is on human trafficking as a transnational crime. Shelley studies human trafficking organizations as business models, showing how the organizational structure and patterns of exploitation vary across regions.

Siegel, Dina, and de Wildt, Roos. *Ethical Concerns in Research on Human Trafficking.* Basel: Springer, 2015.
This edited book contains 15 chapters by leading authorities in the field of research on human trafficking based on various themes: trafficking for labor exploitation, sex trafficking, and trafficking in children and human organs. The reader will come to understand ethical concerns and risks faced by those conducting research on victims of human trafficking. Prominent topics addressed in this collection of chapters are the principle of "first, do no harm," informed consent, privacy, and confidentiality.

Skinner, E. Benjamin. *A Crime So Monstrous: Face-to-Face with Modern-Day Slavery*. New York, London: Free Press, 2008.

Skinner, a journalist, traveled around the world to investigate the sale and purchase of human beings in countries on five continents. He has interviewed trafficked victims and those that traffic them, as well as stakeholders who seek to combat the crime.

Smith, Holly Austin. *Walking Prey: How America's Youth Are Vulnerable to Sex Slavery*. New York: Palgrave Macmillan, 2014.

This former victim of human trafficking describes how America's youth from middle class neighborhoods become targets for sex traffickers. Succumbing to pressure to conform and easy access to social media platforms allows predators to easily identify vulnerable adolescents. Law enforcement often views young women in sex work as prostitutes rather than trafficked victims. Smith advocates for training and resources to prevent the cycle of abusive prostitution of adolescent girls.

Smith, Linda, and Coloma, Cindy. *Renting Lacy. A Story of America's Prostituted Children. A Call to Action*. Vancouver, WA: Shared Hope International, 2013.

Through interviews with teenage survivors of forced prostitution, Linda Smith tells the story of Star and Lacy, two teenagers who are "rented out" for a few hours each night to customers who know they are abusing underage girls. The author describes their abuse at the hands of manipulative pimps and their fight to survive. This revised version includes a discussion guide and suggestions for readers to take action.

Territo, Leonard, and Glover, Nataliya. *Criminal Investigation of Sex Trafficking in America*. Boca Raton, FL: CRC Press, 2013.

This book examines international perspectives on sex trafficking, summarizing the major state and federal laws relevant to sex trafficking investigations. Readers are taught what evidence is necessary for a criminal investigation and how evidence should be collected and preserved. Interrogation methods are introduced. The role and responsibility of prosecutors and measures to develop and sustain a multiagency task force are discussed.

Territo, Leonard, and Kirkham, George. *International Sex Trafficking of Women and Children. Understanding the Global Epidemic.* Flushing, NY: Looseleaf Law Publications, 2010.
This book brings together a collection of essays from leading authorities on sex trafficking and (child) sex tourism published in various international journals. Sex trafficking and tourism on different continents is highlighted in the book.

Yea, Sallie. *Human Trafficking in Asia. Forcing Issues.* New York: Routledge, 2014.
Contributors to this book offer an in-depth analysis and share research methodologies to describe the patterns and forms of human trafficking in a region plagued by the problem—East and Southeast Asia. The authors constructively critique anti-trafficking discourses and campaigns, and provide examples of good practices to combat trafficking within the region.

Dissertations

Curtis, Rachel Rae. *Sex Trafficking: How the Media Portrays Victims and Reflects Legislation.* Iowa State University, 2012. http://lib.dr.iastate.edu/cgi/viewcontent.cgi?article=3312&context=etd
This thesis uses a content analysis of news media articles to determine who is involved in trafficking. Examining trafficking through a "symbolic interactionist lens," the author attempts to gain an understanding of the meanings attached to trafficked victims and whether victims are perceived differently in different states.

Mace, Stephanie. *Child Trafficking: A Case Study of the Perceptions of Child Welfare Professionals in Colorado.* Colorado State University, 2013. http://dspace.library.colostate.edu/webclient/DeliveryManager/digitool_items/csu01_storage/2013/06/19/file_1/207546

> The author uses a qualitative, descriptive approach with semi-structured interviews of child welfare professionals with the aim of establishing the level of awareness of child welfare professionals in Colorado. The study focused on discovering the challenges associated with identifying child victims of trafficking from the perspective of child welfare professionals.

Poucki, Sasa. *The Quest for Root Causes of Human Trafficking: A Study on the Experience of Marginalized Groups, with a Focus on the Republic of Serbia.* Rutgers, The State University of New Jersey, 2012. http://dga.rutgers.edu/wp-content/uploads/2012/10/The-Quest-for-Root-Causes-of-Human-Trafficking-A-Study-on-the-Experience-of-Marginalized-Groups-with-a-Focus-on-the-Republic-of-Serbia.pdf

> The author carries out empirical research in Serbia to examine the root causes of trafficking to include culture, religion, customs, and tradition. The study examines whether marginalized ethnic minorities are more vulnerable than others to becoming trafficked victims. The dissertation examines the extent to which the general public is aware of the phenomenon and whether this contributes to success in the fight against human trafficking.

Sverdlick, Ana R. *Human Trafficking: A Comparative Analysis of Why Countries with Similar Characteristics Have Different Situations.* Rutgers, The State University of New Jersey, 2014. http://dga.rutgers.edu/wp-content/uploads/2012/10/Human-Trafficking-A-Comparative-Analysis-of-Why-Countries-with-Similar-Characteristics-have-Different-Situations.pdf

> This study compares Argentina and Brazil in an attempt to explain why these two countries similar in socioeconomic

and political systems differ in patterns of sex trafficking. The study concludes that "matrifocality" or the woman-centered family may explain why adolescent, single mothers in Brazil are easy targets for traffickers.

Tsai, Laura. *"I Will Help as Much as I Can, but I Can't Give Them Everything": The Financial Lives of Women Who Were Formerly Trafficked into Sex Work in the Philippines.* Columbia University, 2014. http://academiccommons.columbia.edu/item/ac: 168493
This dissertation comprises three studies that describe the economic challenges facing formerly trafficked victims upon their reintegration into their communities in the Philippines. The economic reintegration is analyzed through propensity score matching, a grounded theory study, and a financial diaries study. These findings are discussed with relation to social work practices.

Reports

Amnesty International. *Qatar: 'My Sleep Is My Break': Exploitation of Migrant Domestic Workers in Qatar.* 2014. https://www.amnesty.nl/sites/default/files/public/qatar_my_sleep_is_my_break_final.pdf
This report describes the serious abuses faced by foreign domestic workers in the families and homes of residents of Qatar.

Amnesty International. *China: Exploited for Profit, Failed by Governments: Indonesian Migrant Domestic Workers Trafficked to Hong Kong.* 2013. https://www.amnesty.org/en/documents/asa17/029/2013/en/
Amnesty International sheds light on the mala fide recruitment practices in agencies in Indonesia and Hong Kong that facilitate the exploitation of Indonesian women as domestic slaves in Hong Kong.

Amnesty International. *Amnesty International Policy on State Obligations to Respect, Protect and Fulfil the Human Rights of Sex Workers.* 2016. https://www.amnesty.org/en/documents/pol30/4062/2016/en/

> Amnesty International distinguishes between voluntary prostitution and coerced sex work (human trafficking). The organization calls upon states to protect the human rights of sex workers.

Aronowitz, Alexis A. *Report to the Government of Nepal on the Situation of Human Trafficking: An Exploratory Study.* Technical Report, 2014. https://www.researchgate.net/publication/271507264_Report_to_the_Government_of_Nepal_on_the_Situation_of_Human_Trafficking_An_Exploratory_Study

> This study is based upon interviews with 37 persons from various government and nongovernmental agencies to understand the trafficking process in the country. The Dutch Barrier Model was used and amended to examine its usefulness within the context of Nepal. Good practices and recommendations to improve the situation regarding human trafficking within and from Nepal are made to the government, civil society organizations, and donors.

Aronowitz, Alexis A. "Future Possibilities for the Utilization of EU Statistics on Human Trafficking," in *Counting What Counts; Tools for the Validation and Utilization of EU Statistics on Human Trafficking,* Dijk, Jan van, Leontien van der Knaap, Marcelo Aebi, Claudia Campistol, Tilburg University, The Netherlands, 115–153. https://serval.unil.ch/resource/serval:BIB_4ABA60D21BFD.P001/REF

> This report examines European Union data on human trafficking victims and suspected offenders to determine the interpretation of data, and to which use these data should be put.

Aronowitz, Alexis A., Theuermann, Gerda, and Tyurykanova, Elena. *Analysing the Business Model of Trafficking in Human Beings to Better Prevent the Crime.* OSCE Office of the Special Representative and Coordinator for Combating Trafficking in Human Beings, Vienna, Austria, 2010. http://www.osce.org/cthb/69028?download=true
> Based upon an analysis of case files and interviews with experts, this report examines human trafficking from a business perspective and how this business can be interrupted.

Aronowitz, Alexis A. *Guidelines for the Collection of Data on Trafficking in Human Beings, Including Comparable Indicators.* Austrian Federal Ministry of the Interior and the International Organization for Migration, Vienna, Austria, 2009. http://publications.iom.int/system/files/pdf/guidelines_collection_data_iomvienna.pdf
> This report brings together the thoughts of experts from government, law enforcement agencies, victim service providers, NGOs and international organizations, researchers, and other stakeholders to harmonize comparable indicators on human trafficking.

Australia, Commonwealth of. *National Action Plan to Combat Human Trafficking and Slavery 2015–2019.* 2014. https://www.ag.gov.au/CrimeAndCorruption/HumanTrafficking/Documents/Trafficking-NationalActionPlanToCombatHumanTraffickingAndSlavery2015–19.pdf
> This National Action Plan outlines the goals of the Australian government to combat human trafficking and slavery by addressing the four pillars of prevention and deterrence, detection and investigation, prosecution and compliance, and victim support and protection. The Plan also addresses monitoring mechanisms and measuring progress.

Belkis, Wille. *Yemen's Torture Camps: Abuse of Migrants by Human Traffickers in a Climate of Impunity.* New York: Human

Rights Watch, 2014. https://www.hrw.org/report/2014/05/25/
yemens-torture-camps/abuse-migrants-human-traffickers-climate-
impunity

> This report is based on interviews with 67 people, includ-
> ing Ethiopian migrants, smugglers and traffickers, activists,
> journalists, diplomats, health care workers, and govern-
> ment officials. Their stories paint pictures of corruption
> and human rights abuses of African migrants reaching
> Yemen. Migrants are taken to torture camps where money
> is extorted from their families to ensure passage on to other
> countries.

Belser, Patrick. *Forced Labour and Human Trafficking: Estimating
the Profits*. Geneva: International Labour Office, 2005. http://
papers.ssrn.com/sol3/Papers.cfm?abstract_id=1838403

> The ILO estimates the global profits made from human
> trafficking and forced labor could reach US$44.2 billion
> annually—US$31.6 billion from trafficked victims. Mea-
> sures to combat this lucrative trade should include finan-
> cial investigations and the seizure of assets.

Biffl, Gudrun, Pfeffer, Thomas, and Trnka-Kwiecinski, Aga.
*Handbook for Professionals at the Interface of Police and Health
Authorities*. European Commission DG Home, 2014. http://
www.joint-efforts.org/websites/53/uploads/file/2014_
PAYOKE_TRAINING_MANUAL_USB_low.pdf

> This handbook, following a human rights–based approach,
> focuses on the provision of assistance in an effort to em-
> power victims of human trafficking. Emphasis is placed on
> informing and training professionals in the medical field
> to identify victims of trafficking. Part one of the manual
> provides content material while the second part introduces
> a training curriculum.

Brunovskis, Anette, and Surtees, Rebecca. *Preventing Human
Trafficking: Positive Deviance Methodology in Practice*. Norway: Fafo and the Nexus Institute, 2015. https://nexushuman

trafficking.files.wordpress.com/2015/02/preventing-ht-pd-in-practice-brunovskis-surtees-2015.pdf
This study introduces the concept of Positive Deviance and the link to prevention of human trafficking provides examples of its implementation in Nepal and Indonesia. A pilot project introduced in a town in Albania is explained and the authors discuss the replicability of this model in other settings.

Canada, the Government of. *National Action Plan to Combat Human Trafficking.* 2012. http://www.publicsafety.gc.ca/cnt/rsrcs/pblctns/ntnl-ctn-pln-cmbt/ntnl-ctn-pln-cmbt-eng.pdf
This National Action Plan discusses the government's initiatives in addressing prevention, protection, and assistance to victims; detection, investigation, and prosecution of traffickers; and partnerships and knowledge. The report elaborates on the Canadian anti-trafficking legislation as well as selective anti-trafficking efforts.

Eurostat. *Trafficking in Human Beings.* European Union, 2015. https://ec.europa.eu/anti-trafficking/sites/antitrafficking/files/eurostat_report_on_trafficking_in_human_beings_-_2015_edition.pdf
This second working paper provides statistics on human trafficking victims, suspected traffickers, and criminal justice responses (prosecution of suspected offenders) in all 28 Member States of the European Union.

Human Rights Watch. *Exploitation in the Name of Education: Uneven Progress in Ending Forced Child Begging in Senegal.* 2014. https://www.hrw.org/sites/default/files/reports/senegal0314_ForUpload.pdf
This is a follow-up to HRW 2010 report on forced begging in Senegal's Quranic boarding schools, where rather than studying the Quran young boys are sent out on the streets and forced to beg for long hours each day. Despite

the president's pledge to bring an end to such practices, Human Rights Watch found that young boys are still experiencing such abuses.

International Organization for Migration. *Human Trafficking and Business: Good Practices to Prevent and Combat Human Trafficking*. Geneva, Switzerland, 2010. http://publications.iom.int/system/files/pdf/un.gift_private_sector.pdf
This publication introduces the role that businesses can play in addressing human trafficking in their companies. Following an introduction of key issues, a series of case studies show the practical measures companies can take.

Monzini, Paola, Abdel Aziz, Nourhan, and Pastore, Ferruccio. *The Changing Dynamics of Cross-Border Human Smuggling and Trafficking in the Mediterranean*. Rome, Italy: Istituto Affari Internazionali (IAI), 2015. https://www.researchgate.net/publication/283211751_The_Changing_Dynamics_of_Cross-border_Human_Smuggling_and_Trafficking_in_the_Mediterranean
This report disentangles human smuggling from human trafficking, and discusses the extent to which occurrences in the Mediterranean region have impacted upon regional and transregional migration flows. A description is provided of the two main routes into Europe—the Eastern Mediterranean route and the Central Mediterranean route from Libya to Italy.

Shelley, Louise. *Human Smuggling and Trafficking into Europe: A Comparative Perspective*. Migration Policy Institute, 2014. http://www.migrationpolicy.org/research/human-smuggling-and-trafficking-europe-comparative-perspective
Examining smuggling and trafficking trends and patterns from around the world into Europe, this report profiles the victims and facilitators of this business. Facilitators, ranging from small networks to large-scale international organizations, are aided by corrupt officials.

Simmons, Frances, O'Brien, Brynn, David, Fiona, and Beacroft, Laura. "Human Trafficking and Slavery Offenders in Australia." *Trends & Issues in Crime and Criminal Justice.* Australian Institute of Criminology, No. 464, 2013. http://www.aic.gov.au/media_library/publications/tandi_pdf/tandi464.pdf

This report provides information about the characteristics and motivations, as well as the modus operandi used by offenders to control and exploit their victims.

Surtees, Rebecca. *Traffickers and Trafficking: Challenges in Researching Human Traffickers and Trafficking Operations.* International Organization for Migration and the Nexus Institute. Geneva, Switzerland, and Washington, DC, 2014. http://publications.iom.int/system/files/pdf/nexus_traffickers_and_trafficking_final_web.pdf

This study exposes the limitations in gathering data concerning traffickers and their operations from their victims. Information obtained from victim-derived data sets must be supplemented with data from other sources. A discussion on recent research on trafficking and traffickers is included in the report.

Surtees, Rebecca. *In African Waters. The Trafficking of Cambodian Fishers in South Africa.* International Organization for Migration and the Nexus Institute, Geneva, Switzerland, and Washington, DC, 2014. http://publications.iom.int/system/files/pdf/nexus_africanwaters_web.pdf

This report describes the experiences of Cambodian men who suffered forms of extreme exploitation or were held in servitude by human traffickers on fishing vessels in the waters off the coast of South Africa. For more information on exploitation and human trafficking within the fishing industry, see other reports authored by Rebecca Surtees: *At sea: The trafficking of seafarers and fishers from Ukraine*; *Trapped at sea. Using the legal and regulatory framework to prevent and combat the trafficking of seafarers and fishers*; and *Trafficked at sea. The exploitation of Ukrainian seafarers and fishers.*

United Nations General Assembly. 64/293. *United Nations Global Plan of Action to Combat Trafficking in Persons.* 2010. http://www.unodc.org/documents/human-trafficking/United_Nations_Global_Plan_of_Action_to_Combat_Trafficking_in_Persons.pdf

> The UN Global Plan of Action to Combat Trafficking in Persons was adopted on 30 July by the General Assembly with the aim of urging governments worldwide to take consistent and coordinated initiatives to eradicate trafficking. The Plan calls for long-term measures integrating the fight against human trafficking into the UN's broader programs around the world, to increase development and strengthen security. It encourages the establishment of a voluntary trust fund for victims of trafficking.

United Nations Office on Drugs and Crime. *Global Report on Trafficking in Persons.* http://www.unodc.org/unodc/data-and-analysis/glotip.html

> In 2010, the General Assembly of the United Nations mandated UNODC to produce a report under the UN Global Plan of Action to Combat Trafficking in Persons. UNODC releases a report every two years documenting trends and patterns of trafficking in countries around the world. The report contains information on victims, traffickers, markets of exploitation, movement, and criminal justice and legal responses to human trafficking. The first report was released in 2009, followed by reports in 2012, 2014, and 2016.

United Nations Office on Drugs and Crime. *Protocol to Prevent, Suppress and Punish Trafficking in Persons, Especially Women and Children, Supplementing the United Nations Convention Against*

Transnational Organized Crime. 2000. http://www.osce.org/ odihr/19223?download=true

Human trafficking is defined in Article 3 of the "Trafficking Protocol." The protocol defines the scope of application and the need for criminalization. Additional articles spell out what is expected of Member States with respect to protection of victims of trafficking in persons; prevention, cooperation, and other measures; and final measures.

United States Department of State. *Trafficking in Persons Report.* http://www.state.gov/j/tip/rls/tiprpt/

Since 2001, the Office to Monitor and Combat Trafficking in Persons has produced an annual report on the state of human trafficking in countries with a significant trafficking problem. The report highlights areas of growing concern and presents global law enforcement statistics. The report ranks countries on tiers based on the prevention, protection, and prosecution measures implemented to address the trafficking problem.

Academic Articles and Journals

Anti-Trafficking Review is an open source journal published by the Global Alliance Against Traffic in Women (GAATW). The journal promotes a human rights–based approach to understanding trafficking, focusing on overlooked or emerging themes in the field of anti-trafficking.

Volume 1 (2012): *Where's the Accountability?*
Volume 2 (2013): *Human Rights at the Border*
Volume 3 (2014): *Following the Money: Spending on Anti-Trafficking*
Volume 4 (2015): *Fifteen Years of the UN Trafficking Protocol*
Volume 5 (2015): *Forced Labour and Human Trafficking*
Volume 6 (2016): *Special Issue—Prosecuting Human Trafficking*

All issues can be accessed at http://www.antitraffickingreview
.org/index.php/atrjournal/issue/archive

Acharya, Arun Kumar. "Sexual Exploitation and Trafficking of
Women and Girls in Mexico: An Analysis on Impact of Violence on Health Status." *Journal of Intercultural Studies,* 2014,
35 (2): 182–195.

> The author conducts empirical research, interviewing
> 60 trafficked girls and women, 5 madams, and 3 traffick-
> ers in Mexico City. The paper explores the kinds of men-
> tal, physical, and sexual violence experienced by trafficked
> girls and women in Mexico. The author focuses on how
> various forms of violence affect the physical and sexual
> health of victims of trafficking.

Aronowitz, Alexis A. "The Social Etiology of Human Trafficking: How Poverty and Cultural Practices Facilitate Trafficking,"
Pontifical Academy of Social Sciences, Vatican City, April 17–21,
2015. http://www.endslavery.va/content/endslavery/en/publica
tions/acta_20/aronowitz.html

> This paper analyzes three unusual regional patterns of traf-
> ficking: child trafficking and labor exploitation in West
> and Central Africa; transnational trafficking and labor ex-
> ploitation in the Middle East; and the sexual exploitation
> of young boys in Afghanistan. These patterns of abuse are
> explained by examining the economic, social, and cultural
> practices in these specific regions.

Aronowitz, Alexis A. "Victims of Human Trafficking: A Complex Issue," *Dossier of Analysis: Human Trafficking.* Centro de
Estudios Internacionales—CEI Facultad de Ciencias Sociales
Universidad de los Andes, July 2015. http://cei.uniandes.edu.co/
index.php/component/docman/cat_view/5-dossier?Itemid=

> This article introduces the reader to the complexities of
> identifying victims of human trafficking and how vic-
> tims view their own status. Problems of measurement

and consent contribute to the understanding of this multifaceted problem.

Aronowitz, Alexis A., and Koning, Anneke. "Understanding Human Trafficking as a Market System: Addressing the Demand Side of Trafficking for Sexual Exploitation," *Revue Internationale de Droit Penale, International Review of Penal Law,* 2014/3, 85): 669–696.

Human trafficking must be analyzed as a market system where traffickers generate profit by meeting the demand for services supplied by trafficked persons. Analyzing supply and demand within the context of a market-based transaction, the sex market is examined within the cultural and social contexts that foster demand.

Aronowitz, Alexis A., and Isitman, Elif. "Trafficking of Human Beings for the Purpose of Organ Removal: Are (International) Legal Instruments Effective Measures to Eradicate the Practice?" *Groningen Journal of International Law,* 2013, 1 (2). http://papers.ssrn.com/sol3/papers.cfm?abstract_id=25 93581

This paper discusses the complexity of organ trafficking and examines legal and extralegal instruments to regulate the flow of organs for transplantation.

Barrick, Kelle, Lattimore, Pamela K., Pitts, Wayne J., and Zhang, Sheldon X. "When Farmworkers and Advocates See Trafficking but Law Enforcement Does Not: Challenges in Identifying Labor Trafficking in North Carolina." *Crime, Law and Social Change,* 2014, 61 (2): 205–214.

The researchers examine the perception of labor trafficking among farmworkers, law enforcement, and other stakeholders in North Carolina. They found that when farmworkers had experienced various labor trafficking violations and this was reported by community agencies, there appeared to be a general lack of awareness of the problem by local and state law enforcement agencies. The authors suggest a specialized mechanism be established to detect and combat labor trafficking in the agricultural sector.

Brayley, Helen, and Cockbain, Ella. "British Children Can Be Trafficked Too: Towards an Inclusive Definition of Internal Child Sex Trafficking." *Child Abuse Review,* 2014, 23 (3): 171–184. https://www.researchgate.net/publication/260556238_British_ Children_Can_Be_Trafficked_Too_Towards_an_Inclusive_ Definition_of_Internal_Child_Sex_Trafficking

> Despite legislation, there is uncertainty in Britain in terms of how domestic trafficking differs from other forms of commercial sexual exploitation of children. The authors discuss the definitional problems and debate in Britain regarding whether or not British children can be victims of human trafficking. The authors propose a more clearly delineated and all-inclusive definition of internal child sex trafficking which, if standardized, would facilitate more and consistent data collection and effective multiagency interventions.

Brennan, Denise. "Myths Meet Reality: How We Are Not Fighting Trafficking or Supporting Trafficking Survivors." *New York Law School Law Review,* 2016, 60 (3 and 4): 605–613. http:// www.nylslawreview.com/wp-content/uploads/sites/16/2016/06/ Volume-60.3–4.Brennan.pdf

> Based upon 10 years of ethnographic research with exploited migrant workers, the author argues that deporting trafficked persons does not serve them and discourages them from reporting abuses. Furthermore, restrictions under the T(trafficking)-visa harms victims. Trafficked persons experience a period of economic uncertainty and are often left in a legal limbo. A rights-based, peer-to-peer outreach approach is necessary to effectively assist victims and combat trafficking.

Brennan, Denise. "Trafficking, Scandal, and Abuse of Migrant Workers in Argentina and the United States." *Annals of the American Academy of Political and Social Science,* 2014, 653.

> The author discusses the label of "trafficked" victim and argues that the term is often used when referring to all migrant workers, confounding the definition of trafficking (using the examples of the Dominican Republic and Argentina). In contrast, the politics of immigration in the United States influences the government's trafficking policy to overlook "significant exploitation of labor migrants." The term "trafficked" person has become politicized.

Chong, Natividad Gutiérrez. "Human Trafficking and Sex Industry: Does Ethnicity and Race Matter?" *Journal of Intercultural Studies,* 2014, 35(2): 196–213.

> Due to structural poverty, marginalization and sexual violence, which is prevalent among marginalized men and women, racial and ethnic minorities are more likely to be exposed to human trafficking. The author argues that sexist and racist stereotypes of women are used in the sex industry and that patriarchal culture furthers women's passivity and submission making sexual exploitation a likely outcome for many women.

Chuang, Janie. "Beyond a Snapshot: Preventing Human Trafficking in the Global Economy," *Indiana Journal of Global Legal Studies,* 2006, 13(1). http://www.repository.law.indiana.edu/cgi/viewcontent.cgi?article=1323&context=ijgls

> Rather than focusing on human trafficking as a crime that must be prosecuted, the author seeks to frame trafficking as an immigration issue in response to socioeconomic trends and globalization. Long-term counter-trafficking strategies must target the conditions that drive people to seek dangerous labor migration assignments.

Countryman-Roswurm, Karen, and Shaffer, Victoria. "It's More than Just My Body That Got Hurt: The Psychophysiological

Consequences of Sex Trafficking." *Journal of Trafficking, Organized Crime and Security*, 2015, 1 (1): 1–8. http://www.brown walker.com/ojs/index.php/JTOCS/article/view/36/pdf

The authors discuss the long-term physiological and psychological effects due to stress and trauma and introduce a multidisciplinary practice—the Lotus Anti-Trafficking Victim to Vitality Program model. This evidence-based model is built on collaborative multidisciplinary services and is being used with survivors of sex trafficking.

Farrell, Amy, and Pfeiffer, Rebecca. "Policing Human Trafficking: Cultural Blinders and Organizational Barriers," *The Annals of the American Academy of Political and Social Science*, May 2014, 653 (1): 46–64.

The low number of arrests and prosecutions may be due to the challenges that local police face in identifying cases of human trafficking. Based upon interviews and data from case records, the authors find that the culture and perceptions of police do not support the identification of different types of trafficking cases and victims. Most expertise is concentrated on the identification of minors in sex trafficking making labor trafficking "seem largely nonexistent."

Gallagher, Anne, and Surtees, Rebecca. "Measuring the Success of Counter-Trafficking Interventions in the Criminal Justice Sector: Who Decides—and How?" *Anti-Trafficking Review*, June 2012, 1:10–30. https://works.bepress.com/anne_gallagher/21/download

Counter-trafficking interventions should demonstrate accountability and success and have a positive impact on its target group. This may be determined by who decides what programs to implement and how this decision is reached. Success or failure varies according to who is consulted and their specific role within the program, and the criteria established to measure success and assumptions attached to those criteria.

Gozdiak, Elzbieta. "Children Trafficked to the United States: Myths and Realities." *Global Dialogue*, Summer-Autumn, 2012, 14 (2). https://www.researchgate.net/publication/272508344_ Children_trafficked_to_the_United_States_Myths_and_Realities

> In this study of child victims of human trafficking, the author interviews more than 30 child survivors as well as stakeholders and examines court records. She dispels myths about child trafficking. The group is diverse in terms of age, markets of exploitation, how they arrived in the United States, how they were treated by traffickers, how they perceived their experience, and whether they suffered trauma. How the children were perceived, in terms of agency and expectations, plays an important role in their post-trafficking adjustment.

Huisman, Wim, and Kleemans, Edward R. "The Challenges of Fighting Sex Trafficking in the Legalized Prostitution Market of the Netherlands." *Crime, Law and Social Change*, 2014, 61 (2): 215–228. https://www.researchgate.net/publication/260493897_ The_challenges_of_fighting_sex_trafficking_in_the_legalized_ prostitution_market_of_the_Netherlands

> This paper examines the impact in the Netherlands when Dutch authorities lifted the ban on brothels. Brothels meeting certain licensing conditions became legal. Despite its legitimacy, the licensing conditions and the monitoring of compliance have not eradicated human trafficking in the prostitution sector nor has it driven out organized crime. The authors conclude that fighting human trafficking may be more difficult in the legalized prostitution sector.

Leman, Johan, and Janssens, Stef. "The Albanian and Post-Soviet Business of Trafficking Women for Prostitution." *European Journal of Criminology*, 5 (4): 433–451. https://lirias.ku leuven.be/bitstream/123456789/204177/2/Leman.pdf

> The authors examined 62 court files involving East European trafficking networks, to understand the network

structure and financial modus operandi of the trafficking organizations. Criminal organizations are learning organizations as they develop and adapt to change.

Minaye, Abebaw, and Zeleke, Waganesh. "Re-conceptualizing Human Trafficking: The Experiences of Ethiopian Returnee Migrants." *Journal of Trafficking, Organized Crime and Security*, 2015, 1 (1): 9–23. http://www.brownwalker.com/ojs/index.php/JTOCS/article/view/37/pdf_37a
This study is part of a larger study of return migrants to Ethiopia from the Middle East and South Africa to understand the context in which migration turns into trafficking. Participants in the study reported being exploited by employers within the context of the *kafala* sponsorship system.

O'Connell Davidson, Julia. "Moving Children? Child Trafficking, Child Migration and Child Rights." *Critical Social Policy*, August 2011, 31 (3): 454–477. https://www.researchgate.net/profile/Julia_Oconnell_davidson/publication/254084807_Moving_children_Child_trafficking_child_migration_and_child_rights/links/55e7606908aeb6516262e163.pdf
The author contrasts the concern over children as trafficked victims with the lived experience of migrant children. It contrasts the intense public and policy concern with the suffering of "trafficked" children against the relative lack of interest in other ways that migrant children can suffer, due, for example, to immigration policy and its enforcement. Policy and practice often punishes, rather than protects, children who do not conform to the preconceived norm of what constitutes a "child."

Oram, Sian, Stockl, Heidi, Busza, Joanne, Howard, Louise M., and Zimmerman, Cathy. "Prevalence and Risk of Violence and the Physical, Mental, and Sexual Health Problems Associated with Human Trafficking: Systematic Review." *PLoS Med*, 9 (5):

e1001224. doi:10.1371/journal.pmed.1001224. 2012. http://journals.plos.org/plosmedicine/article/asset?id=10.1371%2Fjournal.pmed.1001224.PDF

This is a systematic review of 19 studies investigating the prevalence and degree to which victims of trafficking (women and girls) of sexual exploitation are exposed to violence, and the prevalence and risk of mental, physical, and sexual health problems, including HIV.

Pandey, Sonal, Kaufman, Michelle, Tewari, Hare Ram, and Bhowmick, Pradip Kumar. "Life in the Red Light: A Qualitative Investigation of the Daily Life of Trafficking Victims in Indian Brothels." *Journal of Trafficking, Organized Crime and Security*, 2015, 1(1): 36–46. http://www.brownwalker.com/ojs/index.php/JTOCS/article/view/39/15–1–1Pandey39a

Thirty survivors of sex trafficking were participants in this study to examine how women adapt to work in Indian brothels. The authors describe the business enterprise of the brothel, survivors' adaptation to the work, their clients, and their earnings. The authors argue that "intricate and client-focused rehabilitation" programs are necessary to help survivors adjust to life outside the brothel.

Siegel, Dina, and de Blank, Syvia. "Women Who Traffic Women: The Role of Women in Human Trafficking Networks—Dutch Cases." *Global Crime*, 2010, 1 (4): 436–447.

Data collected from 89 court files demonstrate that women play active roles in human trafficking networks. The authors analyze the activities, tasks, and roles of female offenders and identify three roles—as supporters, partners in crime, and "madams" or heads of trafficking operations.

Surtees, Rebecca, and de Kerchove, Fabrice. "Who Funds Re/integration? Ensuring Sustainable Services for Trafficking Victims." *Anti-Trafficking Review*, 2014, 3: 64–86. http://www.antitraffickingreview.org/index.php/atrjournal/article/view/65/63

Resources for reintegration services are generally not widely available. This article discusses the importance of reintegration services to trafficked persons as central to an effective anti-trafficking response. Different strategies used within the Trafficking Victims Reintegration Programme (TVRP) in the Balkans are introduced.

Tsutsumi, Atsuro, Izutsu, Takashi, Poudyal, Amod K., Kato, Seika, and Marui, Eiji. "Mental Health of Female Survivors of Human Trafficking in Nepal," *Social Science & Medicine,* 2008, 66: 1841e1847. https://www.researchgate.net/profile/ Atsuro_Tsutsumi/publication/5576066_Mental_health_of_ female_survivors_of_human_trafficking_in_Nepal/links/ 0c9605199defb2a4d8000000.pdf

This article examines demographic variables as well as the mental and physical health of survivors of sex and labor trafficking in Nepal. While both groups of survivors show signs of anxiety, depression, and PTSD, symptoms are more pronounced in victims of sex trafficking.

Weitzer, Ronald. "New Directions in Research on Human Trafficking." *The Annals of the American Academy of Political and Social Science,* 2014, 653: 6. http://s3.amazonaws.com/academia .edu.documents/45250358/ANNALS_R.Weitzer_.pdf?AWS AccessKeyId=AKIAJ56TQJRTWSMTNPEA&Expires=147 0091596&Signature=5l%2F2O22QHP9z8VKFZTmPEI 9fo6c%3D&response-content-disposition=inline%3B%20 filename%3DNew_Directions_in_Human_Trafficking_Rese .pdf

This article examines trends, the international magnitude, and the seriousness of human trafficking relative to other illicit activities. Weitzer finds that most claims are unfounded and not evidence-based or verifiable. The author argues for micro- rather than macro-level research, which can be more easily quantified and is better suited for appropriate policy and enforcement responses.

Weitzer, Ronald, and Zhang, Sheldon. "Human Trafficking: Recent Empirical Research." *Annals of the American Academy of Political and Social Science*, 2014, 653 (1). http://ann.sagepub.com/content/653/1.toc

The topics are diverse and focus on empirical research ranging from policing human trafficking in the United States to issues related to labor trafficking in Asia, Argentina, West Africa, Bulgaria, South Africa, and Cambodia.

Withman, Charlene J. D. "Hitting Them Where It Hurts: Strategies for Seizing Assets in Human Trafficking Cases." *AEquitas*, 2013, 20. http://www.aequitasresource.org/Hitting-Them-Where-it-Hurts-Strategies-for-Seizing-Assets-in-Human-Trafficking-Cases.pdf. Accessed on July 31, 2016.

The seizure of property that is the fruit of or was used to further the criminal enterprise—asset forfeiture—can be used to deter and disrupt traffickers, while compensating trafficked victims or financing victim compensation funds to support all victims of trafficking. Asset forfeiture takes the form of civil or criminal seizures. Civil asset forfeiture can often be pursued, even where there is no criminal case pending and is not dependent on a conviction. This article discusses what measures should be considered and how prosecutors can petition the court for the seizure of assets.

Investigative Journalism

Rankin, Jennifer. "Human Traffickers 'Using Migration Crisis' to Force More People into Slavery." *The Guardian*, May 19, 2016. https://www.theguardian.com/world/2016/may/19/human-traffickers-using-migration-crisis-to-force-more-people-into-slavery. Accessed on July 13, 2016.

Concerns are rising over the number of unaccompanied minors who have "dropped off the radar of official agencies" since having arrived in Europe. It is feared that they may have fallen prey to traffickers. At least 10,000 children have disappeared; Germany reports the disappearance of 4,700 children, while Sweden reports the disappearance of up to 10 children a week.

Vulliamy, Elsa. "Refugees Who Cannot Pay People Smugglers 'Being Sold for Organs.'" *Independent,* July 4, 2016. http://www.independent.co.uk/news/world/europe/refugee-crisis-sold-for-organs-people-smugglers-trafficker-a7119066.html
An arrested smuggler cooperating with Italian police reported that "[m]igrants who are unable to pay people smugglers for their journey from Africa to Europe are killed for their organs . . . migrants who couldn't pay for journeys across the Mediterranean 'were sold for €15,000 to groups, particularly Egyptians, who are equipped for harvesting organs.'"

Academic Collaboration Platforms

Academia.edu
https://www.academia.edu/
By registering for free with this academic website, the researcher can access tens of thousands of academic papers uploaded by authors. A search can take place by topic (e.g., "human trafficking," "organ trafficking," "child trafficking") or by author. A search by author allows the researcher to browse the author's uploaded academic papers.

Researchgate.net
https://www.researchgate.net
Similar to Academia.edu, Researchgate.net is a forum where academics have uploaded millions of academic articles that can be accessed by joining for free.

Videos and Documentaries

Born into Brothels
https://www.youtube.com/watch?v=_kyXFr2g1x8
    This 2004 award-winning documentary shows the lives of the children of prostitutes in Kolkata's red light district.

CNN Freedom Project
    The CNN Freedom Project has produced a number of documentaries on various forms of human trafficking around the world. Some of the documentaries include:
    Branded: Sex Slavery in America
    http://edition.cnn.com/videos/world/2015/09/14/
    spc-freedom-project-sex-slavery-in-america.cnn/video/
    playlists/cnn-freedom-project-human-trafficking/

    Children for Sale
    http://edition.cnn.com/videos/intl_tv-shows/2015/
    07/28/freedom-project-children-for-sale.cnn

    Cocoa-nomics
    http://edition.cnn.com/videos/international/2014/
    03/02/cfp-cocoa-nomics-full.cnn

    Every Day in Cambodia: Documentary
    http://edition.cnn.com/videos/intl_tv-shows/2015/
    04/28/spc-freedom-project-every-day-in-cambodia.cnn

    Nepal's Organ Trail
    http://edition.cnn.com/videos/world/2015/05/06/spc-
    cfp-nepal-organ-trail.cnn

    Operation Hope
    http://edition.cnn.com/2012/12/06/world/freedom-
    project-operation-hope/index.html

Dancing Boys of Afghanistan, The. PBS documentary.
https://vimeo.com/11352212
> This documentary exposes the practice of *Bacha Bazi* in Afghanistan. Young boys are dressed in women's clothing and perform erotic dances in front of all-male audiences. They are often "sold" afterwards to the highest bidder. The boys are owned by wealthy, influential men who use them as pawns in their games of influence and power.

Opium Brides
https://www.youtube.com/watch?v=Rxx_-t_PX3A
> This documentary shows that when opium crops fail and Afghan farmers are unable to repay loans from drug gangs, they are forced to repay their debts by giving their daughters to drug traffickers.

Qatar's World Cup, ESPN, Bluefoot Entertainment, documentary.
https://vimeo.com/95215527
> This 17-minute video introduces the exploitation of Nepali workers in Qatar during the building of the 2022 infrastructure for the World Cup Soccer games. The *Kafala* system is introduced as a facilitator to the exploitation of migrant workers in the Gulf State country.

Sex Slaves, Frontline, 2006, documentary.
https://vimeo.com/14944657
> This 57-minute video introduces survivors of sexual exploitation in Turkey. Women from Moldova and Ukraine are deceived with promises of jobs abroad, only to find themselves sold into sexual slavery. The undercover journalists follow the case of one man trying desperately to find his wife who was sold to a violent pimp. This PBS documentary won an Emmy for outstanding investigative journalism.

Taliban Child Fighters
https://www.journeyman.tv/film/6023
    This documentary introduces us to children in Afghani-
    stan who either are kidnapped and coerced into or will-
    ingly take on the role of suicide bombers. Others are
    primed to carry out attacks on ISAF troops.

NOT IN
OUR
STOP
BUYING
DEFENDERS
OUR
GIRLS
thedefendersusa.org
People's bodie
ARE NOT
commoditie
ARE TRAFFICKED

This chapter provides a chronology of important dates within the field of slavery, forced labor, and human trafficking. The reader will understand the historical development of slavery and how individuals, governments, international and nongovernmental organizations (NGOs) have contributed to eradicating its various forms. These entries, covering the last 6,000 years, are among the most important and interesting.

4000 BCE Slaves in Mesopotamia, taken as spoils of war either as punishment for the transgression of laws or for having taken up arms against the community, were used in agriculture and to contribute to food production, to tend stock, and work in mines.

1792–1750 BCE Slavery is practiced during the reign of King Hammurabi. Distinction was made between chattel slavery—persons who could be enslaved forever—and those who were obtained as a result of debt bondage and could be

People opposed to child sex trafficking rally outside the Washington Supreme Court in Olympia, Washington, on October 21, 2014. On September 3, 2015, the Washington Supreme Court ruled in favor of three young girls who sued Backpage.com, claiming they were sold as prostitutes on the site. The court's ruling says the Communications Decency Act does not protect Backpage from state lawsuits because there is enough evidence to show that it did not just host the ads, but helped develop the content. (AP Photo/Rachel La Corte)

freed by their owners after a period of three years. Male slaves were provided rights that were denied female slaves.

Fifth to the third centuries BCE   Ancient Greece maintained slave societies. Slavery was so pervasive in Ancient Athens that slaves outnumbered freemen by approximately two to one.

594 BCE **onward**   Slaves in Ancient Greece were non-Greek captives of war acquired generally at markets. Women and female children were purchased for the purpose of sexual exploitation.

Between 27 BCE **and 476** CE   Slavery was documented in ancient Rome; the Roman Empire was the largest slave society in the ancient world. Slaves were viewed as property rather than persons. Female slaves were expected to reproduce offspring, who themselves became slaves.

1315   Louis X issues a decree in 1315 claiming that any slave setting foot on French soil should be freed.

1441   The European slave trading begins with the Portuguese transporting people from Africa to Portugal and using them as slaves. The Portuguese are followed by Britain, France, Holland, Spain, Sweden, Denmark, and North America.

1619   The first Africans are brought by Dutch traders to Jamestown, Virginia.

1783   Quaker Anti-Slavery Committees, established in the United Kingdom, presented the first slave trade petition to the British Parliament.

1807   The Abolition of the Slave Trade Act abolished the slave trade in the British colonies and made it illegal to carry enslaved people in British ships.

1833   The Slavery Abolition Act of 1833 abolished slavery in most of the British Empire. The Act was strongly supported by William Wilberforce, moralist and British parliamentarian, who campaigned for the complete abolition of slavery.

1838   Two hundred seventy-two men, women, and children are sold as slaves bound for the plantations of the Deep South.

They are sold by Jesuit priests to help secure the future of the Catholic institution of higher learning—which has now become Georgetown University. Other universities, among them Columbia, Brown, the University of Virginia, and Harvard, were also involved in the slave trade.

1839 The Anti-Slavery Society is formed by Thomas Buxton, Thomas Clarkson, and other abolitionists to campaign against slavery worldwide.

1849 Harriet Tubman, a slave, escapes via the Underground Railroad. Over an 11-year period, she would rescue dozens of slaves and provide instructions to an additional 50–60 fugitive slaves who were able to escape.

1863 Abraham Lincoln issues a preliminary Emancipation Proclamation that took effect on January 1, 1863. It resulted in freeing the slaves in the rebellious states but left those in the states loyal to the Union in bondage.

1865 The Thirteenth Amendment to the U.S. Constitution abolishes slavery and involuntary servitude, except as punishment for a crime. It passes the Senate in 1864 and the House in 1865, and is ratified by the required number of states that year.

1904 The International Agreement for the Suppression of "White Slave Traffic" to protect women from being deceived or forced into prostitution is negotiated in Paris. A total of 26 states ratified the original 1904 treaty, which entered into force a year later.

1910 The Mann Act, also known as the White Slave Traffic Act, is enacted in the United States. This federal criminal statute was not only intended to fight the interstate trafficking of women, but was also used to prosecute men who moved women across state lines for the purpose of consensual prostitution.

1919 The International Labour Organization (ILO) is founded in this year. The ILO addresses, among others, forced labor, human trafficking, and slavery.

1921   The International Convention for the Suppression of the Traffic in Women and Children is adopted under the auspices of the League of Nations. Article 2 of the Convention addresses the trafficking of children of both sexes.

1924   The Council of the League of Nations creates the Temporary Slavery Commission. Its final report called on States to consider the "abolition of the legal status of slavery."

1926   The Slavery Convention is signed at Geneva on September 25, and entered into force a year later. The convention obliged signatories to eliminate forced labor, slavery, and the slave trade in their territories.

1927   The League of Nations changes "white slavery" to "trafficking in women," to emphasize the inclusion of women of all races.

1930   The International Labour Organization Convention Concerning Forced or Compulsory Labour is adopted and entered into force in 1932. It required parties to take effective measures to prevent and eliminate the use of forced labor.

1933   The International Convention for the Suppression of the Traffic in Women of Full Age extends the punishment to include attempted offences and extends the jurisdiction to include the colonies, protectorates, and territories under of the parties concerned.

1946   In the aftermath of World War II, the United Nations General Assembly votes to establish the United Nations International Children's Emergency Fund (UNICEF). The organization, founded in that year, works with development partners, governments, and NGOs on practices that exacerbate children's vulnerabilities to trafficking.

1948   The Universal Declaration of Human Rights is drafted by representatives with different cultural backgrounds from all regions of the world. It establishes fundamental human rights to be universally protected. Article 4 states that "No one shall be held in slavery or servitude; slavery and the slave trade shall be prohibited in all their forms."

1949 Convention for the Suppression of the Traffic in Persons and of the Exploitation of the Prostitution of Others is adopted and entered into force in 1951. This was the first internationally legally binding instrument on trafficking, prescribing procedures for combating international trafficking for prostitution.

1954 The Asia Foundation is founded. This nonprofit international development organization is committed to improving lives across countries in Asia. One of its focuses is on improving the rights of women through projects to counter human trafficking.

1956 The Supplementary Convention on the Abolition of Slavery, Slave Trade, and Institutions and Practices Similar to Slavery updates the 1926 Convention and includes the criminalization of debt bondage, servile marriage, and child servitude.

1960 Terre des Hommes is founded in Lausanne, Switzerland, with the objective of helping children in need in Algeria. The organization will grow to an international confederation of 10 national organizations working for the rights of children around the world.

1978 The Helsinki Watch is created to monitor government compliance of the 1975 Helsinki Accords by "naming and shaming" abusive governments. America Watch will be founded in 1981, followed by Asia Watch (1985), Africa Watch (1988), and Middle East Watch (1989). "The Watch Committees" will become Human Rights Watch in 1988.

1987 First established as the Foundation against Trafficking in Women, the Dutch NGO campaigns to develop and improve national legislation and litigation for addressing trafficking in women and to assist victims. The organization began serving as the central registration for victims of trafficking in the Netherlands.

1989 The United Nations Convention on the Rights of the Child provides rights to protect children from neglect, abuse, and exploitation. Article 35 of the Convention requires governments to take all possible measures to ensure children are not abducted, sold, or trafficked for any purpose.

1990 Advocates from numerous countries in Asia gather in Chiang Mai, northern Thailand, with the goal of putting an end to child sex tourism. This is the birth of ECPAT (End Child Prostitution in Asian Tourism).

1992 The ILO creates the International Programme on the Elimination of Child Labour (IPEC) with the overall goal of promoting a worldwide movement to combat child labor.

1995 A trilateral anti-trafficking project between the Czech Republic, Poland, and the Netherlands results in the formation of La Strada, an international organization addressing trafficking in human beings.

1996 The Stockholm Declaration is adopted at the first World Congress against Commercial Sexual Exploitation of Children held in Stockholm, Sweden.

1996 Shakti Samuha is the first organization in Nepal to be established and run by survivors of human trafficking.

1997 The United Nations International Drug Control Program (UNDCP) and the Crime Prevention and Criminal Justice Division are combined to form the Office for Drug Control and Crime Prevention at the United Nations Office in Vienna. The UNDCP will later become the United Nations Office on Drugs and Crime. Its aim is to assist Member States in their struggle against international crimes such as human smuggling and trafficking.

1997 Gary Haugen launches the International Justice Mission (IJM), a global organization that partners with local authorities to rescue victims of violence, bring criminals to justice, restore survivors, and strengthen justice systems. IJM combats slavery, sex trafficking, police brutality, and other forms of violence in nearly 20 communities throughout Africa, Latin America, South Asia, and Southeast Asia.

1997   The World Tourism Network on Child Protection (formerly the Task Force for the Protection of Children in Tourism) is established. It is a network featuring the participation of a range of tourism stakeholders, from governments, international organizations and NGOs to tourism industry groups and media associations. Its mandate is to prevent all forms of (sexual) exploitation of youth in the tourism sector.

1998   The Global March Against Child Labor, an 80,000-kilometer march crossing 103 countries, raises awareness and carries the message that child labor is unacceptable. The march, one of the largest social movements ever on behalf of exploited children, culminated four and half months later in Geneva at the ILO Conference.

2000   The United Nations Convention Against Transnational Organized Crime represents a major step forward in the fight against transnational organized crime. The Protocol to Prevent, Suppress and Punish Trafficking in Persons, Especially Women and Children, supplementing the Convention, introduces the first internationally recognized definition of human trafficking, which includes forced labor and organ trafficking.

2000   The U.S. Congress passes the Trafficking Victims Protection Act (TVPA). The legislation creates an Interagency Task Force to Combat Trafficking as well as the Office to Monitor and Combat Trafficking. Reauthorizations of this Act followed in 2003, 2005, 2008 and 2013.

2000   The first independent National Rapporteur on Trafficking in Human Beings to report on the nature and extent of human trafficking and the effectiveness of government policies is appointed in the Netherlands.

2001   Fulfilling the mandate of the Trafficking Victims Protection Act of 2000, the U.S. Department of State publishes the first global Trafficking in Persons Report. Annual reports follow.

2001 The countries of the Economic Community of Western African States (ECOWAS) agree on an action plan to tackle slavery and human trafficking in the region.

2002 The Polaris Project is founded in the United States. This leading nonprofit works to stop human trafficking through awareness raising, training law enforcement, advocating for better legislation, and maintaining a national, toll-free hotline.

2003 The UN Protocol to Prevent, Suppress and Punish Trafficking in Persons, especially Women and Children is entered into force. The Protocol contains provisions on criminalization of the act and prevention and protection for victims. It also addresses demand, the exchange of information and training, and measures to strengthen the effectiveness of border controls.

2003 The Organization for Security and Cooperation in Europe establishes the Office of the Special Representative and Coordinator for Combating Trafficking in Human Beings to help participating States develop and implement effective policies.

2004 The Organization of American States (OAS) creates the position of the Anti-TIP Coordinator, with the aim of fostering national action by governments, advancing best practices, implementing new projects and training programs, and gaining new allies for the hemisphere.

2004 The U.S. Department of State introduces the Trafficking in Persons Heroes—individuals, who, through their commitment, have helped pass legislation, establish shelters, and aid victims.

2004 The Association of South-East Asia Nations (ASEAN) joins forces to combat human trafficking and adopts the Declaration Against Trafficking in Persons Particularly Women and Children.

2004 The World Health Assembly urges Member States to take measures to protect poor and vulnerable persons from transplant tourism and to address the issue of international trafficking of human organs and tissues.

2004 A Special Rapporteur on Human Trafficking is appointed by the United Nations.

2005 The Council of Europe Convention on Action Against Trafficking in Human Beings is adopted and entered into force in 2008. It takes a human rights perspective and focuses on victim protection while establishing a monitoring mechanism to control the implementation of obligations contained in the Convention.

2006 STOP THE TRAFFIK, initially launched as a campaign, has become a global coalition to eradicate trafficking through fundraising, education, and advocacy.

2006 The African Union COMMission Initiative against Trafficking (AU.COMMIT) is adopted in Tripoli in November. In the same year, The Ouagadougou Action Plan is adopted by Ministers for Foreign Affairs, ministers responsible for Migration and Development from Africa and EU Member States, and AU and EC Commissioners and other representatives gathered in Tripoli, Libya.

2007 The United Nations Office on Drugs and Crime (UNODC), together with the International Labor Organization (ILO), the International Organization for Migration (IOM), the Organization for Security and Cooperation in Europe (OSCE), the Office of the United Nations High Commissioner for Human Rights (OHCHR), and the United Nations International Children's Emergency Fund (UNICEF), launches the United Nations Global Initiative to Fight Human Trafficking (UN.GIFT).

2008 The U.S. TVPA is reauthorized and renamed the William Wilberforce Trafficking Victims Protection Reauthorization Act of 2008.

2008 In an effort to fight organ trafficking, more than 150 representatives from government officials, the medical and scientific community, and ethicists from 78 countries convene in Turkey to draft the Declaration of Istanbul. This Declaration recommends alternatives to the shortage of organs and addresses principles of practice in organ transplant.

2008   Former slave Hadijatou Mani is the first to take her government to court for failing to protect her from slavery. The case was taken to the Economic Community of Western African States (ECOWAS), which condemned the government of Niger for failing to have met its obligation to defend Mani against slavery. The state was required to compensate her in the amount of US$19,000 for damages caused.

2009   The United Nations Office on Drugs and Crime (UNODC) publishes the first Global Trafficking in Persons report. UNODC will continue publishing reports in 2012, 2014, and 2016.

2010   The United Nations Global Plan of Action to Combat Trafficking in Persons is adopted by the General Assembly. The Plan calls for the establishment of a trust fund for victims of trafficking and aims at integrating the fight against trafficking into the United Nations' broader development programs.

2011   By Presidential Proclamation in the previous year, January is designated National Slavery and Human Trafficking Prevention month in the United States; January 11 is designated National Human Trafficking Awareness Day.

2011   UNODC launches the first global database of human trafficking cases. The database is aimed at assisting policy makers, prosecutors, judges, researchers, the media, and other interested parties by making available details of real cases with examples of how the respective national laws in place can be used to prosecute human trafficking.

2011   CNN launches a humanitarian news media campaign—the Freedom Project Ending Modern Slavery. This project investigates global slavery and raises awareness of the issue.

2011   Directive 2011/36/EU on preventing and combating trafficking in human beings and protecting its victims is adopted by Member States of the European Union. The Directive focuses on the victims and human rights, and requires an integrated, comprehensive approach that is gender-specific.

2011   ILO Convention 189 concerning decent work for domestic workers is adopted in 2011 and will enter into force in 2013.

2011   The California Transparency in Supply Chains Act is enacted requiring major retail and manufacturing firms to disclose the efforts they are making to eliminate human trafficking and forced labor from their supply chains.

2012   The Walk Free Foundation is founded by an Australian millionaire philanthropist aimed at producing research, and mobilizing global activists and businesses to collaborate in ending modern-day slavery. It will release the first Global Slavery Index in 2013, with annual reports in following years.

2012   The International Tourism Partnership brings together the world's leading international hotel companies to raise awareness of social and environmental responsibility in the industry. Partners have developed an anti-trafficking policy addressing supplier codes of conduct and clear procedures for training staff and reporting suspected incidences.

2013   The Reauthorization of the U.S. Trafficking Victims Protection Act is attached as an amendment to the Violence Against Women Act and passes.

2013   At the UN General Assembly, Member States adopt resolution A/RES/68/192 and designate July 30 as the World Day against Trafficking in Persons.

2013   Terre des Hommes in the Netherlands launches "Sweetie," a computer-generated child, to stop webcam sex tourism and catch online child predators. More than 1,000 men offering "Sweetie" money for webcam sex are identified.

2014   Pope Francis and Catholic, Orthodox, and Anglican religious leaders together with representatives from Jewish, Hindu, Muslim, and Buddhist faiths sign a declaration against modern slavery calling it a crime against humanity.

2014 The Protocol of 2014 to the Forced Labour Convention, 1930, is adopted. It will be entered into force in November 2016.

2014 Establishment of the Global Business Coalition Against Human Trafficking, comprising international corporations that aim to mobilize the resources and leadership of the business community to end human trafficking.

2015 The ASEAN Convention on Trafficking in Persons and the ASEAN Plan of Action are adopted.

2015 Human Rights Watch issues guidelines to protect the basic rights of migrant construction workers in the Gulf Cooperation Council countries.

2015 The U.K. Home Secretary appoints the first ever independent Anti-Slavery Commissioner. In the same year, Britain's Modern Slavery Act comes into force. Businesses are required to disclose what action they have taken to ensure their supply chains are free of slave labor and allow authorities to force traffickers to pay compensation to their victims.

2015 The Sustainable Development Goals are created by world leaders with the aim of eradicating poverty by 2030. The new global agenda was adopted by the 193 Member States of the United Nations. The 17 Sustainable Development Goals include targets to end slavery and eradicate forced labor and human trafficking.

This chapter provides definitions for some of the most commonly used terms in the trafficking, anti-trafficking, and slavery literature.

bacha bazi The practice in parts of Afghanistan where prepubescent boys are dressed in women's clothing and forced to dance at parties attended only by men. The boys are kept by masters and are sexually abused.

chattel slavery A form of slavery in which a master "owns" his slave. Slaves are considered the property of the slave owner and can be bought, sold, inherited, or traded.

child sex tourist Preferential child sex tourists travel to a country with the sole purpose of sexually abusing children, whereas situational offenders may take advantage of a situation to have sex with a child. A new pattern involves offenders who, rather than abusing children during short-term travel, establish schools or orphanages in source countries with the purpose of having unrestricted access to children.

child soldiers Persons under the age of 18 are recruited or coerced into joining the ranks of government forces or paramilitary organizations. They may not only be used as combatants, but also for forced labor or sexual exploitation.

commercial sexual exploitation of children (CSEC) The commercial sexual exploitation of a person under the age of 18, but often much younger, by an adult for the purpose of child pornography, prostitution, or child sex tourism.

corruption   The abuse of public office by government officials for personal gain. Corruption can be either (or both) proactive—such as actively assisting traffickers in procuring travel documents—or passive—a failure to react by turning a blind eye.

debt bondage   An illegal practice in which individuals incur a debt. Unable to repay the borrowed money, the person falls prey to the debtor who extracts labor in exchange for the debt. In many countries, debts may be passed down for generations, resulting in the enslavement of entire families.

demand-side approach to combatting trafficking   This approach focuses on targeting the demand side of trafficking by educating consumers about the products they buy or the services they use. In sex trafficking, a demand-side approach targets clients of prostitutes, often with arrest, fines, or educational programs.

domestic trafficking   Refers to the trafficking of citizens within their own country.

extraterritorial legislation   Allows countries to prosecute their citizens who travel abroad and engage in sexual relations with children.

feminization of poverty   In many countries, women are disproportionately poor, marginalized, and excluded from advancement opportunities through deeply rooted gender-based discrimination.

forced labor   All work or service which is obtained under the threat of any penalty and for which the individual has not offered himself voluntarily.

gender inequality   The unequal perceptions or treatment of individuals based on their gender. Women are disproportionately disadvantaged.

human rights–based approach Places the needs and care of the victim at the center of any investigation and prosecution.

human trafficking The illegal recruitment, transportation, receipt or harboring of persons through deception, fraud, coercion, or abuse of a position of vulnerability for the purpose of commercial sexual exploitation, forced labor, or trade in organs.

involuntary servitude Involuntary or compulsive labor, often to satisfy a debt, and under threat of, or actual harm.

National Human Trafficking Resource Center (NHTRC) The U.S. NHTRC provides data on (suspected) cases of human trafficking and maintains a national, toll-free hotline operating 24 hours a day, 7 days a week, 365 days a year to answer calls from anywhere in the United States. Callers can receive information and report tips on human trafficking.

nongovernmental organization (NGO) A legally recognized not for profit organization that operates independently from government entities.

nonpunishment principle Advocates for the nonprosecution and nonpunishment of persons who may have committed offenses as trafficked victims.

organ trafficking The recruitment, transportation, or receipt of persons through fraud, deception, or coercion for the purpose of organ removal. Many persons consent to sell an organ, often times unaware of the nature and consequences of the operation.

The Protocol to Prevent, Suppress and Punish Trafficking in Persons, Especially Women and Children (also referred to as the "Trafficking Protocol" or "Palermo Protocol") The Protocol supplementing the UN Convention Against Transnational Organized Crime is an international, legally binding agreement defining trafficking in persons and establishing guidelines for international cooperation in investigating and prosecuting the crime, and protecting and assisting victims.

push and pull factors Factors, such as poverty, gender inequality, political instability, conflict, discrimination, and marginalization which facilitate the migration (internal or international) out of a region or country (push factors). Persons migrate toward cities or countries that provide economic and political stability (pull factors).

smuggling The facilitation or transportation (usually for a financial or other material benefit) of a person across an international border to further the illegal entry of the smuggled person into a country.

supply chain This is a system of organizations or business cooperating in the production and transportation of goods or services from supplier to customer. Abuses (by subcontractors) in a business' supply chain often results in situations of human trafficking.

T-visa The T-visa, created under the U.S. Trafficking Victims Protection Act, gives temporary nonimmigrant status to victims of severe forms of trafficking, on the condition that they help law enforcement officials investigate and prosecute crimes related to human trafficking.

"3P" paradigm The paradigm is outlined in the UN's trafficking in persons protocol and the United States' TVPA. It stands for protection, prevention, and prosecution. The fourth "P," partnerships, has been added recently.

trafficking survivors Former trafficked victims who have overcome their victimization.

Trafficking Victims Protection Act (TVPA) The U.S. Victims of Trafficking and Violence Protection Act of 2000 (P.L. 106–386), and its subsequent reauthorizations, provide the tools to combat trafficking in persons in the United States and internationally.

victim continuum The degree to which victims are complicit in, or had prior knowledge of what would later happen to them, can be placed on a continuum. On one extreme are victims who are obtained through coercion or force, through complete deception of the nature of their work, to partial deception. On the other extreme, are victims who knew of the nature, but were deceived about the conditions of their work.

White Slave Trade The trade in foreign women across international borders for the purpose of prostitution.

Abolishslavery.org, 187
Abu Bakr al-Baghdadi, 186, 188
Abu Bakr-Shekau, 189
abuse of power, 15, 20, 75
Act, 147
   offender-specific, 102–103
   offense-specific, 102
Action Pour Les Enfants
   (APLE), NGO, 131
adoption, as a form of
   trafficking, 39
AdultFriendFinder, 183
Advanced Human Trafficking
   Training Program,
   125–126
advocacy, to help victims
   119, 237–238, 249,
   257, 269, 271
Afghanistan, different forms
   of human trafficking,
   266–268
   bacha bazi, 38, 92, 267
   forced marriages of
   children, 32–33
   suicide bombers, 85–86,
   92, 94, 131

African Network Against
   Trafficking, 203
African Union, 238
aftercare (program), 241
agencies, recruitment, 25, 55
agency, victim self-
   determination, 18, 76,
   122
AIDS, 41. *See also* HIV/AIDS
Al Qaeda, 189
Albania, 27, 34, 53, 101,
   117, 122, 278, 295
amicus curiae brief, 260
Amnesty International, 17,
   186, 190–191
Amsterdam, Red Light
   district, 76
Anthony, Susan B., 276
Anti-Slavery Campaign,
   233
Anti-Slavery International,
   11, 35, 249
Anti-Trafficking
   Coordination Team
   (ACTeam), 125–126,
   253

About the Author

Dr. Alexis A. Aronowitz received her Masters and PhD in Criminal Justice from the University of Albany, New York. From 1986 to 1994, she served as instructor and Law Enforcement Program Manager in Berlin, Germany, and Law Enforcement Program Coordinator Europe in Kaiserslautern, Germany, for Central Texas College.

Alexis moved to the Netherlands in 1994 and worked as a researcher for the Dutch Ministry of Security and Justice, the International Police Institute Twente (University of Twente) and RADAR, an antidiscrimination bureau in Rotterdam. From December 1999 through March 2002, Alexis conducted and coordinated research on human trafficking at the United Nations Interregional Crime and Justice Research Institute, continuing to serve as a consultant on projects on human trafficking for the United Nations Office on Drugs and Crime. Upon returning to the Netherlands, Alexis served as a project coordinator for the Police Research Program. She currently works as a senior lecturer a University College Utrecht and Leiden University College in the Netherlands.

She continues to work as an independent consultant and has contributed to projects on human trafficking for the United Nations Office on Drugs and Crime, the United Nations Division for the Advancement of Women, the International Organization for Migration, the Organization for Security and Cooperation in Europe, the International Victimology Institute Tilburg (University of Tilburg), Human Rights First, Management Systems International, and Winrock International. Alexis has served as a visiting professor teaching a course on human trafficking at universities in the United States and Germany. She has been invited to speak on human trafficking at the Commission on Crime Prevention and Criminal Justice (United Nations Office on Drugs and Crime), the Vatican, and the European Parliament, and has published extensively on the topic of human trafficking and hate crimes. Her book, *Human Trafficking, Human Misery: The Global Trade in Human Beings*, was published by Praeger in 2009. *Human Trafficking: A Reference Handbook* is her second book.